Indian Drinking

INDIAN DRINKING

Navajo Practices and
Anglo-American Theories

JERROLD E. LEVY

STEPHEN J. KUNITZ

A Wiley-Interscience Publication

JOHN WILEY & SONS, New York · London · Sydney · Toronto

Copyright © 1974, by John Wiley & Sons, Inc.

All rights reserved. Published simultaneously in Canada.

No part of this book may be reproduced by any means, nor transmitted, nor translated into a machine language without the written permission of the publisher.

Library of Congress Cataloging in Publication Data:

Levy, Jerrold Edgar, 1930–
   Indian drinking: Navajo practices and Anglo-American theories.

   "A Wiley-Interscience publication."
   Bibliography: p.
   1. Navajo Indians—Liquor problem. I. Kunitz, Stephen J., joint author. II. Title. [DNLM: 1. Alcohol drinking. 2. Indians, North American. WM274 L668i 1974]

E99.N3L63   362.2'92'09701   73-17173
ISBN 0-471-53163-4

Printed in the United States of America

10 9 8 7 6 5 4 3 2 1

Acknowledgments

The research on which this study is based was begun while we were working with the U.S. Public Health Service in Tuba City, Arizona. Our initial work was supported by NIMH small grant MH 14053 and was sponsored by the Public Health Service Indian Hospital. Dr. John Muth, formerly Service Unit Director of the Tuba City Hospital, Dr. George Bock, Navajo Area Indian Health Service Director, and Dr. Charles MacCammon, Phoenix Area Indian Health Service Director provided helpful support and advice. Mr. Joseph Deffenbaugh, formerly chief of the pharmacy at the Tuba City Hospital, gave us access to records of Disulfiram prescriptions distributed during the time of our study. Dr. Arthur Vall-Spinosa, formerly chief of medicine at the Tuba City Hospital allowed us to interview patients admitted to the hospital for Disulfiram therapy.

During the study, Levy was supported by NIMH Career Development Award 5-K3-MH-31, 184. Kunitz was supported by a grant from the Josiah Macy, Jr. Foundation and subsequently by NIMH Award 1-F03-MH45174-01.

During the several years that our field work was in progress, we were fortunate to have the help of a number of interpreters: Mr. Dennis Parker, Miss Susan Betoney, Miss Dorothy Pete, Mr. Nelson Betoney and Mr. Amos Belone. We are grateful for the high quality of their work and for their interest in the project.

Other people who have provided advice and help are Dr. Charles Odoroff for statistical advice; Dr. Robert L. Berg for moral and financial support; Professors August B. Hollingshead and Jerome K. Myers for reading and commenting on an earlier version of the manuscript; Professors Keith Basso and Michael Everett for useful discussions of drinking patterns and deviant behavior among the White Mountain Apaches; Dr. Edward B. Danson and the staff of the Museum of Northern Arizona for providing us office and library facilities during the course of our work; and Dr. Joseph G. Jorgensen for critically reviewing the finished manuscript.

Acknowledgement is gratefully made to the following authors and publishers who have granted permission to use selections from their publications.

Aldine Publishing Company for quotes from *Drunken Comportment: A Social Explanation* by C. MacAndrew and R. B. Edgerton.

The American Anthropological Association for quotes from "Acculturation, Access, and Alcohol in a Tri-Ethnic Community," by T. D. Graves, reproduced by permission of the American Anthropological Association from the *American Anthropologist,* 69:317–318, 1967; "The Personal Adjustment of Navajo Indian Migrants to Denver, Colorado," by T. D. Graves, reproduced by permission of the American Anthropological Association from the *American Anthropologist,* 72:39, 42, 1970; "A Note on the Navajo Visionary," by B. Haile, reproduced by permission of the American Anthropological Association from the *American Anthropologist,* 42:359, 1940; "Change and Persistence in an Isolated Navajo Community," by M. Shepardson and B. Hammond, reproduced by permission of the American Anthropological Association from the *American Anthropologist,* 66: 1045, 1049, 1964.

College and University Press Publishers for a quote from *Primitive Drinking* by C. Washburne, Copyright © 1961 by Chandler Washburne.

Doubleday and Company, Inc. for quotes from *Asylums, Essays on the Social Situation of Mental Patients and other Inmates,* by E. Goffman, copyright © 1961 by Erving Goffman, Doubleday and Company, Inc.

Michael Everett for quotes from "Cooperation in Change? Western Apache Evidence," by M. Everett, a paper presented at the Annual Meeting of the Society for Applied Anthropology, Mexico City, April, 1969.

Holt, Rinehart and Winston, Inc. for quotes from *Society, Personality and Deviant Behaviour* by R. Jessor, T. D. Graves, R. C. Hanson and S. L. Jessor. Copyright © The Free Press, a corporation, 1960.

Houghton Mifflin Company for a quote from *Patterns of Culture* by Ruth Benedict, Houghton Mifflin Co., Boston.

Macmillan Publishing Company, Inc. for quotes from "Notes on the Sociology of Deviance," by K. T. Erikson in *The Other Side,* by H. S. Becker, editor, the Free Press, New York, copyright © 1964 by the Free Press of Glencoe, a division of the Macmillan Company.

Rutgers University, Rutgers Center of Alcohol Studies, *Quarterly Journal of Studies on Alcohol* for quotes from "American Drinking Practices: Summary of Findings from a National Probability Sample, I Extent of Drinking by Population Subgroups" by D. Cahalan and I. H. Cisin, *Quarterly Journal of Studies on Alcohol, 29:*137; "Problem Drinking Among American Indians" by E. P. Dozier, *Quarterly Journal of Studies on Alcohol, 27:*76–77; "The Use of Alcohol in Three Salish Indian Tribes" by E. M. Lemert, *Quarterly Journal of Studies on Alcohol, 19:*98–99; "Drinking in Iowa, III. A Scale of Definitions of Alcohol Related to Drinking Behaviour" by H. A. Mulford and D. E. Miller, *Quarterly Journal of Studies on Alcohol, 21:*275, 276, 277–278; "Drinking in Iowa, IV. Preoccupation with Alcohol and Definitions of Alcohol, Heavy Drinking and Trouble Due to Drinking" by H. A. Mulford and D. E. Miller, *Quarterly Journal of Studies on Alcohol, 21:*291.

The University of Arizona Press for quotes from *Cycles of Conquest* by E. H. Spicer and *The Albuquerque Navajos* by W. H. Hodge.

The University of California Press for permission to quote short excerpts taken from pages 21 and 97 of *Animal Husbandry in Navajo Society and Culture* by J. F. Downs, University of California Press Publications in Anthropology Vol. I, published 1964. Originally published by the University of California Press; reprinted by permission of the Regents of the University of California.

The University of Chicago Press for quotes from "Navaho" by E. Vogt in *Perspectives in American Indian Culture Change,* edited by E. H. Spicer, copyright © 1961 by the University of Chicago, Published by the University of Chicago Press.

University of Nebraska Press for quote reprinted from *Son of Old Man Hat, A Navajo Autobiography,* 2nd edition, by W. Dyk by permission of University of Nebraska Press and Mrs. Ruth R. Dyk. Copyright © 1938 by Walter Dyk, renewal copyright © 1966 by Walter Dyk.

The University of Oklahoma Press for quotes from *Indian Traders,* by Frank McNitt. Copyright © 1962 by the University of Oklahoma Press, and from *The Navajos,* by Ruth M. Underhill. Copyright © 1956 by the University of Oklahoma Press.

University of Washington Press for quotes from *Ceremonial Patterns in the*

Greater Southwest by Ruth M. Underhill, American Ethnological Society Monograph 13, 1948, University of Washington Press, Seattle.

Utah State University Press and L. J. Arrington for permission to quote from *The Changing Economic Structure of the Mountain West 1850–1950* by L. J. Arrington, Utah State University Press, Logan.

John Wiley and Sons, Inc. for quotes from "A New Cross-Cultural Study of Drunkenness," by P. B. Field in *Society, Culture and Drinking Patterns* edited by D. J. Pittman and C. R. Snyder. Copyright © 1962 by John Wiley and Sons, Inc.

J. E. L.
S. J. K.

Contents

Tables

Indian Drinking

Introduction

Although mankind's "love affair" with alcoholic beverages has persisted for more than 2000 years, the relationship has never become a mundane or boring one. Man, seeking either to justify his involvement or to resolutely break off the liason entirely, somehow manages to keep his interest alive if not always inflamed. Man sees defects in alcohol when in reality he is seeing the defects in himself. Although he also maligns his fellow man, alcohol, has not the voice to talk back. Alcohol thus is a scapegoat for our own deficiencies.

In the United States, the concern about the "drunken Indian" has been with us from the earliest contacts between Europeans and Indians until the present time. Historically, the use of alcohol by most Indian tribes north of Mexico is relatively recent, a direct result of contact itself. But whether our concern is directly related to an objective assessment of the Indians' excessive use of his newly received "gift" or to more subtle involvements between whites and Indians has never been determined.

Our images of the American Indian continue to vary, reflecting not only changes in the contact situation but also those in perceptions of ourselves as a people and our ideas about the nature of society. From an untamed savage who, along with nature, had to be domesticated, the Indian gradually became a noble Red Man destroyed by modern, industrial, alienated society. Regardless of many fairly accurate assessments that may have been made of the nature and condition of the Indian, it can be argued that in all periods of our history the Indian has been used as a screen on which white America has played its own dramatic presentation of America's changing image. The presentation is replete with doubts, internal contradictions, and no little sense of guilt.

1

Since the settlement of the New World by Europeans, our ideas about the nature of alcohol, excessive drinking, and drinking behaviors have changed radically. Although we have constantly maintained that American Indians drink excessively and thus suffer, our explanations of this phenomenon differ appreciably. We believe that the current interest in Indian drinking must be viewed within the larger context of contemporary ideas about the nature of alcohol, alcoholism, the Indian, and society in general because this larger framework of ideas determines the assumptions on which our research is based and many of the questions posed by the research itself.

Although these larger considerations are important, the unfortunate experiences of Indians with the demon rum generally provide the starting point for all discussions of the topic (1) and contemporary statistics do not dispel the image of the drunken Indian that was formed during colonial times.

Indians, for example, have a higher crime rate than any other ethnic group in the nation, and the vast majority of crimes are related to alcohol (2). The death rate from alcoholic cirrhosis for all Indians is more than twice the national average; 26.7 versus 12.1 per 100,000 total population. When the rates are adjusted to include only individuals who are twenty years old and over, the difference becomes even greater because the Indian population is younger than the general population of the United States.

Deaths from accidents are about 160 per 100,000 for Indians and about 55 per 100,000 for all races. Many of the accidents are related to alcohol. Deaths from homicide are about 16 per 100,000 for Indians compared to only 5 per 100,000 for all races. Again, many homicides are considered to be related to excessive drinking (3).

Many tribal leaders view alcoholism as a "number one health problem" (4). The Office of Economic Opportunity has funded programs on reservations to aid in the control of alcoholism. The Indian Health Service of the United States Public Health Service has labeled alcoholism as "a high priority health problem" (5).

Despite the general agreement that Indians tend to drink a lot and to get into trouble frequently as a result, many studies question whether Indian drinking involves a high level of alcoholism. A major reason for this disagreement is the fact that gathering adequate data among Indian populations is extremely difficult, and the interpretation of the data becomes largely a matter of theoretical taste. In another publication (6) we discussed the difficulties that plague the data-gathering process; the confusion that has arisen as a result of imprecise definitions of alcoholism; the problems inherent in the use of Merton's paradigm of anomie (or modification of it) as if it were a proved theorem in all societies rather than a hypothesis yet to be tested in many areas of the world; and the seemingly contradictory results obtained by using different measuring techniques aimed at describing different aspects of the same phenomenon.

Generally, the investigators of Indian drinking have viewed all tribes as having similar problems and have suggested that the etiology of excessive drinking is the same in each tribe. Usually, deprivation and social disintegration or disorganization have been held responsible for the problem. Essentially, drinking is viewed as an anxiety-alleviating and escapist response to an intolerable social environment. According to this view, the contact between Indians and whites has been characterized by rapid and forced social change, which has produced disintegration and disorganization on the societal level as well as disorientation, alienation, anomie, and social and psychopathologies among individuals.

Until recent years, studies of American Indian drinking have been descriptive and impressionistic. Because most of them have been conducted by anthropologists, they have concentrated on determining cultural definitions of drinking and describing normative drinking behavior. For many reasons, little effort has been devoted to the tasks of establishing quantifiable measures of alcohol consumption or measuring actual drinking patterns as opposed to the culturally recognized ones. It is difficult therefore, to make intertribal comparisons, and it is impossible to compare the data collected in studies of non-Indian drinking with the data derived from studies of Indian groups.

This book (in what some might call a foolhardy manner) deals with the larger issues of definition and theoretical taste, and also with the issues of methodology and data gathering. Our research used several data-gathering techniques. We tried to quantify results and then to reexamine more critically the current definitions of alcoholism and the ideas about its etiology. Consequently, the data are varied, and the exposition is sometimes indirect. To facilitate the discourse, we have posed this question throughout: Is Indian drinking best explained by considering it as a retreatist or escapist response to social disintegration, or by viewing it as serving ends that are compatible with preexisting and persisting tribal institutions and values?

Let us emphasize that we pose these explanations as if they were mutually exclusive primarily as a heuristic device, one that gives form and coherence to the narrative. Moreover, we do not claim that our data can be explained by a single theory of drinking. In fact, we carefully discuss what appear to be considerable differences in motivations for drinking in different tribes. We will not deny, however, that we have been impressed by the evidence for the persistence of drinking styles as well as other social pathologies, even though we are aware of the lack of attention paid by many students of Indian society to this aspect of the drinking problem. Our presentation of this evidence is, therefore, forceful. But in making our assertions we do not wish to imply that the contact situation plays no role whatsoever—if nothing else, it was through white contact that alcohol was acquired by most tribes north of the Rio Grande River. Instead, we intend to explore the degree to which aboriginal social organization may explain contemporary drinking patterns, the degree to which acculturation changes these patterns, and in what manner.

The core of the study is the drinking behaviors of four small groups of Navajo Indians living on and adjacent to the westernmost portion of the Navajo Indian Reservation in Arizona. However, to provide a larger perspective, we have conducted a number of epidemiological studies of the Navajo population as a whole and of two neighboring tribes, the Hopi and White Mountain Apache. We think that the cultural determinants of drinking styles can be indicated best by comparing the conditions of the Navajo with those of neighboring tribes of similar and contrasting cultures. Also it is desirable to discuss the history of these tribes and the development of drinking among the Indians and whites in the area.

The much discussed differences between acculturated and traditional Indians led us to select samples of people ranged along a scale from the most traditional to acculturated Navajos successfully adapted to off-reservation life. In order to compare our results with those from studies of non-Indian populations, we quantified our data by the use of interviews already used elsewhere (7) and obtained as much material as possible pertaining to withdrawal symptoms. The ideas about drinking collected from informants and descriptions of drinking past and present have been a great aid in the interpretation of the data, but they have not been the major source of information.

Since so many studies of Indian drinking implicitly rely on a particular set of ideas about the nature of deviant behavior, we have prefaced our material with a discussion of theories of deviance. In Chapter One we delineate the ways in which social theory, ideas of deviance, and ideas of drinking have become inextricably interwoven.

In Chapter Two we outline the history of the three Southwestern tribes for whom we have epidemiological data. This is followed by a detailed history of the Navajo, particularly the western Navajo. A history of the off-reservation community, selected to represent acculturated Navajos, is also included. We hope to provide not only a general orientation but also a description of the differences—social and cultural—that distinguish tribes from each other and that characterize subpopulations within the Navajo tribe itself. By doing this, we can discuss general hypotheses about the types of drinking found in different tribal populations.

The view that drinking among Indians is a response to acculturational stress and that alcohol has a set drug effect (i.e., the release of inhibitions) on whomever uses it, regardless of cultural background, implies that alcohol is used for similar purposes everywhere. In Chapter Three we review the history of alcohol use in the Southwest generally, and particularly among the Navajo, to determine (1) whether drinking patterns have persisted or have changed in response to the changing contact situation, and (2) whether Navajo drinking patterns are peculiar to the Navajo, that is, whether they serve Navajo goals and remain consonant with Navajo values or are escapist and disintegrative in nature.

Part Two presents in detail our data and methods. Chapter Four discusses the methods used in each study, the results of the epidemiological studies of alcoholic cirrhosis, and selected social pathologies among the Navajos, Hopis, and White Mountain Apaches. Our findings support the work of anthropologists such as Field, (8) who claim that public inebriety is positively associated with loosely integrated social organization. We found that homicide and suicide are of this pattern. There is considerable evidence that the pattern is an old one and that suicide and homicide rates have not been rising as a result of culture contact or the effects of increased alcohol use.

Chapters Six and Seven describe the more intensive field study undertaken among several groups of Navajo, ranging from acculturated to traditional. Drinking patterns and the sequelae of drinking, as they are found in these groups, are compared. The major finding of this study was that the most intense form of drinking occurs among the more traditional Navajos. Acculturated Navajos tend to drink in a manner that approximates contemporary white practices. Some of the social factors that influence the incidence of withdrawal symptoms are discussed, and it is suggested that even these physiologic indicators of the presence of alcoholism cannot be used uncritically in comparing levels of alcoholism in different populations with different drinking styles.

We conclude (Chapter Eight) with a discussion of the implications of our findings. An interesting problem is the definition of alcoholism in cross-cultural studies. In several instances, measurements that are most often thought to indicate the presence of severe, addictive alcoholism were found to measure the style of drinking instead of the presence of addiction.

Our presentation of the data might suggest that our investigation began with a clear-cut statement of hypotheses and methods to test them. Since this was not true, we might call this a "pseudoinductive" method of presentation. Actually, our studies started with an attempt to gather data about Navajo drinkers in a manner that was quantifiable and comparable with the work by others in non-Indian populations.

NOTES

1. See, however, C. MacAndrew and R. B. Edgerton, *Drunken Comportment* (Chicago: Aldine, 1969) Chapter 6.

2. O. C. Stewart, "Questions Regarding American Indian Criminality," *Human Organization 23* (1964): 61–66.

3. U. S., Department of Health, Education and Welfare, Public Health Service, Bureau of Medical Services, Division of Indian Health, *Indian Health Highlights* (Washington, D.C., June, 1966), p. 16.

4. Arizona Commission of Indian Affairs, *Reservation Survey of Health* (Phoenix, 1966).

5. Indian Health Service Task Force on Alcoholism, *Alcoholism: A High Priority Health Problem* (Washington, D.C.: U.S. Public Health Service, Indian Health Service, 1969).

6. J. E. Levy and S. J. Kunitz, "Indian Drinking: Problems of Data Collection and Interpretation," in *Research on Alcoholism: I. Clinical Problems and Special Populations,* M. E. Chafetz, ed. (Washington, D.C.: U.S. Government Printing Office, in press).

7. H. A. Mulford and R. W. Wilson, *Identifying Problem Drinkers in a Household Health Survey,* National Center for Health Statistics (USDHEW), PHS Publication No. 1000, series 2, No. 16, Washington, D.C., 1966.

8. P. B. Field, "A New Cross-Cultural Study of Drunkenness," in *Society, Culture and Drinking Patterns,* D. J. Pittman and C. R. Snyder, eds. (New York: Wiley, 1962).

Part One

THE BACKGROUND

Chapter One

THEORIES OF DEVIANCE

The image of the Indian in the mind of Anglo-America has undergone a profound change in the past few centuries (1). The dominant image in the eighteenth and nineteenth centuries was that the Indian was an implacable, savage foe who stood in the way of westward expansion and manifest destiny. American practice in dealing with him was largely rationalized by the theories of the Scottish Moralist philosophers. Wild nature, for most Americans, was not valued in itself but for what could be made of it— "A terrain of rural peace and happiness" (2). Indians were a part of savage nature and, like the wilderness, had to be conquered so that nature could be domesticated. In its wild state, nature is not nearly as bountiful as we sometimes like to think. It is civilized man who domesticates nature and makes it over into productive gardens. Because Indians were a part of untamed nature, they too had to be domesticated (3).

By the time of the American Civil War, a change was taking place in the American consciousness. In response to growing urbanization, immigration, and industrialization, many artists, writers, and intellectuals were becoming aware of the price that was being paid for expansion. With the closing of the frontier, the disappearance of wilderness areas, the penning up of Indians on reservations, and the massive growth of cities by the end of the century, attention was turned to the world that had been lost. The image of the Indian began to change. No longer was he a savage foe to be conquered at all costs. He was now the pitiful remnant of a noble race, which had lived in harmony with nature before the coming of the white man. The Indian had earned his conqueror's philanthropy (4).

In important respects the thinking about Indians closely paralleled the thinking about immigrant groups, which had come to the cities in increasing numbers at the end of the nineteenth century and the beginning of the twentieth century. Many educators and policymakers wanted immigrants to be "Americanized" as quickly as possible so that their Old World traditions would not interfere with their adaptation to the New World.

Many urban reformers, however, felt strongly that Old World traditions were the only factor that would save the immigrant groups from complete disorganization upon their arrival in the New World. Indeed, it was in this context that American sociology became concerned with the concepts of social disorganization, social problems, and deviant behavior. The destruction of peasant communities was thought to have caused a variety of deviant behaviors—excessive drinking, prostitution, participation in juvenile gangs, ward politics, and the rackets—which occurred, in varying degrees, in the urban slums. Many social workers began to reinforce whatever sense of community remained from the Old World and to help establish neighborly attitudes in the city. The settlement house and school center movements, for instance, shared this goal (5).

The concern for the well-being of American Indians was colored by many of the same perceptions. For example, at the Eighth Annual Meeting of the American Sociological Society, devoted to "problems of social assimilation," Robert A. Woods spoke on "The Neighborhood in Social Reconstruction." Robert E. Park spoke on "Racial Assimilation in Secondary Groups," W. I. Thomas spoke on "Prussian-Polish Assimilation," and F. A. McKenzie spoke on "The Assimilation of the American Indian" (6).

The point of McKenzie's talk and of the speakers who followed was that attempts to "Americanize" the Indians by breaking up their communally held reservations into privately held homesteads (by the Dawes Act of 1887) had thus far failed to lead to the assimilation of the Indian into the larger society. The appropriate method of dealing with Indians, as it was for the urban immigrants, was to establish schools in their midst: "Adjusted to what they know, made responsive to their tribal standards, articulated with their family and vocational activities, and supported by teachers and helpers who would minister in the direction of building up ideals and practices in domestic and agricultural work" (7). Problematic behavior by Indians and immigrants came to be viewed as part of a much larger phenomenon, social disorganization, which was thought to result from forced, rapid acculturation to the dominant Anglo-American society.

Although anthropology did not develop directly from the urban reform movement as did American sociology, it shares many of the same assumptions concerning the nature of community and the origins of deviant behavior in the contact situation. The two fields appear to converge, especially in regard to American Indians. We have discussed elsewhere the career of John Collier, Commissioner of Indian Affairs under Franklin Roosevelt, and the continuity in his social thought from his early years in the urban reform movement to his later years in Indian affairs (8). Collier, like many other reformers, had been concerned with the destruction of the sense of community that was experienced by immigrants to the cities. As an early social worker, he had attempted to recreate the *gemeinschaft* way of life in the urban slums. The urban reform movement had failed, but Collier discovered among American Indians perhaps the last place in the western world where the *gemeinschaft* way of life persisted; and he felt it his duty to protect that way of life from the shattering impact of the *gesellschaft* way of life (9).

One of Collier's projects as commissioner was to encourage the intensive study by anthropologists of a number of Indian tribes in order to better understand them and their needs and therefore to serve them better. A series of important books was produced in this endeavor. Collier's view was essentially a functionalist view of society, and this was shared by many of his consultants. For instance, Thompson and Joseph commented on the Hopis:

> Contemplating the complex and dynamic character of the Hopi nature-culture-personality configuration, we are arrested by its essential consistency. In fact, no detail as revealed in our findings, whether of ecology, social organization, religion, symbolism or personality— fails to fit into the general scheme (10).

Kluckhohn and Leighton stated that, whereas Navajo culture had been a "patterned mosaic," it was now, under the stress of white contact, "becoming an ugly patchwork of meaningless and totally unrelated pieces" (11). One of Alexander Leighton's recommendations from his study of Japanese war relocatees in Poston, Arizona during World War II (a camp administered by the Bureau of Indian Affairs under Collier) was:

> Never forget that people are dependent on their social organization, and that no matter how inadequate or superfluous a particular set of customs and practices seems, it may still be interconnected with ways of doing things that are necessary for the security and capacity of the people (12).

Leighton and Adair, in criticizing Benedict's picture of Zuni as the archetypal Apollonian society, did not say that it was wrong but said that it did not account for culture change under the impact of white contact (13). MacGregor's discussion of the Sioux explained their aggressive behavior as being a result of their frustration in being unable to practice their skills as warriors (14). The major point of these studies was that contact with white society led to social disorganization and that social disorganization was the cause of personal pathologies and deviant types of behavior.

In contemporary studies of American Indians, as in the past several generations, deviant behavior is generally attributed to social disorganization and the stress of acculturation. Many sociologists concerned with the study of deviant behavior have begun to question, however, whether social disorganization in itself can explain deviant behavior. Instead of social disorganization, Sutherland suggested the idea of "differential social organization" as a means of explaining behaviors that are considered deviant by the dominant society (15). Subsequently, a number of sociologists have elaborated on this idea and have explained that a variety of behaviors are attributable to participation in deviant subcultures, but not as a result of social disorganization per se (16).

These studies of the origins of subcultures and the introduction of new members have caused deviance to be considered from another perspective as well: that is, the idea that deviant behavior is behavior that someone or some group has labeled as deviant. Labeling theory (as it has come to be called) really does not involve deviant behavior but the reactions to deviance (17). It rests on the assumption that all sorts of behaviors are normally generated by a society but that certain groups—moral entrepreneurs—that happen to have power are able to label other groups as deviant (18). Deviance, according to Erikson, is socially defined and not "a property *inherent in* certain forms of behavior" (19).

Let us make two points about labeling theory, which is more of a perspective than a theory: (1) it assumes that society is pluralistic and composed of many subcultures, each with its own particular values and not necessarily sharing any or all of the values of the larger society; and (2) it does not deal with the origins of behavior as much as with the effects of labeling some behaviors as deviant. This is what Lemert has called secondary deviance (20).

These aspects of labeling theory raise problems that we will discuss in detail in subsequent chapters. We will merely state the problems here. First, it is not clear—as many observers have noted—to just what degree U.S. society may be considered as pluralistic. To what degree, for instance, do various social classes, ethnic groups, races, and regions share a common set of values and goals? And to what extent do the differences that exist determine behavior in other than trivial ways? Second, by assuming that the effects of labeling are more important in the study of deviant behavior than the study of the origins of the originally labelled behavior, a large area of important inquiry is neglected. As we shall point out later, we regard this area of inquiry—primary deviance—as being of crucial importance in the study of Indian drinking.

A second influential theory of deviant behavior is based on an important essay by Robert Merton, published in the 1930s (21). Merton enunciated what has come to be called a structural theory of deviance. He declared that deviant behavior represented a variety of responses to blocked access to the generally accepted goals of American society. In his paradigm of anomie, he outlined these deviant responses as retreatism, ritualism, rebellion, and innovation. It is significant that this theory was first clearly stated during the Depression of the 1930s when limited access to economic success became a severe problem for the middle class. Since then, it has become a generally accepted theory in the sociological literature.

The theory has been criticized on a number of counts. It assumes a general consensus on what the values of the total society are, and it does not allow for subcultural differences. Also, it assumes that a clear distinction can be made between means and ends: Is money an end in itself or a means to an end? Finally:

> The "anomie" theory may help us appreciate the various ways in which people respond to conditions of strain, but it does not help us differentiate between those people who infringe on the letter of the norm without attracting any notice and those who excite so much alarm that they earn a deviant reputation in society (22).

More recently, Cloward and Ohlin attempted to combine Sutherland's theory of differential social organization and Merton's "anomie" theory (23). These authors call their theory the "theory of differential opportunity systems." This theory states that patterns of deviant behavior are determined not only by access to the legitimate means of success within society but also by access to illegitimate means of success. The case of "retreatism" is an example.

In Merton's formulation, retreatism included such behaviors as alcoholism, drug addiction, and mental illness, all of which were considered to be possible outcomes when access to the legitimate means provided by society was blocked and the individual involved withdrew from further attempts to achieve success. Cloward and Ohlin point out that the same response may occur when, for instance, a lower class boy is denied access to illegitimate means of success, such as participation in rackets that are institutionalized in his particular subculture. Thus, the alcoholics and drug addicts in slum areas would be expected to be the individuals who are double failures: people who are neither successful in the larger society nor in their own subsociety. This formulation also maintains that the goals of the dominant society may not be internalized by an individual or group.

Feldman (24) has questioned whether Cloward and Ohlin's theory provides a full explanation for so-called retreatist behavior, even in urban slum areas. Observing the entry of narcotics into a slum neighborhood in Manhattan's Lower East Side, he noted that the persons who first became addicted were high status leaders of youth gangs who regarded the use of narcotics as risk-taking behavior. They felt that their status would be enhanced by taking drugs and not becoming addicted. As the leaders became addicted, lower status individuals began to use drugs, too, reasoning that they would gain status if they could resist addiction when the high status leaders could not.

Despite the fact that a variety of studies based on sources such as the Human Relations Area Files have shown that drinking behavior varies between societies, most observers of American Indian drinking practices do not consider those practices to be a reflection of different types of social organization. These observers, unlike many sociologists who consider deviant behavior as a reflection of subcultural differences, generally view Indian drinking as a reaction to sociocultural disorganization, deprivation, or anomie.

Dozier, for instance, has listed a number of deprivations that have caused many Indians to feel inadequate: "Confinement on reservations, attempts to make him an agriculturist, the prohibition of liquor, and subjection to countless indignities and humiliating experiences through the years. Perhaps the greatest blow was Federal wardship." And, he continues, "Alcoholic beverages have been the easiest and quickest way to deaden the senses and to forget the feeling of inadequacy" (25).

Among the Pueblos of New Mexico and Arizona, where aboriginal controls still exist and where white contact has not seriously disorganized the tribal members either socially or economically, Dozier maintains that alcoholism is not as serious a problem as it is elsewhere. However, where the aboriginal institutions of social control are breaking down, alcohol is becoming a serious problem. We shall reexamine the subject of drinking among the Pueblos in Chapter Five.

Anomie theory is relied on much more explicitly in two extensive studies of drinking behavior by Jessor and associates in a triethnic community in southern Colorado and by Graves and associates among Navajo migrants to Denver, Colorado (26). In each case, Cloward and Ohlin's elaboration of Merton's paradigm of anomie is utilized, although in a somewhat modified form.

> Access to illegitimate means, socially patterned and differentially distributed, can refer to far less structured and organized illegitimate means (than juvenile gangs—SJK and JEL). That is, it can usefully refer to differences in exposure of individuals to the everyday manifestations of deviant behavior by other individuals in the environment, or to differences in daily, even fortuitous, opportunities to transgress. This more general view of the idea of access to illegitimate means makes possible an account of deviance which is not necessarily institutionalized in gangs or organized over time (27).

Thus, these investigators postulate: *"The magnitude of deviance rates at a given location in society will vary directly with the degree of value-access disjunction, anomie, and access to illegitimate means characterizing that location"* (28). Value-access disjunction refers to an increased pressure toward the use of illegitimate means; anomie refers to attenuated control against the use of illegitimate means; and access to illegitimate means refers to attenuated control against the use of illegitimate means. Generally, these factors vary together and are usually found in the lower classes.

In a paper from the triethnic study, Graves summarized and explained some of the findings. Among the Spanish-Americans, deviance (i.e., excessive drinking) was low in the acculturated group with high economic access. Deviance was high in the acculturated group with low economic access. For the Indians, deviance was high in the following groups: those who were acculturated but with low economic access, and those who were unacculturated irrespective of economic access. Deviance was low only for those who were acculturated and had high economic access. These differences were explained as follows.

> Unacculturated Spanish-Americans displayed the strong social and psychological controls that have been reported ethnographically and that we would expect in a settled agricultural group. Of particular im-

portance are the controls of family and church, which apparently have
been strongly internalized. By contrast, unacculturated Indians displayed weak social and psychological controls, which have also been
noted in the ethnographic literature. Furthermore, a semi-nomadic
hunting-and-gathering economy would be expected to give rise to independence of thought and action and to a reluctance to intervene in
the lives of others. As a consequence, when acculturative pressures are
strong upon both groups, destroying the means for their attainment of
traditional goals and giving rise to intense feelings of alienation and
relative deprivation, it is among the Indians and not among the Spanish that excessive amounts of heavy drinking and related social-
problem behavior are to be found. By contrast, among the acculturated
members of both groups a convergence in social and psychological
controls is found. The influence of family and church begins to break
down as the Spanish-Americans move toward the more secular American norm, whereas the Indians, whose nonacculturated background is
socially anomic, become mapped into new control structures. These
structural changes are paralleled by psychological changes. As a result
of this convergence little difference between the two groups is to be
found in *controls* and internal differences in *pressures* can thereby
give rise to parallel differences in rates of social-problem behavior (29).

Since some of our findings for the Navajos are similar to the findings reported above, we shall mention a point that will be elaborated on in later
sections. Anomie theory assumes that drinking is a form of retreatism.
However, we maintain that alcohol use is, among other things, a means of
achieving power and is compatible with the values of seminomadic hunting-
and-gathering groups. We do not think that this is necessarily true for
the tribe dealt with by Jessor and associates because their contact situation
may have been different from that of the Navajos. Nevertheless, the assumption on which the anomie theory's explanation of heavy drinking is
based—that it is a form of retreatism—is just that, an assumption. It
is not proved by the data. Retreatism may be one reason that some people
have for drinking, but it may not be the only or most important reason.

Graves has objected to anything specific in Navajo culture or values that
might influence the Navajos' use of alcohol.

> It is my contention that the vast majority of Indian drunkenness can
> be explained purely in terms of structural and psychological variables
> relatively independent of their particular cultural tradition, and that
> any residue of difference between them and other minority groups

which remains may as well be accounted for by the limitations of our theory and measurement as by some Indian "cultural predisposition" (30).

He hypothesizes that the people in the best position to avail themselves of economic opportunities in the city will have the lowest rates of drunkenness, as measured by arrest rates (31).

The major structural pressure to drink experienced by Indians in U.S. society derives from their marginal economic position. The theoretical basis for this statement is to be found in the work of Merton and others. When goals are strongly held for which society provides inadequate means of attainment, in the view of these theorists, the resulting means-goals "disjunction" produces pressures for engaging in alternative, often non-approved adaptations, of which excessive drinking is one common form (32).

These statements are from one of a series of studies of Navajo migrants to Denver, Colorado. In this migrant group, it was found that persons with fathers who had been wage workers had fewer arrests than persons whose fathers had not been wage workers. Migrants with more than eight years of education plus some vocational training had fewer arrests than migrants without such educational experience. People with exclusively Navajo friends had more arrests than people who also had non-Navajo friends. According to Graves, this Navajo peer group develops from the fact that people who are doing less well economically seek solace and friendship with other people like themselves. The arrest rate is also higher for persons who are single than for married persons.

Thus, Navajo drinking groups off-reservation constitute deviant subcultures in much the same way as drug users and delinquent gangs form deviant subcultures (33). And the formation of these groups is part of the same larger social phenomenon: limited access to the goals of the dominant society.

One question raised in the present study is: Can one totally abandon the idea of some "cultural predisposition" in explaining the findings? Our own findings will point out that the fact that persons who are less deviant tend to be better educated and to have been exposed to nontraditional role models may mean not only that they have better access to the goals of the dominant society but that they have internalized the goals more strenuously than persons with traditional models and less education. Indeed, we maintain that peer-group drinking is a typical phenomenon for unacculturated, on-reservation Navajos and that it is transported off-reservation when these individuals migrate for part-time or full-time work. Clearly, this is deviant behavior by the criteria of off-reservation observers, but it is not clear that it is deviant on-reservation.

Unfortunately, as we shall discuss later, our work is not as comparable to Graves' work as we would like it to be. For example, our off-reservation informants were all long term residents of the off-reservation town. Almost by definition, then, they were successful migrants and would be expected to be very different from the migrants who left town after a somewhat shorter stay. Without commenting on the differences between migrants who had lived in town ten or more years—the ones who ultimately formed one of the groups described in the present study—and migrants who had lived in town less than ten years [which we have described elsewhere (34)], we mention here that the present study and Graves' study in Denver are not precisely comparable in these respects: (1) the way informants were selected, and (2) the fact that border towns and large, distant cities differ in the kind of migrant attracted to each; large cities tend to get BIA assisted relocatees.

Methodological differences do not entirely explain the different results and interpretations reported by Graves in his study of Navajo migrants to Denver and our own work on and adjacent to the reservation. Theoretical tastes and personal experience explain a large part of the difference. Since the theoretical differences will become apparent in subsequent chapters, we shall not discuss them here. Differing personal experiences—primarily on-reservation in our study and off-reservation in Graves' study—may also color our views. These are the issues:

1. Anomie theory, even as modified by Cloward and Ohlin and Jessor and associates, assumes that drunkenness is a retreatist response to lack of access to valued goals, whether of the larger society or a subsociety.
2. American Indians represent the most deprived segment of American society—deprived both in terms of achieving in the larger society or in their own tribal societies—and hence they have the highest rates of alcoholism.
3. Peer group drinking represents a deviant response to lack of access to valued goals just as drug addiction, juvenile gangs, and other deviant subcultures do.

Clearly, these are not separate issues. We maintain that: (1) drinking may be viewed not only as a retreatist response (which it may at times be), but also as a means of achieving socially valued goals; (2) although Indians are very deprived, judging by a variety of conventional indexes, it is difficult to say exactly what this deprivation means when comparing wage-work and subsistence economies; and (3) peer group drinking has existed since the early reservation period in areas that, until today, were isolated from contact with the dominant society.

As we have suggested above, despite the fact that a number of cross-cultural surveys have demonstrated varying drinking practices in different societies, most observers of American Indians have attributed their drinking patterns to anomie, deprivation, and acculturation. We have pointed out, however, that this position may be an anthropological conventional wisdom stemming from a sentimental view of Indian life. At least, alternative hypotheses ought to be considered, if for no other reason than to be able to reject them intelligently. Usually, however, alternate hypotheses are not considered.

Since alcohol was not generally known in North America before the coming of Europeans, its use is a product of the contact situation. Furthermore, since written records are only available from the postcontact period, we cannot get a clear picture of deviant behavior in the pristine, aboriginal state. Thus we can attribute all forms of deviance to the only reality we are able to observe or for which there are data. If we should discover a high prevalence of drunkenness, homicide, or suicide in the early reservation period, we suggest that it was at a particularly disruptive time. If evidence should come to light that these behaviors were common even before the reservation period, we suggest that the period of turmoil and warfare before final conquest was especially disorganizing. In essence, then, every period for which there is historical documentation involved social disorganization, acculturation, and debauchery. Ironically, there is no test of the connection between deviance and social organization for if a tribe does not manifest a variety of misbehaviors, it is claimed that somehow it has not suffered the ravages of the contact situation.

Now let us review a number of cross-cultural studies and suggest alternate hypotheses to the usual explanations of Indian drinking. We forewarn, however, that this is not as scientific an operation as we would like it to be. First, the societies that we shall discuss in subsequent chapters are often included in the samples analyzed in the cross-cultural surveys. Thus, we shall engage in the questionable practice of using some of the same data to prove our hypotheses as we used in framing them. Second, most of our hypotheses were developed after we embarked on our field work. Obviously, it is a questionable procedure to examine data for interesting and potentially significant results and then perform tests of significance only when it appears that the results will be significant. We have tried to avoid this, but we may not have been entirely successful.

Nevertheless, by presenting our argument in the form of hypothesis-testing, we hope (1) to give our work a scientific aura; and (2) to help the reader to follow and evaluate our argument more easily in later chapters.

Horton's study (35), the first and most often cited cross-cultural study of drinking, concluded that the level of insobriety in a society was related to the amount of anxiety. This was found to bè related to both acculturation and subsistence. If acculturation were removed from consideration, it was found that the societies with the most primitive economies were the ones in which drinking was the heaviest. This was considered to be a response to subsistence anxiety, and it was most common in hunting-and-gathering groups.

This interpretation has been questioned by McClelland, and associates (36), by Field (37), by Washburne (38), and by MacAndrew and Edgerton (39). Washburne, for instance, has pointed out that:

> Alcohol should not be thought of as typically allowing the discharge of unsocialized aggression. An important area of human life, like aggression, is not left without social norms to regulate it. The behavioral data on the societies in the present study give the impression that the effect of alcohol upon the personality of the individual is not all that relates drinking to aggression, but that the norms of society encourage and direct this relationship. . . .
>
> In one society after another it can be seen that aggression is highly patterned, indicative of the norms governing behavior. . . .
>
> Not only are the methods socially controlled, but the objects of aggression are limited. We do not have good information of this point, but how many persons become involved in physical aggression with parents when drinking? In some societies, like the Cuna, women are never the objects of physical aggression by drinking men. In other societies, like the Ainu or some African tribes, men are likely to beat their wives when drunk (40).

Field, reanalyzing the societies in Horton's sample, suggested that it is not the level of anxiety but social organization that determines drinking behavior.

> The most important single conclusion was that the degree of drunkenness at periodic communal drinking bouts is related to variables indi-

cating a personal (or informal) rather than a corporate (or formal) organization, but is substantially unrelated to the level of anxiety in the society.

Following are some of the variables found to be positively correlated with relative *sobriety* in primitive tribes: (a) corporate kin groups with continuity over time, collective ownership of property, and unified action as a legal individual; (b) patrilocal residence at marriage; (c) approach to a clan-community organization; (d) presence of a bride-price; (e) a village settlement pattern (rather than nomadism). It was suggested that societies with these features are likely to be well organized, to have a high degree of lineal social solidarity, and to have interpersonal relationships structured along hierarchical or respect lines. It was hypothesized that these factors in turn controlled extremely informal, friendly, and loosely structured behavior at drinking bouts. This interpretation was supported by the fact that the sober tribes were shown to control aggression severely in their children, while the drunken tribes are relatively indulgent with their children and permit disobedience and self-assertion (41).

McClelland and his associates elaborated on this theme in an analysis of the folk-tale content of tribes with different drinking patterns. They concluded that loosely organized societies demand that a man conform to social norms at the same time he is expected to be assertive. The individual put into such a bind finds in alcohol the means to become "powerful in a primitive, non-instrumental impulsive way . . . (42)." Alcohol is used to break through the social restraints rather than to help the individual conform to them.

The subject of all of these studies is group drinking—behavior that is readily observable. It is this behavior that correlates with the variables listed above, not other patterns of drinking that are less easily observed. This is a serious issue, discussed in Chapter Five. Although we should remember that easily observable drinking behavior does vary in a consistent fashion between societies, there are other, less easily observed patterns that also appear, but they are not recorded in these cross-cultural surveys. Thus, while Navajos, Apaches, and other tribes are considered to be flamboyant, excessive drinkers, the Hopis are considered to be nondrinkers. Actually, as we shall see later, the Hopis are heavy drinkers but, since their style is covert, it is assumed they have no difficulties with alcohol.

We think that people drink for a variety of reasons. In the case of tribes like the Navajos and the Apaches, who drink in highly visible groups, drinking may facilitate the expression of some socially approved values. With respect to the Hopis, who drink more covertly, drinking may be a response to living in a society that is tightly controlled and highly stratified.

MacAndrew and Edgerton concluded in their cross-cultural and historical study "that the way people comport themselves when they are drunk is determined not by alcohol's toxic assault upon the seat of moral judgment, conscience, or the like, but by what their society makes of and imparts to them concerning the state of drunkenness" (43). The tribes that we shall deal with later do impart to their members differing expectations of what alcohol can do to and for them, and we shall explore these differences.

Lemert points out in his study of alcohol use in three Northwest Coast tribes that drinking behavior derives partly "from the cultural pattern of the potlatch, which in attenuated 'feast' form is still observed by these natives. The prestige function is most apparent where the drinker or party giver is able to secure distilled spirits" (44).

> From the standpoint of collective behavior the drinking party can be viewed as one of the few ways, in addition to religious ritual, through which the Homalthko can feel a sense of social solidarity in the presence of white man's society. It is also one way—apart from feasts, which are rather costly and now rarely given—through which continuity can be established with the old culture. This is done through the telling of myths and stories and the singing of drinking songs (45).

Drinking for these Indians also facilitates aggressiveness. Lemert states that this is related partly to frustrations encountered by the Indians in their dealings with whites, partly from their warlike past, and partly from intragroup hostilities. With the disappearance of warfare, the handling of aggression becomes an anxiety-provoking problem. However, aggression and assertiveness are not things that just happen to people when they get drunk. It can just as plausibly be suggested that people get drunk in order to be assertive (46). Indeed, in a tribe with a warrior tradition and a positive value placed on assertiveness and aggression, the state of drunkenness may be approved precisely because it facilitates the conduct that the society basically values. In other words, although alcohol was first introduced to most North American Indians by whites, it may or may not have been well accepted, depending on the preexisting values of the particular tribe. The cross-cultural studies, previously cited, seem to indicate that in hunting-and-gathering groups where a premium is placed on individual skill, luck, and daring and where social controls are weak, alcohol may be valued because people under its influence do what the tribe already values anyway.

Thus far, we have not discussed alcoholism but, instead, we have discussed drinking patterns and styles. Throughout this book we shall avoid a definition of alcoholism, although we have observed elsewhere that alcoholism is usually defined by behavioral manifestations (47). Keller, for instance, identifies the central manifestation of alcoholism as being the consistent inability of the alcoholic to control either the start of drinking or its termination (48). He points out, however, that any operational definition used in epidemiological studies must rely on a set of additional behaviors or signs that are associated with alcoholism and that will allow for the identification of the alcoholic. The additional behaviors frequently mentioned in operational definitions include chronicity of "excessive" drinking along with a number of undesirable characteristics such as antisocial behavior and the ill effects of drinking on the alcoholic's health and social and economic well-being. Alcoholism, then, is usually defined as a chronic disease whose manifestation is the loss of control. Loss of control is manifested by a variety of undesirable events.

The use of such an operational definition in cross-cultural research creates many problems. First, it is tautologous (49). A sensible, healthy individual would not engage in undesirable behavior. If he does, he must be unhealthy, and he must be suffering from some sort of illness. If someone drinks in a manner that damages the family economy, for instance, he must be sick; that is, he must be an alcoholic.

Here is another related problem: all of the manifestations of alcoholism have come to our attention through experience with heavy drinkers in our own and other western societies, and there is no guarantee that a similar association will prevail in another culture. Moreover, since the diagnosis must be made on the basis of the manifestations, there is no method readily available for testing the validity of the association in other cultures.

Finally, all of the manifestations are more or less culturally defined and determined, especially the ones that are used as indicators in most epidemiological investigations. The economic ill effects of drinking are defined and measured by western standards as are the social effects of broken homes and overt aggression, for example. In an Indian society where divorce was common in aboriginal times, where economic opportunities are limited for drinkers and nondrinkers alike, and where arrests are made for breaches of white rather than aboriginal norms and laws, it is difficult to determine whether these behaviors are caused by drinking, whether they cause drinking, or whether they are fortuitiously associated because they occur frequently in many Indian communities.

Another reason for avoiding a definition of alcoholism is that it might not be useful to define all heavy drinking as either deviant behavior or disease. If we did this early in our inquiry, we would predetermine our results. Although it is common nowadays to define alcoholism as a disease, this is a relatively new way of viewing the phenomenon of heavy drinking. As our ideas of the Indian have changed, so have our conceptions of drinking and drunkenness. As the Indian, through much of our history, was viewed as an ignoble savage, so was drunkenness viewed as a pernicious vice. The changed definition of alcoholism from vice to disease, and of the alcoholic from culprit to patient, parallels the changed view of the Indian from ignoble savage to pathetic victim.

Earlier writers attributed the Indian's proclivity to drunkenness to his level in the evolutionary scheme. Without resurrecting that debate, we point out that our changed view results from a profound ideological change. Although this ideological change may spring partly from humane motives, it pervades current discussions of drinking to such an extent that the suggestion that heavy drinking among Indians may not be pathological shows a lack of common sense. Common sense nowadays tells us that people who drink a lot are sick in some way. Since sick personalities are assumed to result from sick or disorganized societies, we infer from heavy drinking the existence of personal and social disorganization. But this common sense view may lead us to infer the presence of social disorganization when, actually, we have no indicators other than the presence of heavy drinking.

As we previously pointed out, labeling theory and the perspective from which it developed do not pay sufficient attention to the problem of so-called "primary deviance." In the case of Indian drinking, however, we think that much of the behavior is learned; that is, is cultural, and this, in turn, is largely determined by the ecological adaptation of the tribe in question. We maintain that drinking behavior is mainly a reflection of traditional forms of social organization and cultural values instead of a reflection of social disorganization.

In the next chapter we shall describe the history of the three tribes with which we are concerned in this study, especially the Navajos with whom most of our work was done. We shall consider the social organization of each tribe and place it on a scale, as suggested by Field (50), in order to predict the levels of public drinking that ought to be found.

In later chapters we shall explore the following hypotheses.

1. Highly visible group drinking is socially acceptable in loosely organized rather than tightly integrated tribes, and the patterns of resulting medically definable pathologies can be accounted for by the type of social organization.
2. In a tribe with a positive value placed on individual prowess and magical power, the mind-altering effects of alcohol will not be rejected or denied.
3. The pattern of alcohol use differs, depending on the degree of acculturation. To be like a white man means, in part, drinking like one.
4. Who does and who does not become acculturated depends largely on where they are located in the traditional Navajo stratification system. Poorer people, in Navajo terms, have more incentive to adopt white ways than people who are wealthier.

———————— NOTES ————————

1. R. H. Pearce, *Savagism and Civilization* (Baltimore: Johns Hopkins University Press, 1967). W. E. Washburn, "Philanthropy and the American Indian," *Ethnohistory, 15* (1968): pp. 43–56.

2. L. Marx, *The Machine in the Garden* (New York: Oxford University Press, 1964), p. 142.

3. S. J. Kunitz, "Benjamin Rush on Savagism and Progress," *Ethnohistory, 17* (1970): pp. 31–43.

4. R. H. Pearce, *Savagism and Civilization*.

5. J. Collier and E. M. Barrow, *The City Where Crime is Play* (New York: The People's Institute, 1914); R. A. Woods, *The City Wilderness, a Settlement Study* (Boston: Houghton, Mifflin, 1898); R. Hunter, *Poverty* (New York: Harper and Row Torchbook, 1965; 1st ed., 1904); J. Addams, *Twenty Years at Hull House* (New York: Macmillan, 1927); C. S. Smith, *Working with the People* (New York: A. Wessels Co., 1908); A. F. Davis, *Spearheads for Reform; The Social Settlements and the Progressive Movement 1890–1914* (New York: Oxford University Press, 1967).

6. American Sociological Society, *Proceedings of the Eighth Annual Meeting of the American Sociological Society* (Chicago: University of Chicago Press, 1914).

7. J. M. Gillette, "Discussion of F. A. McKenzie's Paper, 'The Assimilation of the American Indian,'" in *Proceedings of the Eighth Annual Meeting of the American Sociological Society* (Chicago: University of Chicago Press, 1914), pp. 64–65.

8. S. J. Kunitz, "The Social Philosophy of John Collier," *Ethnohistory, 18* (1971): 213–229.

9. J. Collier, *From Every Zenith* (Denver: Sage Books, 1963).

10. L. Thompson and A. Joseph, *The Hopi Way* (Chicago: University of Chicago Press, 1945), pp. 131–132.

11. C. Kluckhohn and D. C. Leighton, *The Navaho* (Cambridge: Harvard University Press, 1946), p. 237.

12. A. H. Leighton, *The Governing of Men* (Princeton: Princeton University Press, 1968; 1st ed., 1945), p. 327.

13. D. C. Leighton and J. Adair, *People of the Middle Place* (New Haven: Human Relations Area Files Press, 1966), p. 141.

14. G. MacGregor, *Warriors without Weapons* (Chicago: University of Chicago Press, 1946), p. 220. Other books in this series were: A. H. Leighton and D. C. Leighton, *The Navaho Door* (Cambridge: Harvard University Press, 1944); D. C. Leighton and C. Kluckhohn, *Children of the People* (Cambridge: Harvard University Press, 1948); and A. Joseph, R. Spicer, and J. Chesky, *The Desert People* (Chicago: University of Chicago Press, 1947).

15. E. H. Sutherland and D. R. Cressey, *Principles of Criminology* (Philadelphia: Lippincott, 1966), pp. 77–83 are reprinted in D. R. Cressey and D. A. Ward, eds., *Delinquency, Crime, and Social Process* (New York: Harper and Row, 1969), pp. 426–432.

16. H. S. Becker, *Outsiders, Studies in the Sociology of Deviance* (New York: The Free Press, 1966).

17. E. M. Schur, "Reactions to Deviance: A Critical Assessment," *American Journal of Sociology, 75* (1969): 309–322; E. M. Schur, *Labeling Deviant Behavior* (New York: Harper and Row, 1971); J. I. Kitsuse, "Societal Reaction to Deviant Behavior: Problems of Theory and Method," *Social Problems, 9* (1962): pp. 247–256; J. P. Gibbs, "Conceptions of Deviant Behavior: The Old and the New," *Pacific Sociological Review, 9* (1966): pp. 9–14.

18. H. S. Becker, *Outsiders;* W. Buckley, *Sociology and Modern Systems Theory* (Englewood Cliffs, N.J.: Prentice-Hall, Inc., 1967), pp. 166–167. It is perhaps significant that labeling theory is the product of a generation that came to maturity during the late 1940s and 1950s in a period when blacklisting—that is, labeling—was not an uncommon phenomenon.

19. K. T. Erikson, "Notes on the Sociology of Deviance," *Social Problems, 9* (1962): pp. 307–314, especially p. 308.

20. E. M. Lemert, "Social Structure, Social Control, and Deviation," in *Hu-*

man Deviance, Social Problems and Social Control, by the same author (Englewood Cliffs, N.J.: Prentice-Hall, 1967).

21. R. K. Merton, *Social Theory and Social Structure* (New York: The Free Press, 1968), see especially Chapters VI and VII.

22. K. T. Erikson, "Notes on the Sociology of Deviance," revised version reprinted in *The Other Side,* H. S. Becker, ed. (New York: The Free Press, 1967), p. 10.

23. R. A. Cloward and L. E. Ohlin, *Delinquency and Opportunity: A Theory of Delinquent Gangs* (New York: The Free Press, 1960). See also, R. A. Cloward, "Illegitimate Means, Anomie and Deviant Behavior," *American Sociological Review, 24* (1959): pp. 164–176.

24. H. Feldman, "Ideological Supports to Becoming and Remaining a Heroin Addict," *Journal of Health and Social Behavior, 9* (1968): pp. 131–139.

25. E. P. Dozier, "Problem Drinking Among American Indians; the Role of Sociocultural Deprivation," *Quarterly Journal of Studies on Alcohol, 27* (1966): pp. 72–87; see pp. 76–77.

26. R. Jessor, T. D. Graves, R. C. Hanson, S. L. Jessor, *Society, Personality, and Deviant Behavior: A Study of a Tri-Ethnic Community* (New York: Holt, Rinehart and Winston 1968). T. D. Graves, "The Personal Adjustment of Navajo Indian Migrants to Denver, Colorado," *American Anthropologist, 72* (1970): pp. 35–54.

27. R. Jessor et al., *Society, Personality and Deviant Behavior,* p. 68.

28. Ibid, p. 78.

29. T. D. Graves, "Acculturation, Access, and Alcohol in a Tri-Ethnic Community," *American Anthropologist, 69* (1967): pp. 306–321; 317–318.

30. T. D. Graves, "Personal Adjustment of Navajo Migrants," p. 39.

31. Ibid, p. 40.

32. Ibid, p. 42.

33. Ibid, pp. 50–51. Other reports from the Navajo Urban Relocation Project are: P. Z. Snyder, "The Social Environment of the Urban Indian;" R. S. Weppner, "Urban Economic Opportunities: the Example of Denver;" all of which appeared in J. O. Waddell and O. M. Watson, eds., *The American Indian in Urban Society* (Boston: Little, Brown and Company, 1971).

34. S. J. Kunitz, J. E. Levy, and C. L. Odoroff, "A One Year Follow-up of Navajo Migrants to Flagstaff, Arizona," *Plateau, 42* (1970): pp. 92–106.

35. D. Horton, "The Functions of Alcohol in Primitive Societies," *Quarterly Journal of Studies on Alcohol, 4* (1943): pp. 199–320.

36. D. C. McClelland, W. Davis, E. Wanner, and R. Kalin, "A Cross-Cultural Study of Folk-Tale Content and Drinking," *Sociometry, 29* (1966): pp. 308–333; D. C. McClelland, W. Davis, R. Kalin, and E. Wanner, *The Drinking Man: Alcohol and Human Motivation* (New York: The Free Press, 1972).

37. P. B. Field, "A New Cross-Cultural Study of Drunkenness," in D. J. Pittman and C. R. Snyder, eds., *Society, Culture and Drinking Patterns* (New York, Wiley, 1962).

38. C. Washburne, *Primitive Drinking* (New Haven: College and University Press Publishers, 1961).

39. C. MacAndrew and R. B. Edgerton, *Drunken Comportment* (Chicago: Aldine, 1969).

40. Washburne, *Primitive Drinking,* pp. 261–262.

41. Field, "A New Cross-Cultural Study," p. 72.

42. McClelland et al., "Folk-Tale Content and Drinking," pp. 331–333.

43. MacAndrew and Edgerton, *Drunken Comportment,* p. 165.

44. E. M. Lenert, "The Use of Alcohol in Three Salish Indian Tribes," *Quarterly Journal of Studies on Alcohol, 19* (1958): pp. 90–107, 98.

45. Ibid, p. 99.

46. C. MacAndrew and H. Garfinkel, "A Consideration of Changes Attributed to Intoxication as Common-Sense Reasons for Getting Drunk," *Quarterly Journal of Studies on Alcohol, 23* (1962): pp. 252–266.

47. J. E. Levy and S. J. Kunitz, "Indian Drinking: Problems of Data Collection and Interpretation," in *Research in Alcoholism: I. Clinical Problems and Special Populations,* M. E. Chafetz, ed. (Washington, D.C.: U.S. Public Health Service, U.S. Government Printing Office, in press).

48. M. Keller, "Definition of Alcoholism," *Quarterly Journal of Studies on Alcohol, 21* (1960): pp. 125–134.

49. C. MacAndrew, "On the Notion that Certain Persons Who Are Given to Frequent Drunkenness Suffer from a Disease Called Alcoholism," in *Changing Perspectives in Mental Illness,* S. C. Plog and R. B. Edgerton, eds. (New York: Holt, Rinehart and Winston, 1969).

50. P. B. Field, "A New Cross-Cultural Study of Drunkenness."

Chapter Two

THE SETTING

Each of the hypotheses mentioned in Chapter One requires a preliminary discussion of (1) where the Hopi, Navajo, and White Mountain Apache tribes fit on a scale of social organization ranging from the least to the most integrated; (2) the nature and extent of contact and acculturation experienced by each tribe; (3) the degree to which the Navajo Society may be considered as a stratified society rather than an egalitarian or homogeneous one. In the present chapter we shall give the historical background of the three tribes and discuss the topics just mentioned.

Our discussion is divided into three parts. The first part deals with the history of the Southwest and of the three tribes. We shall compare their social organizations, assess the degree to which the tribes are isolated from intense contacts with white society, and review social stratification among the Navajos. The second part examines the western portion of the Navajo Reservation where our field interviews were conducted. Let us emphasize here that many aspects of the reservation system perpetuate rather than destroy traditional institutions. Finally, we shall give a short history of Flagstaff, Arizona, the off-reservation town in which we interviewed an acculturated group of Navajos.

Off-reservation towns of this kind have provided wage-work opportunities for Navajos for almost a century. Conversely, of course, the Navajos have provided local white entrepreneurs with numerous money-making opportunities over the years so that a symbiotic relationship between the reservation and the towns has become an important element in the economies of each. Of particular interest to the study is the fact that a border town such as Flagstaff provides two distinctly different forms of employment to Navajos.

On the one hand, the large amount of seasonal employment of non-skilled laborers allows the traditional reservation Navajo to circulate between his home and the town with little need to adopt new values or modes of life. On the other hand, a smaller number of permanent positions, primarily with federal agencies, are occupied by Navajos who were already educated before leaving the reservation and who, in order to succeed as skilled workers, had to adopt the life styles and values of the surrounding white community. It is an oversimplification to think of town life as having the same meaning for all the Navajos who live there.

──────── THE HISTORY OF THE NAVAJO, HOPI, ────────
AND WHITE MOUNTAIN APACHE

The area occupied by these three tribes is in the "four-corner" states of Utah, Colorado, New Mexico, and Arizona. In this area, during the eighth century A.D., various hunting-and-gathering groups began to establish sedentary horticultural communities wherever there was land suitable for farming. About the same time, the climate began to shift from winters of heavy snow and dry summers to relatively dry winters and summers with short, high-energy rainstorms (1). These climatic changes gradually forced the people to develop more sophisticated farming techniques and to move their settlements as the heavy summer rains began to erode the available arable land. By the end of the thirteenth century, these horticulturists had abandoned much of their former habitat and had withdrawn to areas in which permanent water was available. These new locations were primarily in the drainages of the Rio Grande and Little Colorado rivers. Nomadic invaders, drought, and disease have also been suggested as reasons for the decline of the horticultural peoples. The Pueblo Indians of today are generally considered to be the descendants of the earlier societies. The Hopis, presently settled on three mesas in the Little Colorado River drainage, are the westernmost Pueblo tribe.

During the sixteenth or seventeenth century, groups of Athabaskan-speaking Indians began to move into the Southwest from the north, probably utilizing a route along the eastern foothills of the Rocky Mountains. These hunting-and-gathering nomads were able to subsist in an area that could no longer support intensive farming and moved into the ecological niche vacated by the Pueblos.

During this early period, Athabaskan social organization was markedly different from that of the Pueblos. The Athabaskans were loosely organized groups living at what Steward (2) called a family-band level of organization. Leadership positions were acquired rather than inherited, and lines of authority were weak. Descent most probably was reckoned bilaterally, and corporate lineage groups were absent. By contrast, the Pueblos lived in permanent compact settlements with clearly marked hierarchies of authority and inherited positions of leadership. Among the western Pueblos, unilineal descent and corporate lineages were developed.

The association between sobriety and a highly integrated social organization posited by Field (3) should apply to the Hopis, with the loosely organized Athabaskans representing the other end of the scale. But the picture is not clear. Over time, several Athabaskan groups adopted numerous Pueblo traits until the contrast between the two types of social organization was considerably lessened. It should be emphasized, therefore, that Field does not posit a direct causal relationship between elements of social organization and the degree of sobriety or public drinking in a society. Instead, it is assumed that social institutions mold personalities and that personality type predisposes an individual to drink in a particular manner. Thus, the highly organized society emphasizes social solidarity, respect, and control of aggression. The social ideal is cooperativeness within the group. By contrast, the loosely organized societies foster individuality and self-assertion and tend to permit displays of aggression. Let us outline the changing forms of Athabaskan social organization and examine other cultural elements that influence the types of personalities developed in these societies.

During the seventeenth century, the Spaniards were able to distinguish between a number of Athabaskan-speaking peoples who had come to be known as Apaches. To the west, the "Apaches de Navajo" were recognized by the fact that they did more farming than the other Apache groups. The Apache groups to the east practiced marginal forms of horticulture. The tribes that came to be known as the Western Apaches, a grouping that includes the White Mountain Apaches, relied on farming less than did the Navajos (4). Unlike the Pueblos, neither tribe made sedentary pursuits the core of subsistence.

It is believed that the adoption of farming by the southern Athabaskans was borrowed from the Pueblos and that the Navajos had more sustained interaction with the Pueblos than did the Western Apaches. Nevertheless, it is hard to describe the differences in the social organization of the Navajos and the Western Apaches as they are reconstructed for the Spanish and early American periods.

Neither the Navajo nor the White Mountain Apache developed permanent villages or a tribal political organization. In this respect, social organization is loose and akin to that of the hunting-and-gathering period. However, matrilineal descent, matrilineal clans, and matrilocal residence after marriage were characteristic of both tribes and appear to be related to the adoption of horticulture and Pueblo contact. But if the social organizations of the two tribes are almost indistinguishable, there are still reasons to believe that Navajos somehow became more Puebloized than their Apache neighbors, even though they retained a basic Athabaskan individualistic orientation.

The southern Athabaskans were related to the Athabaskan-speaking tribes of Canada and Alaska and very likely practiced, at one time, a religion similar to that of their northern kinsmen. This religion probably was vision oriented, shamanistic, and individualistic. At the end of the seventeenth century, contact between the Navajos and Pueblos had intensified. In 1680, the Pueblos had rebelled against the Spaniards and expelled them from what is now New Mexico. A decade later, the Spanish returned, and many Pueblos fled to the Navajos for protection. The religious life of the Navajos appears to have undergone a major transformation as a result of this contact.

Ruth H. Underhill, in her discussions of ceremonialism in the Southwest, has distinguished two basic patterns:

> In spite of the complex intertwining of ideas, two separate lines of religious practice can, I think, be followed out. Oversimplified, they are as follows: The agriculturalists tend to develop communal ceremonies, the hunters, personal religious participation (5).

The agriculturalists, perhaps because they must work together, have communal ceremonies in which the whole group prays for rain and sun. This leads to a "standardized ritual with a hereditary officiant, whose power does not result from a vision but from memorizing a formula, both in words and behavior" (6).

Hunting peoples practice a more solitary skill, which demands great courage and luck. "In this solitary struggle with Nature, each man seeks his own contact with the supernatural, finding his answer in the vision" (7). In the Southwest, the vision quest is not the rigorous event that it is in other areas, for instance, on the Plains. Instead, it is a stereotyped experience. The Athabaskans practiced just this sort of individualistic religion. Navajo religion was more formalized, however, as a result of the Navajos' contact with the Pueblos.

According to Ruth Underhill:

> Pueblo ceremonies are community affairs conducted by a hierarchy of priests to bring rain and blessing on the whole village. The Navajo hunters thought little about rain. . . . What they cared about was the hunter's own health and well-being, his one sure possession. Heretofore, this had been secured through a medicine man, whose vision took him to a spirit village where powerful songs and rites were taught him. With these as his only therapy, the visionary came back to sing over one who was sick or unfortunate and thus to effect a cure.
>
> The Navajos kept this idea. The medicine man still sang over a single patient, who paid his fee. But all who heard of the ceremony were invited, fixed their thoughts on good things, and shared in the blessing. The medicine man, instead of a single vision, had now learned some elaborate stories which intertwined elements of Pueblo myth with others from the north. . . .
>
> The chanter who recited such rituals during nine days of exacting ceremony was no longer a mere medicine man, but a priest, whose training required years and was scrupulously paid for (8). (From *The Navajos,* by Ruth H. Underhill, Copyright 1956 by the University of Oklahoma Press.)

Significantly, the role of the shaman, the seer, seems to persist in Navajo religion, not in the form of the singer, but in the form of the diagnostician or diviner to whom one goes to be told what ceremony is needed in a particular case. It sometimes occurs, however, that the diagnostician and the singer are the same person (9).

The Navajos and the White Mountain Apaches are closely related (10), but their ceremonial structure is quite different, although the Apache tribe described below has a more standardized ritual than some of the others.

> They have thirty-two ceremonies, brief and simple but still learned by heart and unalterable. A man learns these by paying his teacher but some gain added value by "dreaming" additional songs. The ceremony to guard against lightning is the only one which must be wholly dreamed.
>
> The Navajo have not been mentioned among vision recipients, yet it seems probable that, at one time, they shared a simple vision con-

cept with the Apache. If so, they have taken a further step in elaborating and crystalizing a once spontaneous experience. Today, their contact with the supernatural is in the form of group ceremonies, conducted by a paid specialist. These conform vaguely to a Pueblo model, often occupying nine days and involving offerings, purification, the exhibition of sacred objects, sand paintings, songs, prayers and impersonations. The only reminiscence of the vision area lies in the fact that this elaborate performance is, in first intention, for the health and welfare of an individual (11).

Kaplan and Johnson suggested that the unique feature in Navajo culture is the intermingling of the Puebloan and Apachean traditions (12). It is usually the Puebloan tradition that has received the most attention from anthropologists, but Kaplan and Johnson maintain that the Apachean tradition is equally important in understanding the Navajo.

Thus, according to these authors, much that is characteristic of Navajo personality is shaped by institutions and values deriving from the individualistic, older and, today, the more covert Apachean tradition.

In light of these considerations, we can place the Navajo between the Hopis and the White Mountain Apaches on a scale of relative social organization. We would expect the Hopi to conform to Field's description of the sober society and the White Mountain Apaches to be flamboyant and overt drinkers.

─────────────── POSTCONTACT DEVELOPMENTS ───────────────

By the beginning of the eighteenth century, the Navajos were becoming more like they are today. They had obtained much from the Pueblos but had rejected their settled village life. They had obtained horses, sheep, and cattle from the Spaniards. As a result, they became seminomadic herdsmen and shepherds who raided the settled Pueblo villages and the New Mexican ranches. Downs maintains that this way of life allowed the Navajos to remain more isolated than the other American Indian tribes (13). They did not raid to eat what they captured but to build up their herds and flocks. Then they could retreat, with their livestock, into the inaccessible areas of northern Arizona when they were pursued by Spaniards or Anglo-Americans.

This pattern persisted through the Spanish period until the late 1840s when the Anglo-Americans gained control of what is now the American

Southwest. As Vogt pointed out, this pattern resulted in an open but stratified society.

The *ricos* owned many sheep and horses; the *pobres* without sheep attached themselves to the encampments of the *ricos* and worked for them; the slaves were non-Navaho captives. Since the *ricos* could easily lose their sheep in retaliatory raids, the *pobres* could build up herds by raiding, and the descendants of slaves were free, the system was not rigid. But it may have been important in the dynamics of the raiding complex — the *ricos* wanted peace to maintain the herds they had; the young *pobres* wanted raids to build up their herds of horses and sheep (14).

During the Anglo-American period, Navajo raids had become less tolerable and, in 1864, Colonel Kit Carson and his New Mexico volunteers rounded up the Navajos for four years of captivity at Fort Sumner, New Mexico.

This period has been described by Underhill (15) and others, and need not be repeated here. The attempt to turn Navajos into sedentary agriculturists at Fort Sumner was a failure because of drought, depredations by other Indians and, probably, the unwillingness of the Navajos themselves to be so converted. In 1868 they were allowed to return to part of their homeland, which had been set aside for them by treaty as a reservation.

The reservation was not the first area that was settled by the Navajo in the Southwest. As Hester has pointed out, the Navajos, throughout their history in the Southwest, have gradually moved south and west from their original homeland in northwestern New Mexico (16). It is agreed, however, that they were not west of the Hopi towns, permanently and in significant numbers, until after their return from Fort Sumner. The area from the Hopi villages west to the Colorado and Little Colorado rivers was used by many other tribes before that time, including the area near what is now Tuba City where a perennial stream (Moenkopi Wash) and the outcroppings of a porous layer of rock, now called Navajo sandstone, made farming possible (17). Indeed, in the late autumn of 1776, Father Escalante on a journey from Santa Fe to Salt Lake and back stopped near what is now Moenkopi Wash at a Paiute camp where he heard of some Havasupai Indians camped not far away. The Navajos at this time were east of the Hopi villages, which were east of where Father Escalante found the Paiutes and Havasupai (18).

Within the next 100 years, the Hopi Village of Oraibi established a summer farming community on the Moenkopi Wash only a few miles from what is now Tuba City. Subsequently, this community has become a permanent village (19). To help protect them from the Navajos, who had begun penetrating the area in the 1860s, the Hopis invited the Mormons to build a settlement near Moenkopi. In the early 1870s, Tuba City was established as a Mormon settlement and named after Tuve, the Hopi leader who had dealt with the Mormons. Not only was this settlement advantageous to the Hopis but it was also advantageous to the Mormons: "Hamblin could see that a town so located would be a strategic link in President Young's chain of settlements between Utah and Mexico" (20).

At this time, the Mormons were being subjected to increased attacks, the primary issue being polygamy. However, "The frictions that made headlines were caused by a conflict of social orders and of cultures and not by a conflict over polygamy alone" (21). Very likely, there was a good deal of apprehension within the federal government over the extent of Mormon influence in the Southwest. At any rate, in 1896 Utah became a state and four years later the Navajo Reservation was extended, by executive order, to include Tuba City. Whether it was intentional or not, the effect was to drive a wedge into the chain of Mormon colonies that had spread south from Utah through Arizona. By 1903, all of the Mormon claims had been paid and Tuba City had been set aside as a site for a Navajo school. To this day it remains the headquarters for numerous government and tribal agencies on the western side of the Navajo Reservation and provides one of the relatively few places on the reservation where wage-work opportunities for Navajos are available. We shall discuss this point again in Chapter Four.

There has been disagreement about the effects on the Navajos of their four years of captivity at the Bosque Redondo. Downs, for instance, has said:

> I feel it profoundly changed Navajo culture by so disorganizing the older social and political forms that they were never completely revived. Moreover, much of the material culture of what we now call "traditional" Navajo was introduced at this time. The need for these new material elements forced the Navajo to create new institutions through which livestock products could be exchanged for white manufactured goods without the necessity for the individual Navajo to interact with the wider white society (22).

Vogt, on the other hand, has stated:

> It is clear that the Fort Sumner experience did effectively bring the Navahos under the authority of the U.S. Government and eliminate

the raiding complex—the only major change in Navaho culture resulting from their five-year captivity (23).

He also points out that there "is a resistant institutional core at the heart of Navaho culture composed of a system of social relationships, ecological adjustments, and values that has formed a coherent and distinctive Navaho pattern at least since about 1700."

The crucial features of this institutional core include: the scattered settlement pattern; the matrilocal extended family and matrilineal exogamous clans; a material culture complex composed of a nuclear family hogan (sometimes now a house), a sweat house, and a sheep corral with openings to the east; political leadership based upon a local headman; a ceremonial system focused upon individual curing; ghost and witchcraft patterns as means of managing hostilities and aggression; values stressing "harmony," with bodily illness being an important manifestation of "disharmony" and "motion"; Navaho as a primary language; and a combination of farming and sheep husbandry, supplemented by weaving and, more recently, silversmithing as the basic economic pursuits (24).

He has called this an "incorporative" model of social change, and clearly the theory on which the present study is based is more in line with Vogt's argument than with Downs' argument.

One of the things that has allowed the Navajos to retain so much of their old style of life has been the fact that, until fairly recently, their reservation has been continually expanded, although not rapidly enough to keep up with their growing population and often at the expense of other tribes. It was suggested above that the Navajos may have been allowed, even encouraged, to move west of the Hopi towns because the Hopis at the end of the nineteenth century had allied themselves with the Mormons, who at that time were perceived as a threat to the federal government. They were also fortunate in having land that whites did not want. In the areas in which there was good land for ranching (for instance, near Flagstaff), there were conflicts with whites and, with few exceptions, the Navajo reservation has not been extended into these areas. By the time oil and minerals were found on Navajo land, the reservation was protected by the federal government so that it could not be stolen in the way that other Indian lands had been stolen.

This does not mean that the reservation period was not difficult. After the Navajos' return from Fort Sumner, they were issued livestock and were encouraged to rebuild their flocks, even though they did not need encouragement. By the 1930s, however, as a result of overgrazing and erosion, much land that had once been able to support flocks was rendered useless. Therefore, John Collier, Commissioner of Indian Affairs under Franklin D. Roosevelt, ordered the Bureau of Indian Affairs to go ahead with stock reduction in a somewhat ruthless fashion (25).

This was a tragic situation for Collier and the Navajos. Since the Commissioner is a political appointee, and since, in the middle 1930s, Collier did not know how long Roosevelt would be president, he wanted to accomplish the reduction before he left office so that the work could not be undone. The job was all the more pressing because of Collier's passionate commitment to the Indians and to the cause of conservation. Therefore, he completed the stock reduction without obtaining the full consent of the Navajo people, thereby violating a basic principle of his administration and causing a great deal of bitterness among the Navajos.

The effect of stock reduction was to disrupt the established system of stratification. In fact, Aberle has demonstrated that persons with large pre-reduction holdings were more likely than persons with small holdings to become members of the Native North American (peyote) Church after the period of stock reduction (26). And Downs has suggested that stock reduction was "the prime mover in the amazing shift in Navajo attitudes after World War II":

> Many writers have credited the experience of Navajos who served in the armed forces and who were employed in war work off the reservation as being the important factor in changing Navajo attitudes toward progress and the acceptance of white culture. It is my belief that this experience alone would have had no more impact than military service in World War I had on many of my older informants. The important factor, I believe, was that the Navajo of World War II was no longer able to depend on his herds for an adequate income. Many veterans lost all their grazing rights during their absence. Faced with this, they had no alternative save to find new means of livelihood, usually occupations requiring a higher degree of participation in White society and culture (27).

The present situation on the Navajo Reservation, in some respects, is similar to the situation in other southwestern tribes. About 49 percent of the labor force is employed (28) compared to 47.3 percent at Fort Apache (White Mountain Apaches), 39.1 percent on the San Carlos Apache reservation, 40.0 percent at Acoma Pueblo, 47.3 percent at Laguna Pueblo, 30.3 percent on the Papago reservation, and 59.4 percent for the general United States population (29).

In a sense, these figures are misleading. They consider the labor pool as being all persons who would take a wage-work job if one were available. For the Navajos, at least, unemployment does not necessarily mean doing nothing. Many individuals who would take a job if one were available have plenty to occupy their time: sheep herding, hauling wood and water, and many other activities that are necessary in such an environment. There are various possible sources of income, but all of them, by themselves (except possibly a steady job), are inadequate to support a family. As Aberle has said:

> Three hundred years of history leave the Navajo in one sense exactly where they started: In the 1660's they depended on multiple, fluctuating resources—the farm, the herd, the hunt, the raid, and in the 1960's the sources have only partly changed—the farm, the herd, the hunt to a small extent, the job, the wool, rug, silver, and pinon nut market, and the welfare check (30).

We have not provided employment figures for the Hopis because there are none available. However, there is no reason to believe that a significantly higher percentage of Hopis is employed than is found in the other tribes: "Employment is presently at an all-time low. The Hopis need employment on the reservation; however, some of them will and do accept employment within a 200-mile radius" (31).

In some ways the recent history of the White Mountain Apaches resembles that of the Navajos more than the history of their close neighbors, the San Carlos Apaches. In the late 1870s, most of the Western Apaches had been collected and placed on the San Carlos Reservation. However:

> By 1890 two thousand Coyoteros (later distinguished by ethnologists as the White Mountain and Cibecue bands of the Western Apaches) had returned to the northern reservation and taken up pretty much their old life, namely, hunting, gathering, and intensive small-scale agriculture. They remained peaceful and were self-supporting, as they had been before their removal to San Carlos. At San Carlos it was a different matter. The land that could be irrigated for farming was far from sufficient for the support of the Indians and hence rations were necessary. A whole generation of Apaches grew up in this period accustomed to going regularly to the agency and there receiving the rations of beef, flour, beans, sugar, and coffee (32).

As Everett has pointed out:

> The breakdown in economic autonomy and subsequent social distance that occurred at San Carlos was experienced to a much smaller degree

by White Mountain Apache. Local groups were able to maintain internal mechanisms for promoting cooperation and solidarity. In the late 1930's, this was true of economic and social sanctions, and is still seen today in major religious ceremonies and witchcraft activity (33).

And Taylor and O'Connor have written that "The White Mountain Apache does not appear to be nearly as mobile to off-reservation places as members of some other tribes. This apparent immobility is largely explained in terms of the extent of nonfarm employment opportunities on the reservation and an elaborate system of income sharing" (34).

Despite the fact that the White Mountain Apaches have continued to live in the areas that they occupied aboriginally, and despite the fact that their relations with the Anglo world have been less conflict-ridden than the relations of many other tribes, it is still true that their society is undergoing many profound changes. One of the most significant changes "has been the emergence of the *gowa,* or nuclear household, as the primary economic unit and the decline in this capacity of extended kin groups, most notably the family cluster" (35).

Eggan has said that "The Hopi preserve more of their aboriginal character than the other western Pueblos" (36). This is mainly because they were well beyond the range of direct Spanish control during the seventeenth, eighteenth, and early nineteenth centuries. When the Southwest came under Anglo-American dominance in the latter half of the nineteenth century, Hopi contacts with whites began to increase. It is primarily during the present century that contact with Anglo-Americans has become intense.

Factionalism and the splitting of villages seems to have been known in Hopi society as a means of dealing with disputes long before the contact period but, within this period, it may have increased (37). Although we shall not enumerate the various splits that have occurred among the Hopis, we point out that they are along lines labeled (somewhat erroneously) "progressives" and "conservatives." The progressives are the people who favor working more closely with Anglo-Americans within the structure of rules established by the dominant white society. They are allied with the tribal council faction. The conservatives are more interested in maintaining traditional Hopi values, methods of social control, and social structure, for example. This does not mean that they necessarily are opposed to some of the conveniences of the Anglo-American world, such as plumbing and automobiles. It means that they reject the right of the federal government to make laws telling them how to govern themselves, how to deal with their land problem, and so on (38).

The Hopi tribal council was established on the reservation (as was the practice among many other tribes) in the 1930s as a result of the Wheeler-Howard Act. A provision of this act was to empower tribes to elect democratically representative councils that could deal with the federal government and other agencies as the tribe's official spokesman. Among the Hopis, this method of choosing representatives was a direct threat to the already established theocracy. Nevertheless, the council was established, and the major dichotomy in the tribe at present is between the pro- and anti-council factions. We have estimated that the distribution of the *on-reservation* Hopi population is about two thirds in procouncil villages and one third in anticouncil villages (39).

The new villages that have developed since the contact period are less well organized and integrated than the older, parent villages (40). In them the Anglo-American institutions of courts and police have replaced the more traditional methods of social control that exist in the anticouncil villages. Although reintegrative forces are at work, "These are not yet sufficient to even the losses" (41). We shall discuss this issue further in Section Four in connection with the results of our comparative record surveys.

THE WESTERN NAVAJOS

All of our on-reservation work was done in the western end of the Navajo Reservation. As previously mentioned, this area of the Navajo domain became part of the reservation somewhat later than the eastern portion. Although there were probably some Navajos throughout what is now the western end of the reservation prior to the four years of captivity at Fort Sumner, intensive settlement began after that period.

As Levy has described it:

> The area dealt with in this study, and called the Western Navajo throughout, is bounded by the Colorado and Little Colorado Rivers on the north, west, and south, and by the longitude 111° 30′ on the east. . . . It is about 170 miles from north to south at its longest point and some 70 miles from east to west. The terrain varies from desert to steppe and includes five major geographic divisions and parts of two others (42).

And he continues:

> Gregory's survey divided the largest portion of the Western Navajo Reservation into four geographical provinces: Moenkopi Plateau, Kaibito Plateau, Rainbow Plateau, and the Painted Desert. The

latter may be subdivided, with the Little Colorado River forming the southern boundary of a distinct sub-province here called the Northern Painted Desert (43).

Furthermore, certain clans predominated in certain of the geographical provinces. Later on, we shall be primarily concerned with groups on the Kaibito Plateau and in Tuba City. Here, however, we merely give a general picture of this area.

The Western Navajo Reservation contains the spectrum of communities to be found on the entire Reservation—from extraordinarily isolated communities to so-called transitional communities. Transitional communities are those such as Shiprock, New Mexico, and Window Rock, and Tuba City, Arizona, which are on-reservation and are administrative centers for various federal agencies and the Navajo tribe. In centers such as these, wage work is found most readily; shopping centers, hospitals, and legal services are available; and modern conveniences such as running water and electricity are easily obtained. Hodge has written that:

> These transitional communities are the places where urban resident Anglo-modified Navajos hope to live, and where many such Navajo now live. They offer Anglo-modified Navajos a range of material comforts, education, and medical facilities generally inferior to those available in the city. However, they lack many of the city's disadvantages, and hence they are perceived as desirable.
>
> The capacity of these communities to absorb additional Navajos is limited or non-existent. An increased capacity would seem to depend upon increased industrialization. This, in turn, hinges around the interest of private capital and the skill of tribal and federal officials in attracting industry. The current industrial development of the reservation is at best minimal (44).

Although transitional communities are centers of wage work and represent a fairly high level of acculturation, the traditional networks of kin relations have not entirely broken down. In the case of Tuba City, it is not clear that a real community exists in the sense that we think of it in Anglo-American towns of comparable size. There are several reasons for this. The town now contains between 800 and 1000 people. About half of them are Anglos who are employed by various federal agencies. Even though some of these people have lived in the area for more than 20 years, the majority are transients. In general, the Anglos make up several subcommunities depending on the agency that employs them, either the Public Health Service, the Bureau of Indian Affairs, or the Arizona Public School

System. The entire Anglo population has little to do with the Indian population, which lives primarily in an area called South Tuba.

It is not clear that a real sense of community yet exists in the population of South Tuba itself, although this may be changing.

> Series of related camps are found in South Tuba. These are sometime extensions of preexisting outfits in the hinterland. They may also be complete outfits in miniature, with negligible relationships with relatives in rural areas. In any event, the prevalence of wage work appears to be lessening the frequency of traditional inter-camp cooperation, although it would be incorrect to say that inter-camp cooperation is necessarily on the wane.
>
> The population appears to be divided into three major groupings: (a) families of early settlers from the eastern part of the reservation, (b) families related to and actively cooperating with rural outfits of the Bitter Water Community centered around Coppermine and (c) families coming from other areas of the western part of the reservation (45).

Not only wage work but the zoning of South Tuba into individual lots and the completion of a federally financed low-cost housing development probably will increase the trend toward the development of nuclear families. However, during our field work, many of the ties with rural families had not been broken and, even within Tuba City itself, many forms of inter-camp cooperation still existed as they do in the hinterland.

At the other end of the spectrum are communities such as the ones on Kaibito and Rainbow Plateaus. Later, we shall examine the group with whom we worked on Kaibito Plateau. Now, let us describe a larger but comparable group on Rainbow Plateau. This area includes Navajo Mountain, a place to which a number of Navajos retreated during Kit Carson's campaign. They were never captured, and this area retains a reputation as a prototype of the traditional Navajo community.

Shephardson and Hammond, in their diachronic study covering a 25-year interval (1938–1963), found that little had changed on Rainbow Plateau that would indicate the disappearance of the society as it had traditionally existed (46). Although the population has increased and there are more goods (such as radios and pick-up trucks), residence patterns, ceremonial participation, and cognitive orientation, for instance, have remained essentially unchanged. There is no desire to be anything other than Navajo: "They do not wish to be White men, therefore they do not see themselves as deprived" (47).

These authors make another important point that we shall discuss later: the system of federal subsidy and support helps to maintain the traditional economy, not to destroy it. As Aberle pointed out, Navajo income has always depended on multiple fluctuating sources (48). On Rainbow Plateau, these include livestock, agriculture, federal employment (both steady and seasonal), migrant labor, welfare, and social security (49). Without being whimsical, we suggest that migrant labor may be a contemporary form of the raiding complex that was abolished when the reservation period began.

As already mentioned, raiding among the Navajo was carried out to build up flocks and was an activity of the *pobres*—persons who were somewhat worse off in the traditional stratification system. Uchendu has stated that Navajo migrant laborers demonstrate a "complementary" response to the job situation. This "combines traditional economic activities with the new job opportunities in such a way as to achieve not only a higher income level, but maintain their cultural identity" (50). He points out that most migrants are people in what he calls the "primary phase" of the Navajo family cycle.

This phase is created by marriage when a young couple "depends on their respective families for economic support" (51). During this time the Navajo man undergoes a relatively stressful period, since he usually leaves his own family to be with his in-laws and follows the advice and direction of the oldest, active man in the camp. Whatever income he makes is often given to his wife's family until he divorces his wife or gains the respect and perhaps even the leadership of her family. This pattern is very close to what seems to have happened aboriginally and, in itself, does not indicate a destruction of the traditional Navajo way of making a living.

Our point is not that federal policies have always been in the best interests of the Indians or that migrant labor is an inherently good form of work. Rather, our point is this: in traditional communities the various sources of income may be compatible with a more traditional way of life and may, in some cases, support it. As Shepardson and Hammond state:

> Rainbow Plateau meets acculturative stress, especially the threat of absorption into another society, with a normative system in which change is neither valued in itself nor rejected per se. It has a social structure which is sufficiently flexible to permit the incorporation of new action systems as alternates and supplements. Secondly, the particular contact situation has not presented the community with an either/or choice in basic economic orientation. Supplementary systems serve to cushion stress and assist in preserving the structure

which met the functional requisites of Rainbow Plateau as a distinct and self-sufficient system of action (52).

Thus the setting within which the on-reservation Navajo lives includes a spectrum from very traditional, unacculturated communities to communities that are more transitional and that appear to be approaching the off-reservation wage-work community pattern. Let us now consider the off-reservation community in which one of our groups of respondents lived.

A SHORT HISTORY OF FLAGSTAFF

According to Spicer, Spanish domination of Arizona was never as complete as it was in New Mexico (53). Despite several expeditions and numerous attempts at settlement and pacification, the Spaniards and, after them (in the early nineteenth century) the Mexicans, were never able to subdue the Apaches. When the Americans assumed control over Arizona and New Mexico with the treaty of Guadalupe-Hidalgo in 1848, they attempted to keep the Apaches from raiding southward into Mexico. In this the Americans were unsuccessful, and they themselves were soon brought into conflict with the Apaches.

As a result of American westward expansion, particularly after the gold strikes in California in the late 1840s, it became important to open lines of transportation and communication between the East Coast and the West Coast. Numerous surveying parties passed through Arizona searching for the best routes for railroads. The most promising routes were considered to be along the thirty-second or thirty-fifth parallels (54). Flagstaff lies near the thirty-fifth parallel and into this region in the 1850s came several parties of army engineers: in 1851, Lieutenant Sitgreaves and his party; in 1853, Lieutenant Whipple; and in 1858, Lieutenants Ives and Beale in separate expeditions (55).

In 1866 the Atlantic and Pacific railroad was chartered to build along the thirty-fifth parallel. Because of financial troubles, this company was acquired by the Santa Fe railroad in 1890. In 1902 the Atcheson, Topeka and Santa Fe railroad gained control. Despite these financial difficulties, the road was built. Flagstaff was established in 1880 when a sawmill was built to cut ties for the railroad, which reached it in 1882.

Mormon settlement began intensively in northern Arizona in the late 1870s, and John Young, one of Brigham Young's sons, established a fort (Fort Moroni) near what is now Flagstaff in 1882. They were engaged in cutting timber for the railroad and raising cattle. Flagstaff, being at the foot of the San Francisco peaks, is at a high elevation (7000 feet) and is surrounded by Ponderosa pine forests. Lumbering has continued as a major enterprise in the area.

The history of Flagstaff, since then, is typical of the history of the state. Its establishment was a part of the expansion of railroads westward and, as Lamar has pointed out, many of the earlier settlers were primarily interested in gaining riches quickly by exploitation instead of in satisfying a land hunger (56). In southern Arizona, this meant the extraction of valuable minerals, mainly gold and silver. In the north, lumbering and ranching became important. Furthermore, much of the development of Arizona and the rest of the West was not accomplished by rugged, individualistic entrepreneurs, but by individuals heavily financed by eastern interests. No doubt there were many frontiersmen like Bill Williams and Kit Carson, but most of the development of the area was engineered and financed from the outside (57).

Clearly the founding of Flagstaff was dependent on outside capital, especially the railroad. The sawmill that was established to cut most of the railroad ties and to provide lumber for the building of the town was financed by a Chicago businessman. The wealthiest family in town consisted of five brothers from Ohio, three of whom married sisters—the daughters of a Cincinnati millionaire who supported them until their various enterprises became successful (58).

Flagstaff is typical of the entire Mountain West with respect to the pattern that its economic development has taken. In the early period of settlement, extractive industries such as mining, lumber, and cattle were the most important ones. As Arrington has mentioned, their importance has diminished in the course of a century: "From 39 percent dependence on export in 1860 the Mountain West had declined to 13 percent by 1950." According to him, there have been four qualitative changes since 1940 that account for this development:

1. The climate and scenic attractions of the region have now become a major industry. This is particularly true of Nevada, Arizona and New Mexico, where tourism and entertainment have mounted to fantastic heights.

2. There is far less dependence than previously on mining and agriculture. The exhaustion of hitherto productive mines and rising costs of operation, and the mechanization of agriculture and the progress of consolidation into larger farm units, have occasioned a

reduction in the dependence on the traditional staples of Western life.

3. For the first time in its history the Mountain West now has manufacturing on a significant scale. Of particular note are the steel complexes in Utah and Colorado and several missile plants of magnitude.

4. The Mountain West, in a special sense, has been the beneficiary of the enormous outlays for defense of the federal government. These included not only army bases but many factories for defense work (59).

Let us add that the government employed many people not only in defense work but in other federal agencies. For instance, a large percentage of the land in Arizona is national forest, national park, or Indian reservation. The people who administer these various areas are all federal employees.

Finally, the population of the entire Southwest has increased dramatically over the past century, especially during the past 20 years, as has the population of Flagstaff, indicated by the following figures:

1900	1,271
1910	1,663
1920	3,186
1930	3,891
1940	5,080
1950	7,663
1960	18,250
1970	28,000 (estimated)

These statistics are an indication of the rapid growth of Arizona's population: among all states, it ranks first in the growth of manufacturing employment, second in growth of population, first in growth of bank deposits, second in growth of personal income, second in growth of life insurance in force, and first in growth of passenger-car registration from 1956 to 1966 (60).

Tables 2.1 and 2.2 highlight the points of similarity and difference between the Flagstaff area and the rest of Arizona. The data are for the entire county of which Flagstaff is the seat. This county is geographically the second largest in the nation, and Flagstaff contains about 51 percent of the population.

Table 2.1 indicates that Coconino County shows essentially the same em-

Table 2.1 Arizona Employment Profiles Comparing the State to Coconino County (Annual Averages Estimated for 1967)

	State		Coconino County	
	Frequency	Percent	Frequency	Percent
Total nonagricultural wage and salary	443,800	81.14	13,300	87.78
Manufacturing	78,500	14.35	1,500	9.90
Mining and quarrying	13,200	2.41	100	.66
Contract construction	23,300	4.26	850	5.61
Transportation, communication, and public utilities	26,300	4.80	800	5.28
Wholesale and retail trade	102,400	18.72	3,650	24.09
Finance, insurance and real estate	23,000	4.20	300	1.98
Services	73,300	13.40	2,300	15.18
Government	103,800	18.97	3,800	25.08
All other nonagricultural (proprietors, unpaid family workers, and domestics)	65,200	11.92	1,650	10.89
Agricultural	37,900	6.92	200	1.32
Totals	546,900	99.95 *	15,150	99.99 *

Source: Arizona State Employment Service, *Arizona Basic Economic Data*, Research and Information Series No. ECO-2-68, Phoenix, April, 1968, p. 67.
* Does not equal 100 percent because of rounding.

Table 2.2   Coconino County Employment
by Industry (1960 and 1968 Compared)

	1960		1968		Approximate Percent Change
	Fre-quency	Per-cent	Fre-quency	Per-cent	
Total nonagri-cultural wage and salary	12,200	87.76	15,350	85.99	+ 25.8
Manufacturing	1,100	7.91	1,250	7.00	+ 13.6
Mining and quarrying	300	2.15	50	.28	− 83.3
Contract construc-tion	2,400	17.26	950	5.32	− 60.4
Transportation, communication, and public utilities	500	3.59	850	4.76	+ 70.0
Wholesale and retail trade	2,500	17.98	3,325	18.62	+ 33.0
Finance, insurance, and real estate	300	2.15	275	1.54	− 8.3
Services	1,300	9.35	3,350	18.76	+158.0
Government	3,800	27.33	5,300	29.69	+ 39.5
All other non-agricultural (pro-prietors, unpaid family workers, and domestics)	1,500	10.79	2,300	12.88	+ 53.3
Agricultural	200	1.43	200	1.12	0.0
Totals	13,900	99.94 *	17,850	99.97 *	+ 28.4

Source: Arizona State Employment Service, *An Arizona Resource Study, Flagstaff, 1969,* Research and Information Series No. ECO-3-69, Phoenix, May, 1969, p. 15.
* Does not equal 100 percent because of rounding.

49

ployment profile as the rest of the state with a few exceptions: there is less mining and manufacturing in the Flagstaff region than for the state in general, and more people are involved in providing services and in government work than in the rest of the state. Also, there are proportionately fewer agricultural workers than elsewhere.

Table 2.2 compares the employment profile of Coconino County in 1960 with the profile in 1968. Clearly mining and construction have declined, whereas manufacturing, wholesale and retail trade, transportation, communication, public utilities, services, government, and other nonagricultural workers have all increased.

These patterns reflect the overall changes in the Mountain West previously described: increased tourism, declining dependence on extractive industries, increase in manufacturing, and an increasing dependence on government employment. These same patterns also highlight an interesting irony of Southwestern history. Perhaps no place more than the Southwest has been under the spell of the romance of the frontier. With many towns in Arizona settled for less than 100 years, the frontier is still a living memory. However, there are few places in the country that rely as heavily on direct government employment as the Southwest.

As Table 2.1 shows, services provide more employment opportunities in Coconino County than in the rest of Arizona. This is chiefly because the tourist potential in Flagstaff is unparalleled in the state and, conceivably, in the nation. Flagstaff itself is in high pine country at the base of the San Francisco Peaks. It is pleasantly cool in the summer and unpleasantly cold in the winter, although it offers good skiing. It is within an easy drive of the South Rim of the Grand Canyon, Monument Valley, the Hopi and Navajo reservations, the White Mountains, Oak Creek Canyon, many scenic areas on the western end of the Navajo Reservation, and, of course, the Indians themselves are considered as a tourist attraction. It is serviced by an airline and a transcontinental railroad. It is at the junction of a north-south highway leading south through Phoenix and Tucson to Mexico and north to Salt Lake City, and an east-west interstate from Chicago to Los Angeles. The tourist potential has not been overlooked by local developers who count on this as perhaps the major source of expanding revenue in the years to come (61).

This increasing dependence on tourism ties Flagstaff intimately to the national economy because, in a recession, tourism would be one of the first industries to suffer (62). Perhaps serving to balance this, there is a growing reliance on government employment, which is probably less sensitive to fluctuations in the business cycle.

Although we have thus far minimized the importance of the frontiers-
man in the development of the Southwest, these individuals played a role
that should not be neglected. In 1884 the *Arizona Champion,* Flagstaff's
newspaper, wrote that:

> On the 23rd instant, Shadick, a sporting character, called George
> Phelps, a stage driver, out of a saloon and shot him, the victim dying
> instantly. There was a strong threat of lynching, but the prisoner was
> finally lodged safely in jail. A fast woman was the cause.

Commenting on the cowboys around Flagstaff, the newspaper stated:

> They are bragging, whiskey drinking bummers who delight in six-
> shooters, fine horses, saddles and fast women. Their aim in life seems
> to be to have a good time. They delight in disconcerting the eastern
> tenderfoot. Nearly all die with their boots on, and no one mourns
> their death (63).

There was also a major range war southeast of Flagstaff in the 1880s that
resulted in over twenty persons known dead and an unknown number pre-
sumed dead. This was the country and the period about which Zane Grey
wrote, and much of what he wrote was evidently based on fact.

There was never much fighting with the Indians in the Flagstaff area,
but the fear of Apache raids prompted the Mormons to build Fort Moroni.
There was, however, a good deal of apprehension over the Navajos. As already stated, the Navajos do not seem to have been west of the Hopi towns
before their captivity at Fort Sumner in the mid-1860s. It is probable, however, that a number of them moved west to escape Kit Carson. Certainly,
many more of them moved west after their return from Fort Sumner and,
from time to time, they hunted in the area around what was to become
Flagstaff. This caused conflicts with whites as the area was settled and
opened for ranching, and at least one armed conflict resulted in which lives
were lost on both sides (64).

Although accounts differ, one Anglo informant who remembers the
event said that the Navajos feared contacts with the Anglos because of the
violence they thought would result. According to him, the specific armed
conflict was started by some cowboys who found a group of Navajos hunting near Flagstaff. In the ensuing fight, two Navajos and one Anglo were
killed. The leader of the Navajo party was tried for murder in Flagstaff and
was acquitted. The defense tried to obtain a change of venue, contending
that prejudice against the Navajos was so great in Flagstaff that a fair trial
could not be held. The court records indicate that many of the leading citi-

zens of the town testified that this was not true. Aside from this one incident and a few others that did not result in deaths, there seems to have been little overt hostility between the Anglo settlers and the Navajos. Indeed, a symbiotic relationship seems to have developed but, over the years, the Anglos have retained the upper hand.

Adams pointed out that it is through the local Anglo trader that Navajos have gained much of their knowledge of the white world as well as many of the items that have now become important for maintaining themselves (65). This is essentially a relationship based on long-term credit. For most traders, this means that they either must have enough capital to maintain their operations or they must depend on credit extended to them by wholesalers. A number of the sizable off-reservation towns (including Farmington, Gallup, and Flagstaff) have become headquarters for such mercantile companies. The Babbitt Brothers Mercantile Company began in Flagstaff in the early years of the present century. The Babbitts originally had been involved in ranching and had a hardware store. The mercantile company was started later.

The Babbitt company is unusual because it owns or has controlling interest in a number of trading posts on the western end of the reservation. These trading posts seem to have been obtained by extending credit to the trader and then assuming control of the trading post when he could not meet his obligations. According to Adams:

> Entry of the Babbitt company into the Navajo retail field emphasized the growing importance of the mercantile wholesaler in 20th-century Navaho trade. This development has been an inevitable outgrowth of the credit system at the retail level. Since most traders have little in the way of capital reserves they have themselves become heavily dependent upon wholesale credit. The measure of Navaho economic dependence upon the trader is commonly, in modern terms, the measure of the latter's dependence upon his own suppliers. If the trading post is the only institution able to grant long-term unsecured credit to the Navaho individual, the off-reservation general wholesale house is equally the only institution able to carry the trading post on the same terms. The modern Navaho market economy is thus underwritten ultimately by the wholesale house (66).

Until recently, trading posts have had almost a monopoly on the Navajo Reservation because the lack of roads and adequate transportation made it impossible for isolated Navajo families to do their shopping in border towns where prices were lower. Clearly, this has been a lucrative business for the mercantile houses that could absorb the credit risks—as the Babbitt company could—and has meant that a good deal of money has flowed from the reservation to towns like Flagstaff.

In return, of course, the trading posts played an important role in mediating between the Navajos and the dominant society. Although many traders have engaged in questionable practices, they have made it possible for many Navajos to maintain themselves in a more traditional manner than might otherwise have been possible (67). As roads have improved and as more and more Navajos have obtained pickup trucks, it has become easier for families to shop off reservation. However, the trading posts and mercantile companies are still important institutions on the reservation.

Generally, the relationship between the reservation and border towns has, in some ways, been symbiotic. However, the reservation is in many ways a colonial domain whose resources flow outward and are controlled by interests outside the reservation (68). In this respect, the reservation's relation to the off-reservation areas is analogous to the relationship between the Southwest and the East at the beginning of the present century.

Flagstaff is predominantly an Anglo town: 77.2 percent of the population is Anglo; 14.1 percent, Mexican-American; 3.8 percent, Negro; 3.4 percent, Indian; 0.8 percent, other nonwhite; and 0.7 percent is of unknown ethnicity (69). The proportion of Indians in the population has remained constant since the end of World War II. A survey by the Bureau of Indian Affairs in 1953 found that the Indian population was between 3.6 and 4 percent of the total population (70). It is not clear just how many of these people were Navajos, but they appear to have been the majority.

Navajos began doing steady wage work in the 1870s and 1880s on the railroad as it moved west from Fort Wingate near the New Mexico-Arizona border. Since then, they have become increasingly involved in the wage economy as their population grew, but their land base remained fixed and a ceiling was placed on the amount of livestock that could be safely maintained on their ranges. As we shall discuss in Chapter Six, it was the people with less traditional wealth who were forced off first—the *pobres*. In recent decades, increased population and fixed resources have led to an increase in this class. Relatively fewer people can now afford to lead a traditional kind of life.

There have been many recent studies of urban Navajo migrants (71). Generally, they agree that Navajos are the least acculturated of the tribes represented in off-reservation cities; they are the most clannish; they tend most often to return rapidly to the reservation; and they are the least likely to participate in pan-Indian organizations. Elsewhere we have presented the results of a census of Navajo migrants to Flagstaff (72). Let us summarize those results.

Not unexpectedly, most Navajos in Flagstaff are from the western end of the Navajo reservation. This trend is not constant over time, however. Sixty-eight percent of those who had lived in Flagstaff ten years or more came from the western end of the reservation, whereas 80 percent of those who lived in Flagstaff less than ten years came from the western end. Likewise, when we compared those who stayed and those who left Flagstaff over a one-year interval, 66.6 percent of the stayers and 95.9 percent of the leavers were from the nearby western end. This indicates that people from nearby areas use Flagstaff as a place for intermittent, migrant labor and generally have no large investment in staying off reservation.

Since Flagstaff's economy is based primarily on tourism, and since tourism is a seasonal industry, if a Navajo migrant should remain in town for a prolonged period of time, this means that he needs to get a job that is not subject to the fluctuations of the tourist trade. For most Navajos who have been in town 10 years or more, this means a federal government job with civil service protection. In Chapters Four and Five we shall discuss the effects of this filtering mechanism in connection with the group of informants with whom we worked in Flagstaff.

Flagstaff, as we pointed out before, is growing at a very rapid rate. In 1968, 29 percent of the total population had lived there for less than three years (73). Among the Navajos surveyed at the same time, the comparable figure was 41 percent. Similarly, of the 113 Navajo households located in Flagstaff in the summer of 1968, only 61 (54 percent) were still in town a year later. Both of these findings indicate a very rapid turnover rate of the Navajo families living in town.

This rapid turnover probably results from two factors: (1) the opportunities for steady employment in Flagstaff, and (2) the ability of some Navajos to find and keep jobs that will allow them to establish longterm residence in town. Although the opportunity structure is beyond the scope of this book, we think that it is not good for anyone looking for long-term, steady employment unless they find a civil service job. Here, we focus primarily on the variations between individuals on and off reservation to see how the variations affect the style of life and drinking behavior of different people.

To complete the description of the setting within which our research was done we shall give a brief outline of the history of alcohol use in the Southwest in the next chapter. Here, it is appropriate, to recapitulate the major points made in the historical discussion thus far.

1. We have noted that the Hopis satisfy most of Field's criteria for classification as a well organized tribe and we would expect them to be sober in public. Both the White Mountain Apaches and the Navajos adopted agriculture and, as a result, developed a number of Pueblo-like institutions in common. Despite the similarities of their social organizations, however, we have maintained that the Navajos practiced agriculture more intensively than the Apaches, developed more religious forms along Pueblo lines, generally had more intense contacts with the Pueblos, and should, therefore, be placed somewhere between the Apaches and the Hopis on Field's spectrum of social types. We expect, therefore, that both Navajos and Apaches will drink in a manner that conforms to our expectations for loosely organized groups but that the Navajo generally will be less flamboyant and aggressive than the Apache.

2. All three tribes have maintained a core of traditional institutions and values. The Hopis appear to be the least changed of all the Pueblos. The White Mountain Apaches and the Navajos also appear to have escaped intense contact and major changes in social organization and values. Thus we can expect to find traditional attitudes that place positive value on individual prowess and magical power. Our second hypothesis leads us to expect that Navajos and Apaches, to an even greater extent, will neither reject nor deny the mind-altering effects of alcohol.

There is another implication for the methodology of the study, however. Since all of these tribes have been isolated from intense contact with whites, we expect to find a greater emphasis on the persistence of traditional traits than we might have found if we had studied a tribe whose land base had been fragmented by white encroachment, for instance. Thus, although we gain by holding constant the factor of social disorganization or change, we are unable to say definitely what effect social disorganization may have had on drinking behavior if we had held constant the type of social organization and allowed the type of contact experience to vary.

Nevertheless, since the Navajo population interviewed was selected in order to represent both traditional and acculturated individuals, to the extent that drinking behavior varies with level of acculturation we shall be able to comment on the drinking behaviors of the acculturated individuals.

Moreover, if our description of the stratification of Navajo society is correct, we ought to find that definite subpopulations of the Navajos tend to become acculturated earlier than others.

NOTES

1. J. Schoenwetter and A. E. Dittert, Jr., "An Ecological Interpretation of Anasazi Settlement Patterns," *Anthropological Archaeology in the Americas* (Washington, D.C.: The Anthropological Society of Washington, 1968).
2. J. H. Steward, *Theory of Culture Change, the Methodology of Multilinear Evolution* (Urbana: University of Illinois Press, 1955).
3. P. B. Field, "A New Cross-Cultural Study of Drunkenness," in D. J. Pittman and C. R. Snyder, eds., *Society, Culture and Drinking Patterns* (New York: Wiley, Inc., 1962).
4. E. H. Spicer, *Cycles of Conquest* (Tucson: University of Arizona Press, 1962).
5. R. Underhill, *Ceremonial Patterns in the Greater Southwest*, Monograph 13 of the American Ethnological Society (Seattle: University of Washington Press, 1948), p. viii.
6. Ibid, p. viii.
7. Ibid, p. viii.
8. R. Underhill, *The Navajos* (Norman: University of Oklahoma Press, 1965), pp. 51–52.
9. G. A. Reichard, *Navaho Religion, A Study of Symbolism*, Bollingen Foundation, No. XVIII (second edition) (New York: Pantheon Books, 1963), p. 101. For a description of how a Diviner proceeds, see pp. 99–100.
10. K. H. Basso, *Western Apache Witchcraft*, No. 15, Anthropological Papers of the University of Arizona (Tucson: University of Arizona Press, 1969), p. 9.
11. Underhill, *Ceremonial Patterns*, p. 4.
12. B. Kaplan and D. Johnson, "The Social Meaning of Navaho Psychopathology and Psychotherapy," in *Magic, Faith and Healing*, A. Kiev, ed. (New York: The Free Press, 1964), pp. 204–205.
13. J. F. Downs, *Animal Husbandry in Navajo Society and Culture*, University of California Publications in Anthropology, Vol. 1 (Berkeley and Los Angeles: University of California Press, 1964).
14. E. Z. Vogt, "Navaho," in *Perspectives in American Indian Culture*

Change, E. H. Spicer, ed. (Chicago: University of Chicago Press, 1961), p. 306. See also D. F. Aberle, *The Peyote Religion Among the Navaho* (Chicago: Aldine Publishing Co., 1966), p. 200.

15. Underhill, *The Navajos.*

16. J. J. Hester, *Early Navajo Migrations and Acculturation in the Southwest,* Museum of New Mexico Papers in Anthropology, No. 6 (Santa Fe: Museum of New Mexico Press, 1962).

17. J. W. Harshbarger, C. A. Repenning, and J. T. Callahan, "Part IV: The Navajo Country, Arizona-Utah-New Mexico, of the Physical and Economic Foundation of Natural Resources," *Interior and Insular Affairs Committee, House of Representatives, United States Congress,* 1953.

18. R. C. Euler, "Havasupai Ethnohistory," A Report Prepared for Marks and Marks, attorneys, Phoenix, 1960.

19. S. Nagata, *Modern Transformations of Moenkopi Pueblo* (Bloomington: University of Indiana Press, 1970).

20. B. I. Judd, "Tuba City, Mormon Settlement," *The Journal of Arizona History,* 9 (1968): 37–42, p. 38.

21. H. R. Lamar, *The Far Southwest, 1846–1912, A Territorial History* (New Haven: Yale University Press, 1966), p. 409.

22. Downs, *Animal Husbandry in Navajo Society,* p. 97.

23. Vogt, "Navaho," p. 315.

24. Ibid, p. 327.

25. Underhill, *The Navajos,* L. C. Kelly, *The Navajo Indians and Federal Indian Policy, 1900–1935* (Tucson: University of Arizona Press, 1968), pp. 18–19. Downs, *Animal Husbandry in Navajo Society.* D. Aberle, *The Peyote Religion Among the Navaho* (Chicago: Aldine, 1966). C. Kluckhohn and D. C. Leighton, *The Navaho,* R. W. Young, *The Navajo Yearbook* (Window Rock, Arizona: The Navajo Agency, 1961). Collier, *From Every Zenith* (Denver: Sage Books, 1962).

26. Aberle, *Peyote Religion.*

27. Downs, *Animal Husbandry in Navajo Society,* p. 21.

28. R. M. O'Donnell, "Program Design Study for the Navajo Tribe" (Window Rock, Arizona: Harmon, O'Donnell and Hennrige, Associates, Inc., 1968), pp. 12–13.

29. B. J. Taylor, "Indian Manpower Resources: The Experience of Five Southwestern Reservations," *Arizona Law Review,* 10 (1968): 579–596. See also B. J. Taylor and D. J. O'Connor, *Indian Manpower Resources in the Southwest: A Pilot Study,* Bureau of Business and Economic Research, College of Business Administration (Tempe: Arizona State University, 1969).

30. D. F. Aberle, "A Plan for Navajo Economic Development," in *Toward Economic Development for Native American Communities*, a compendium of papers submitted to the subcommittee on Economy in Government of the Joint Economic Committee, Congress of the United States (Washington, D.C.: U.S. Government Printing Office, 1969), p. 245.

31. M. L. Mizen, *Federal Facilities for Indians: Tribal Relations with the Federal Government*, Report to the Committee on Appropriations, United States Senate (Washington, D.C.: U.S. Government Printing Office, 1966), p. 676.

32. Spicer, *Cycles of Conquest*, p. 256.

33. M. W. Everett, "Cooperation in Change? Western Apache Evidence" (paper presented at the Annual Meeting of the Society for Applied Anthropology, Mexico City, April 6–15, 1969), p. 12.

34. Taylor and O'Connor, *Indian Manpower*, p. 31.

35. Basso, *Witchcraft*, p. 20.

36. F. Eggan, *The American Indian: Perspectives for the Study of Culture Change* (Chicago: Aldine, 1966), pp. 122–123.

37. D. F. Aberle, "The Psychosocial Analysis of a Hopi Life-History, in *Personalities and Cultures*, R. Hunt, ed., American Museum Sourcebooks in Anthropology (Garden City, N.Y.: National History Press, 1967). See also F. Eggan, *Social Organization of the Western Pueblos* (Chicago: University of Chicago Press, 1950), especially pages 123–138 for a history of the Hopis using archaeological reconstruction as well as contemporary sources.

38. A. Rubenstein, J. Boyle, C. L. Odoroff, and S. J. Kunitz, "Effect of Improved Sanitary Facilities on Infant Diarrhea in a Hopi Village," *Public Health Reports, 84* (1969): 1093–1097.

39. S. J. Kunitz, J. E. Levy, C. L. Odoroff and J. Bollinger, "The Epidemiology of Alcoholic Cirrhosis in Two Southwestern Indian Tribes," *Quarterly Journal of Studies on Alcohol, 32* (1971): 706–720.

40. F. Eggan, *Social Organization of the Western Pueblos*, p. 138.

41. Ibid, p. 138.

42. J. E. Levy, "The Community Organization of the Western Navajo," *American Anthropologist, 64* (1962): 781–801, p. 781.

43. Ibid, p. 789.

44. W. H. Hodge, *The Albuquerque Navajos*, Anthropological Papers of the University of Arizona, No. 11 (Tucson: University of Arizona Press, 1969), p. 27.

45. J. E. Levy, "Community Organization," pp. 797–798.

46. M. Shepardson and B. Hammond, "Change and Persistence in an Isolated

Navajo Community," *American Anthropologist, 66* (1964): 1029–1050.

47. Ibid, p. 1045.

48. Aberle, "A Plan for Navajo Economic Development," p. 245.

49. Shepardson and Hammond, "Change and Persistence," p. 1037.

50. V. C. Uchendu, *Navajo Harvest Hands: An Ethnographic Report* (Stanford, California: Food Research Institute, Stanford University, February, 1966), p. 5.

51. Ibid, p. 14.

52. Shepardson and Hammond, "Change and Persistence," p. 1049.

53. Spicer, *Cycles of Conquest.*

54. Lamar, *The Far Southwest,* p. 416.

55. R. E. Euler, "An Economic History of Northern Arizona During the Territorial Period, 1863–1912" (Flagstaff, Arizona: M. A. thesis, Arizona State College, 1948).

56. Lamar, *The Far Southwest,* p. 418.

57. W. H. Lyon, "The Corporate Frontier in Arizona," *The Journal of Arizona History, 9* (1968): 1–17.

58. J. G. Babbitt, *The Babbitt Brothers Trading Company* (Flagstaff, Arizona: privately published, 1967).

59. L. J. Arrington, *The Changing Economic Structure of the Mountain West, 1850–1950,* Monograph Series, Vol. X (Logan Utah: Utah State University Press, 1963), pp. 22–23.

60. Valley National Bank, *Arizona Statistical Summary,* Phoenix, 1967, pp. 4–5.

61. H. E. Robison, *Some Economic Implications of the Tourist Industry for Northern Arizona* (Phoenix: Stanford Research Institute, Mountain States Division, 1954), and Welsey and Ham (Planning Consultants and Economic Research Associates) (Flagstaff, Arizona: Flagstaff, Arizona, Planning Reports, 1967).

62. S. J. Kunitz, J. E. Levy, P. Bellet, and T. Collins, "A Census of Flagstaff Navajos," *Plateau, 41* (1969): 156–163.

63. *Arizona Champion* (Flagstaff, Arizona), March 1 and September 20, 1884.

64. G. Hochderffer, *Flagstaff Whoa! The Autobiography of a Western Pioneer* (Flagstaff: Museum of Northern Arizona, 1965).

65. W. Y. Adams, *Shonto: A Study of the Role of the Trader in a Modern Navaho Community,* Bureau of American Ethnology, Bulletin 188 (Washington, D. C.: U. S. Government Printing Office, 1963).

66. Ibid, p. 155.

67. Kluckhohn and Leighton, *The Navaho.*

68. Aberle, "A Plan for Navajo Economic Development."

69. Arizona State Employment Service, *An Arizona Resource Study, Flagstaff, 1969,* p. 18.

70. E. L. Lautzenheiser, S. H. Kerr, and E. J. Lincoln, "Flagstaff and Bellemont, Arizona," in *Indians in Non-Indian Communities* (Window Rock, Arizona: Bureau of Indian Affairs, Welfare Placement Branch, 1953).

71. A partial list includes: W. H. Hodge, *The Albuquerque Navajo;* R. E. Kelly and J. O. Cramer, *American Indians in Small Cities,* Rehabilitation Monograph No. 1 (Flagstaff: Department of Rehabilitation, Northern Arizona University, 1966); H. W. Martin, "Correlates of Adjustment among American Indians in an Urban Environment," *Human Organization, 23* (1964): 290–295; T. D. Graves and M. Van Arsdale, "Values, Expectations and Relocation: The Navaho Migrant to Denver," *Human Organization, 25* (1966): 300–307; J. A. Price, "The Migration and Adaptation of American Indians in the San Francisco Bay Area: Social Interaction and Indian Identity," *Human Organization, 23* (1964): 296–304; T. D. Graves, *The Personal Adjustment of Navajo Indian Migrants to Denver, Colorado, American Anthropologist, 72* (1970): 35–54; R. E. Gardner, "The Role of the Pan-American Church in Urban Indian Life," *Anthropology UCLA, 1* (1969): 14–26.

72. Kunitz, Levy, Bellet, and Collins, "Flagstaff Navajos," and S. J. Kunitz, J. E. Levy and C. L. Odoroff, "A One Year Follow-up of Navajo Migrants to Flagstaff, Arizona," *Plateau, 42* (1970): 92–106.

73. Arizona State Employment Service, *An Arizona Resource Study, Flagstaff, 1969,* p. 20.

Chapter Three

THE USE OF ALCOHOL
IN THE SOUTHWEST

The predominant view of Indian drinking in the Southwest relates the seemingly constant increase in the use of intoxicants to a corresponding intensification of culture contact, social disintegration, and acculturation. When drinking is defined as a response to acculturative stress, tribal differences in alcohol use and fluctuations in the source of supply become incidental to the overall picture of dissolution and despair.

This chapter outlines the initial contacts of the various Indian tribes with alcohol and gives especial attention to the development of drinking among the Navajo. We discuss (1) the availability of intoxicants through the years; (2) the types of drinking behavior displayed by non-Indians, which served as learning models for Indians; (3) Indian responses to the introduction of alcohol (e.g., the degree of acceptance and the reasons for drinking); and (4) the development of characteristically Indian patterns of drinking.

THE DEVELOPMENT OF
AN ADEQUATE SUPPLY

The Aboriginal Period. Generally, the areas in which alcohol was used in precontact times correspond to the areas of agriculture because "the liquors were made primarily from domesticated plants" (1). Although the process varied from place to place, the beverages that were fermented probably had an alcoholic content of 3 to 5 percent. Thus they were really beers or wines instead of liquors.

In the Southwest, alcohol was used from southern Arizona into Mexico. The Pimas and Papagos, living near what is now Tucson, Arizona, used it for ceremonial purposes. The Yumans, Apaches, and Zunis only used it informally and secularly (2). The Western Apaches are thought to have made a cactus beer before their initial contacts with the Spanish, although maize beer diffused northward probably about a century ago (3). In any event, the manufacture of a fermented beer and its secular use was noted as an important problem among the Western Apaches immediately after the establishment of the reservation by early administrators (4).

By contrast, the Hopis, Navajos, and Rio Grande Pueblos probably did not use alcohol prior to its introduction by the Spanish, even though all of these tribes were agriculturalists. We might wonder why the use of alcohol had not spread further north by the time of the Spanish conquest but, here, the pertinent fact is that only one of the three tribes that we studied had used alcohol aboriginally.

The Spanish Period, 1540–1846. According to Brown, the introduction of wine and brandy into the Upper Rio Grande region during the two centuries following the Coronado expedition was a gradual process. The supply was so scarce, in fact, that it was often difficult to fill the needs of the church. Therefore, some of the Pueblos were encouraged to develop the art of vitaculture. In 1776, only about 10 liters of wine were needed annually for church use at the Taos mission (5).

In 1786, Bernardo de Galvez, Viceroy of New Spain, suggested that the trade of "intoxicating liquors" should be encouraged among the Apaches and the "tribes of the North (6)." The intention was to make the warlike Apaches dependent on the Spaniards for a supply of distilled liquors such as brandy and mescal. This practice not only would be a profitable undertaking for the merchants but it would also be a way to lessen Apache hostilities and to make them more amenable to Spanish direction. The degree to which the policy affected the various tribes is not clear. For most of the Apaches, the contacts were degrading and the persons who gathered around the *presidios* ". . . not only became debauched but also to a great extent objects of scorn on the part of the Spaniards (7)."

The policy did not affect the Navajos or the Hopis. The Coyoteros (subsequently known as White Mountain Apaches) remained free of this type of contact. Brown believes it possible that the policy included the Comanches who traded at the Taos Fair (8). If, in fact, distilled beverages were traded at Taos, the Rio Grande Pueblos would certainly have had the opportunity to become acquainted with them, and the Navajos also might have had their initial contact at this time.

There are indications of Navajo participation in the Spanish slave trade prior to the nineteenth century. McNitt states that trade with the Navajos, prior to 1775, is indicated by the skill in speaking Navajo displayed by Pedro Cisneros, a trader who Escalante, in 1776, referred to as *alcade major* of Zuni (9). In 1694, Navajos who had made slave raids into Nebraska traded Pawnee captives to the Spanish (10). Again, in 1699, Navajos were at the Taos Fair with slaves and other goods (11). It appears that Navajos, in small numbers, had an opportunity to trade for alcohol, although the supply was so limited that it did not play a significant role in these early contact experiences.

During the 1820s, a number of related events combined to alter the situation radically. This was the time that Anglo-American traders penetrated the region. The penetration involved (1) an increase in the total amount of trade goods coming into the area, (2) the coming of the "mountain man" or fur trapper, (3) the establishment of Anglo-owned trading forts, (4) the importation of grain whiskey from the United States, and (5) the establishment of Anglo-owned distilleries in New Mexico. These developments resulted directly from a shift in trade policy when Mexico became a sovereign nation in 1821. Prior to that time, Spain had banned American trade from her possessions. The government of Mexico, however, sought to foster good relations and to stimulate commerce with her neighbor to the north.

During the 1820s the slave trade continued. Mexican merchants traded whiskey, guns, tobacco, and knives, to the Navajos and Utes for horses. The horses were traded to the Sevier Valley Paiutes for slaves. This trade cycle was at its peak from 1800 to 1850 (12). A number of Mexican villages and Indian Pueblos were the centers of Mexican trading with the Indians. Taos has already been mentioned. Abiquiu, Cebolleta, and Cubero were important points of trade between Navajos and Mexicans. Jemez and Zuni pueblos became centers of trade with Navajos and other tribes (13). At these pueblos, Navajos mixed with Pueblo Indians in peace and friendship. Zuni became a center of trade with the Western Apaches to the south as well as with Hopis and Navajos. By the 1840s, whiskey had become an important and ubiquitous item in the Indian trade.

Anglo trading forts on the south plains and in Utah were built between

1829 and the late 1830s for the Indian trade and to supply the fur trappers. These "mountain men" also attended the Taos fairs as early as 1821 (14). The trading forts were stocked with the imported American whiskey and Taos "mountain dew," or *aguardiente,* distilled in New Mexico. The Anglo-Americans were fond of whiskey for its effect, but they also relied on it to foster their trading relations with the Indians (15).

The first distillery in New Mexico was established in 1824 near Taos by four Anglo-Americans (16). After that ". . . considerable quantities of whiskey have been made there, particularly in the vicinity of Taos . . ." (17). By the middle of the nineteenth century, "Taos lightning" was well known and well regarded, by some people, as the staple alcoholic beverage of New Mexico.

Just before New Mexico's annexation by the United States, the supply of distilled liquor had become guaranteed, and its use in the Indian trade was ubiquitous. The few descriptions of Indian drinking away from the major trading centers probably resulted from the fact that the Mexican traders who penetrated into Navajo or Apache country were not interested in writing memoirs.

The Anglo-American Period 1847–1970. After the establishment of New Mexico as a territory of the United States, the number of reports of Indian drinking escalated precipitously. It is doubtful that this was a sudden response, on the Indians' part, to the disintegrating effects of the new administration. Very likely it was the result of the administration's attitudes toward the illicit liquor trade with the Indians and the fact that there were special Indian agents who wrote reports directly to Washington.

The Mexican trade patterns, just described, continued under the new territorial government and, actually, these traders dominated the Indian trade until the 1860s (18). The Indian agents tried to eliminate the slave trade and the sale of liquor to Indians. Thus, numerous complaints, made by the agents in Santa Fe, give an idea of the extent of the liquor trade at this time. In 1850 and 1851, agent Calhoun mentioned that the Rio Grande Pueblos purchased whiskey from shops located in the pueblos themselves. He found also that these Indians were moody if one did not give them sugar, coffee, and whiskey (19). The economy of many Mexican settlements depended on getting the Indians drunk (20).

Authorized trade with the Navajos started in 1852. Traders traveled into Navajo country in small parties. By 1883 the Navajos were well supplied with guns by traders in the San Juan area. Permanent trading posts in and adjacent to the Navajo country were not established until 1868 when the Navajos were settled on a reservation. Most licensed traders refrained from selling liquor to the Indians, although there were notable exceptions (21).

Although the whiskey supply had been improving steadily between 1824 and 1870, it was still a high-priced, luxury item. In 1850, a gallon of whiskey sold at wholesale, in Fort Leavenworth, Kansas, for $0.52. It was resold in Santa Fe for $1.53 and was retailed there for $3.50 a gallon. In 1851, straight alcohol sold for 10 to 15 cents a gallon. After a 50 to 75 percent dilution, it could bring from $2 to $4 a pint (22).

After 1870 the westward expansion of the railways brought liquor to the Navajos' doorstep, and a new highly visible era of Navajo drinking was born. By 1881 the Atlantic and Pacific Railroad came through Wingate, New Mexico. The railway construction camps and station towns spawned innumerable saloons that sold whiskey openly to the Indians and to neighboring army units, construction gangs, cowboys, and riffraff. Most of the towns that bordered on the southern part of the Navajo Reservation were railway towns—Grants, Thoreau, Gallup, Holbrook, Winslow, and Flagstaff. The term "drunken railroad Indian" was coined about this time. (From *Indian Traders,* by Frank McNitt. Copyright 1962 by the University of Oklahoma Press) (23). Around 1880, observers reported open drunkenness in these towns from Albuquerque to Gallup as well as in the Mexican settlements. Drunken Navajos were a daily occurrence in San Mateo, Cubero, and other places. One observer said "I don't think I have ever made a trip without seeing drunken Indians" (24).

Also, during this period, there were the first Navajo accounts of their own drinking in the interior of the reservation. In the area between Black Mesa and the San Juan River whiskey was being consumed at Squaw dances between 1871 and 1888. "Lots of drunken men" were reported at Squaw dances near the San Juan in 1892" (25).

By the beginning of the century, bootlegging on the reservation had become a profitable business. In 1884 a Navajo bootlegger was apprehended by agency police and, according to some of our informants, one Navajo who was becoming prominent in the 1900s built up a considerable portion of his wealth by bootlegging. The practice of women bootlegging at Squaw dances is also reported prior to 1910 (26).

A number of our older informants in the western portion of the reservation date their first experiences with alcohol to the period 1890–1920. According to these informants, riders dispatched by wealthy Navajos brought liquor to the reservation from a variety of sources: ranches north of

Flagstaff and south of Winslow and a still run by Mormons north of Lee's Ferry. All of them remarked on the uniformly high price of whiskey, the usual cost being one yearling calf for a gallon of whiskey. At these prices only a rich man could afford to drink, a circumstance that we believe had an important influence on Navajo attitudes toward drinking.

A home brew called *tol'pai* also seems to have been made at this time. It was brewed from corn in the fall and spring and was supposed to have been quite intoxicating. The Franciscan Fathers report that it was already less popular in the eastern portion of the reservation by 1910, although its use as late as 1954 in the Shonto area has been reported by Adams (27).

An elderly Hopi informant maintained that it was the Navajos who introduced the Hopis to alcohol. He recalled Navajos selling bootleg liquor to Hopis near Keams Canyon in 1915 (28). In the same year, the Indian agent at Keams Canyon (Hopi Agency) said: "It must be reported that while the Hopi continues a sober tribe, absolutely opposed to the use of intoxicants, the Navajos of the reservation have been procuring more and more liquor" (29).

By the 1900s the eastern end of the reservation was well acquainted with alcohol. Gallup was the principal supplier and established a reputation for illicit liquor sales and a considerable display of public drunkenness. The off-reservation towns along the San Juan River and the Atlantic and Pacific Railroad differed only in degree, however. In the *McKinley County Republican* (Gallup) of October 5, 1901, five bootleg convictions were listed for a single week. Thirty cases were before the grand jury in Gallup in October, 1913 (30).

By contrast, accounts from the western end of the reservation date the appearance of noticeable drinking on-reservation as late as the 1930s. Although there were fewer Whites in this more isolated portion of the reservation, it is also possible that a generally poor clientele helped to keep down the level of drinking. An elderly Anglo informant, who had lived for many years near Tuba City, maintained that she had not seen any drunken Navajos until around 1917 and, even then, it was so uncommon that she had to be told what was wrong with the man. Another Anglo informant, a trader who had grown up on the western end of the reservation, stated that drinking became more common in the 1930s as a result of stock reduction. It was not the loss of stock that drove people to drink rather this was the first time many people had the cash with which to buy liquor.

It appears that neither the national prohibition, which lasted from 1918 to 1933, nor the depression (1930–1940) had an appreciable effect on the steadily increasing use of alcohol. With respect to prohibition, the Navajos had always been denied the legal use of liquor. Insofar as the depression was concerned, the lessened availability of cash may not have had the same economic results among a people who had never lived in a cash economy. Thus, the shifts toward the use of cash were more directly related to the purchase of alcohol than the depressed prices of sheep during those years. In 1939 the report of the Phelps Stokes Fund states:

> The use of intoxicants by the Navajo Indians is approaching serious social and economic proportions. This has been aggravated by a network of good roads leading to Gallup and other liquor sources. . . . Navajo economy has been changing from barter to cash. Many new and second hand automobiles are being purchased on time payment plans. The Navajo in the interior now has the opportunity to reach liquor sources within a few hours time. Then follows trade, cash in the pocket, purchase of liquor, arrest for intoxication, loss of money and possible venereal complications (31).

The report also states that the major concern of the Navajo police force had shifted to cases involving alcohol, which required most of their effort. In 1873, for instance, Navajo stock thieves were the major concern of the police. In the 1900s the bringing of Navajo children to school took up the energies of police officers. In 1937, however, the majority of arrests made by the Navajo police were for drunkenness or possession of alcohol (32).

The increased availability of cash, the improved network of roads, and the growing experiences of Navajos off reservation during the war years continued until 1953 when Indian prohibition was repealed by President Dwight D. Eisenhower. From then until the present, the economic picture has changed appreciably. Now, even poor Navajos have some cash and the manufacture of cheap, fortified wines has made intoxicating beverages available to all who want it at a very modest price. The reservation road system improves each year, and the number of Navajos who own motor vehicles keeps apace. There is public drinking everywhere, even at ceremonials in the remotest areas. More than 80 percent of on-reservation arrests are made for alcohol-related offenses.

Improved access and enhanced supply have proceeded steadily for almost two centuries, and proportionately more Navajos today not only are exposed to liquor but are able to drink as much as they choose, which was not the case in the past. However, we have no concrete evidence that the effects of drinking are worse now than in the nineteenth century when liquor was called the curse of the tribe, and drunken Navajos were seen in all the off-reservation towns. And it is not clear that drinking has increased primarily in response to "hard times" or periods of desperation and despair. A plausible view is that the Navajos are fond of drinking and that the level of drinking is associated with the accessibility of alcohol itself.

LEARNING MODELS

In the same way that the newly acquired techniques of equestrianism had to be learned, it is possible that various Indian tribes observed and emulated the drinking behaviors of the whites who introduced them to the use of alcohol. In fact, MacAndrew and Edgerton devote a considerable portion of their book, *Drunken Comportment,* to this aspect of Indian drinking (33).

For those tribes who did not have a knowledge of alcohol, the first contact with it produced a variety of reactions ranging from distaste to euphoria to stuporousness. During the early years of contact with alcohol, the untoward effects, that is, violence and the lowering of inhibitions, were only infrequently seen. In a relatively few years, however, a more uniform pattern of Indian drinking emerged, one that included group orgies, drinking to stuporousness, boisterousness, aggressiveness, sexual promiscuity, and violence. MacAndrew and Edgerton maintain that this form of drunken comportment was modeled after white drinking behavior. The early descriptions of drinking by troops, trappers, and traders coincide with descriptions of Indian drinking of the debauched or orgiastic type. MacAndrew and Edgerton conclude:

> Thus, across a continent, the Indian observed the dramatic transformation that alcohol seemed to produce in the white man; and reaching into his repertoire of available explanations, he concluded, as the historian A. G. Bailey put it, that "Brandy was the embodiment, or was the medium through which an evil supernatural agent worked." Thus it was that the Indian came to see that changes-for-the-worse were to be expected during drunkenness, for at such times the drinker was temporarily inhabited by an evil supernatural agent. And from this, the Indian reached the entirely reasonable conclusion that since he was thus "possessed," his actions when drunk were not his own and he was not responsible for them. After all, the Indians' precontact cultures already contained an ample array of *time out* ceremonies and supernatural agents (e.g. witchcraft, dreams, spirit possession, etc.) under whose "influence" a man became less than strictly responsible for his

actions. What is more, the notion that the state of drunkenness was excusing of those transgressions committed while "under the influence" was entirely consonant with the model the white man provided, for in regard to his own drunken transgressions and those of his fellows, the white man, too, ignored much and forgave still more on the grounds that when drunk one is "under the influence." In sum, so vivid were the examples of drunken mayhem and so well did such changes-for-the-worse mesh with precontact notions that it is difficult to imagine how a consciously conceived program for instruction about alcohol's "influence" on conduct could possibly have improved on the "lesson plan" that the Indians' white tutors provided (34).

We do not know exactly how the Spanish and Mexicans drank in New Mexico and, although we have good descriptions of trappers' drinking habits, we do not know how many Navajos were afforded the opportunity to observe the frontier prototype of drunken comportment. Nevertheless, the trappers' annual rendezvous at a trading fort became established in northern New Mexico, Colorado, and Utah after the 1820s. A report of this behavior, as seen in 1833–1834 in Fort Hall, Idaho, is typical.

> The consequence was a scene of rioting, noise, and fighting during the whole day; some became so drunk that their senses fled entirely, and they were therefore harmless; but by far the greater number were just sufficiently under the influence of the vile trash, to render them in their conduct disgusting and tiger-like. We had gouging, biting, fisticuffing and "stomping" in the most "scientific" perfection; some even fired guns and pistols at each other, but these weapons were mostly harmless in the unsteady hand which employed them. Such scenes I hope never to witness again . . . (35).

Similar debauches were reported from such forts as Fort Wintey, near Navajo country, in 1842 (36). Here Canadians, Spaniards and Indians were together. Nor was the drinking behavior of the U.S. Army significantly better (37).

This type of drinking did not change much after 1880 when railway towns became the center of attention. Troops, cowboys, construction workers, and assorted outlaws would turn towns such as Coolidge, New Mexico into an indescribable bedlam.

> Troops of Fort Wingate, fourteen miles distant, mingled with the Indians, ranchers and cowboys, found their fun instead in the saloons of Coolidge. Of these . . . there were fourteen. . . . Outlaws and drun-

ken Navajos purchased intoxicants openly. Eventually a series of killings terminated in the execution of seven outlaws. (From *Indian
Traders* by Frank McNitt. Copyright 1962 by the University of Oklahoma Press) (38).

Upon one occasion, the town's justice of the peace sent off a "frantic in-
coherent wire for help to the officers at Wingate." (From *Indian Traders* by
Frank McNitt. Copyright 1962 by the University of Oklahoma Press) (39).

Desperadoes had taken over the town, stolen a wagonload of beer
from the railroad company, and paralysed any semblance of civil law.
It seems that when Wingate troops were not engaged in tearing Coolidge apart, they were being summoned there to keep others from
doing the same thing. . . . The Atlantic and Pacific threatened to recall "the whole construction gang of several hundred men" and to
level the town unless the stolen barrels of beer were returned. (From
Indian Traders by Frank McNitt. Copyright 1962 by the University of
Oklahoma Press) (40).

Add to these group scenes the descriptions of traders who were heavy
drinkers on the reservation and it becomes apparent that the Navajos were
observing a world quite unknown to the contemporary white, middle class
observer.

The opportunity to observe and emulate milder forms of drinking did
not present itself to a significant number of Navajos until World War II
when many young Navajo men and women interacted with a variety of
Anglos in the armed services and in defense factories. Nevertheless, the pattern of heavy drinking by on-reservation Anglos has persisted. In addition
to the drinking of traders, there was drinking by federal employees and anthropologists. Indeed, one of our Anglo informants remarked that many
Anglos working on the reservation felt that the only way to have a good
time was to get drunk. Especially in remote areas, many people would buy
liquor from the Navajos' or sell it to them. When Anglo drinking companions were lacking, these people would also drink with the Navajos. This
same informant told us stories of alcoholic traders and an entire trading
family being decimated by alcoholism. Similar stories concerning federal
employees can be added from our own experiences. Older anthropologists
have described their own summer drinking patterns while doing archeolog-
ical field work on the reservation during the 1930s. In all instances, Navajo employees have had the opportunity to observe the behavior and to
compare it with the public statements concerning drinking.

On the other hand, of course, there were many government employees, traders, and missionaries who were total abstainers. It appears that well into the present century, the Navajos were presented with an either-or model of behavior in regard to the use of intoxicants. Although more moderate models have been learned subsequently, many of the earlier patterns persist with some frequency and visibility on the reservation today. It was not surprising that current patterns described by on-reservation informants involve either a considerable amount of heavy drinking or none at all.

NAVAJO RESPONSES

Although the Indians' response to a first taste of liquor and to the displays of white drunkenness was usually one of dismay, several things caused them to persevere until drinking in the white mode had become institutionalized. Initially, of course, is the fact that a number of individuals found the first experience pleasurable and therefore were induced to drink again. Second, it soon became clear that the white man insisted on his Indian clients drinking. It has often been observed that the Indian trade relied on the free flow of alcohol. Without it, the Indian was all too likely to drive a hard bargain. Thus, a major contact point with whites required the use of alcohol and the Indian, desirous of the benefits of trade, was not fully free to withdraw. Finally, the effects of alcohol were often consonant with a number of features within the precontact cultures themselves (41).

We have already mentioned that the Navajos, despite a degree of Puebloization at the time of initial white contact, still retain much of the general Apachean tradition oriented to individual powers and the possession of magical power. They are—to use Ruth Benedict's notion—still more Dionysian than Appollonian:

> The basic contrast between the Pueblos and the other cultures of North America is the contrast that is named and described by Nietzsche in his studies of Greek tragedy. He discusses two diametrically opposed ways of arriving at the values of existence. The Dionysian pursues them through "the annihilation of the ordinary bounds and limits of existence"; he seeks to attain in his most valued moments escape from the boundaries imposed upon him by his five senses, to break through into another order of experience. The desire of the Dionysian, in personal experience or in ritual, is to press through it toward a certain psychological state, to achieve excess. The closest analogy to the emotions he seeks is drunkenness, and he values the il-

luminations of frenzy. With Blake, he believes "the path of excess leads to the palace of wisdom." The Appollonian distrusts all this, and has often little idea of the nature of such experiences. He finds means to outlaw them from his conscious life. He "knows but one law, measure in the Hellenic sense." He keeps the middle of the road, stays within the known map, does not meddle with disruptive psychological states. In Nietzsche's fine phrase, even in the exaltation of the dance he "remains what he is, and retains his civic name" (42).

To the extent that a society may be called Dionysian, the mind-altering effects of alcohol might be positively valued as many North American tribes have valued the effects of datura, peyote, and a variety of native tobaccos. The attainment of dream and vision states is facilitated and thereby the attainment of supernatural power. It is not clear, however, to what extent Dionysian values and orientations persist among the Navajos. On the one hand, the prowess of the individual on the raid and in the hunt and, later, in the dispersed settlement patterns of the pastoralist persisted into contact times. Also the use of trance states and the power to "see" have persisted in attenuated form in the role of the hand trembler or diagnostician. On the other hand, years of contact with the Appollonian Pueblos led to the adoption of agriculture, a matrilineal clan system, and a reorientation of the religious institutions away from the shamanistic and toward the priestly. Navajo value statements classify all states of excess (*tsi'ndida*) as forms of sickness not to be desired. Nevertheless, Kaplan and Johnson suspect that many of the individualistic, Dionysian value orientations persist on a covert level (43).

It is interesting that among the earliest Navajo drinkers mentioned by name, there are two of the highest ranking chiefs of the early reservation period: Manuelito and Ganado Mucho. The fact that men of high status drank conforms to the notion that drunkenness was a desirable state as well as a boost to the illicit liquor trade. The fact that some have also interpreted drunkenness as indicating the extreme despair felt by prominent chiefs after the establishment of the reservation must also be taken into account. And the fact that Manuelito and Ganado Mucho drank is attested to by their own statement complaining of agent Eastlake (44).

Ganado Mucho, insofar as may be ascertained, never became a heavy drinker. Manuelito, however, drank steadily and became a problem drinker by 1873 at approximately 50 years of age (45). According to Underhill, Manuelito was frequently in the guardhouse for drinking and died there, presumably from drink, in 1884 (46). Underhill adopts a retreatist explanation, believing that Manuelito drank during a period of great stress and in response to a disappointment at not being employed on the Navajo police force after 1873 (47).

According to other sources, Manuelito did not die in 1884 but was deposed as head chief by agent Riordan for possession of slaves and for drinking. It would appear that he died in 1893 at approximately 73 years of age from measles, complicated by pneumonia after treatments in the sweathouse and perhaps the liberal use of whiskey (48). The fact that Manuelito's followers were reported to have sold their sheep for whiskey further detracts from the very personal interpretation given by Underhill and lends credence to the idea that drinking was the proper thing to do for people who could afford it.

We gathered from our own informants many statements concerning the positive side of alcohol use. All informants emphasized the prestige status of whiskey. Only the *rico* could afford to drink, and as youths they always desired to emulate their social betters and ultimately to achieve wealth themselves.

The fact that alcohol facilitated conviviality in social settings was mentioned by almost all informants. It seemed to be a desirable state among a widely dispersed pastoral people who could get together socially only infrequently. Several men mentioned that when they drank with other males, alcohol promoted a feeling of solidarity; and this gave the individual a sense of power and fearlessness.

A number of informants mentioned that alcohol made them better speakers in public gatherings and that many Navajo politicians would drink before addressing large audiences. One of the desired qualities of a Navajo leader is that he be able to speak well and persuasively. The Navajo word for leader, *naat'aani,* means speaker or exhorter, and the initiation ceremony for a leader involved the anointment of his lips with pollen from the four sacred mountains to enable him to make "powerful speeches" (49).

The association of alcohol with ceremonialism and supernatural power was never made directly by informants. It was mentioned tangentially in a number of ways, however. Alcohol is frequently mentioned in association with peyote. Although they have similar effects, peyote is considered as constructive and a medicine. Alcohol, by contrast, is said to have only illusory benefits and cannot heal the body. The opposition between the two suggests the need to deny alcohol a ceremonial status. A ceremonialist once told us (Levy) that he could pray and perform his chants more effectively when he had something to drink. And an informant related how a cere-monialist had once asked him to drink at a healing ceremony so that he could "devote" his songs. In this context, the references appear to refer, even if vaguely, to some facilitation of supernatural power.

Reasons for drinking that may be labeled retreatist were also mentioned frequently. Informants said that with drunkenness their troubles "fell away," that they "forgot their cares," and that they became less shy and constrained. The bad effects of alcohol (social, physical, and economic) were mentioned frequently, but as generalities, and always referred to the after effects and not to the intoxicated state.

The Navajos are midway between the Appollonian and Dionysian poles in their attitudes toward drink and in their social organization. This lack of a clear "official" attitude has been mentioned by several authors. The Fran-ciscan Fathers, in 1910, note that the Navajos are "very fond" of whiskey and purchase it at almost any price. Furthermore, they state: "Ordinarily, a drunken person is not abused or molested and no disgrace seems to attach to habitual drunkenness. . . . Offenses given in drunkenness are not taken seriously as a rule and damages done are repaired or paid with admirable equanimity" (50).

At the present time, tribal law prohibits the use and possession of alco-hol on the reservation, although there is a growing debate over the possi-bility of repealing these laws. Stated Navajo opinion is also varied and di-vided. It is probable that, as Navajos adjust more to the prevailing modes of Anglo drinking, the diversity in attitudes will grow. It is also conceiv-able that the Navajos are undergoing a reevaluation of their own drinking habits much as the Anglos did in the years after prohibition. We should not overlook, however, the fact that many statements concerning the na-ture of alcohol may be simply repetitions of what Anglos have been heard to say on the matter and do not reflect deep inner convictions. There is also considerable resentment of what is thought to be hypocritical behavior on the part of the white man. The Navajos are quick to perceive that the very people who drink are quite likely to be the people who preach against the evils of Indian drinking. Although Indians are prosecuted regularly for li-quor violations on reservation, whites generally are not. Some Anglos who are known to be steady drinkers have been in a position to fire Navajos or to deny them jobs without themselves suffering any of the legal conse-quences of their violations of tribal laws or civil service regulations. Thus, if there were any ambivalence of attitudes toward drinking in the past, it has only increased during recent years.

The present-day role of economics in the furtherance of Indian drinking is difficult to assess. We have already noted that the early Indian trade relied on alcohol to a large extent, and that during the early years of the reservation, many small non-Indian communities relied on the illicit sale of liquor to the Indians of the southwest for a sizable portion of their livelihood. At the present time it is unlikely that any sizable segment of the Anglo economy is dependent on the Indian liquor trade for its success. At the same time, however, the reluctance of liquor dealers and law enforcement agencies to change their practices vis à vis the Indian drinker is worthy of comment. Local law enforcement agencies are underbudgeted and rely, to some extent, on the labor and fines of arrested drunks for revenue. Liquor dealers who depend on the seasonal influx of tourists also say that the Indian customer is important during powwow time. It is interesting to speculate what the economic and social ramifications would be if the Navajos were to become teetotalers overnight. They would then be able to compete more effectively for jobs in an area where employment is scarce and depends largely on tourism and recreation. Although much research remains to be done on the economics of Indian drinking, it is our opinion that Anglo practices are generally less based on economic necessity than on a reliance upon older stereotypes of the drunken Indian as a means to keep the Indian in an inferior status unworthy of budget outlays or social attention.

——— OBSERVABLE PATTERNS OF DRINKING ———

Most studies of Indian drinking and perhaps all of our ideas of the Indian as a drinker are based on the observed drinking behaviors that occur primarily in public places. Thus, the correlation of social integration with drinking, mentioned earlier, has been based on estimating the level of public drunkenness in various cultures and their differing characteristics. Today the public drinking behaviors of the Navajo are at a considerable variance with the accepted forms of drinking in the dominant white society.

Male, Peer Group Binge Drinking. The most commonly observed and commented upon style of Navajo drinking is that undertaken in public places by groups of males of approximately the same age (51). Frequently it takes the form of a binge where large quantities of liquor and, more recently, wine are consumed as rapidly as possible. The drinking continues until the participants pass out or the supply is exhausted. In the off-reservation setting, this takes place in and about bars, in back alleys, vacant lots and in fields. On the reservation it is most easily observed at large public gatherings: rodeos, in the public parts of such healing ceremonies as the Enemy Way (Squaw dance), Night Way (*Yei be chai* dance) and the Mountain Top Way (Fire dance). It may also be observed behind the trading posts immediately adjacent to the reservation where liquor is sold legally. One of us (Levy) has also identified a few "favorite" drinking spots far from habitation where group drinking may proceed undisturbed by neighbors or the police. At one of these, a six-foot high pyramid of empty wine bottles had been carefully constructed over a period of time, forming a commemorative edifice.

In many respects, this form of drinking is analogous to the group drinking seen on skid rows. The consumption of inexpensive, fortified wine and a general sharing of the supply make it possible for the young, less-wealthy Navajo to be assured of a chance to drink even when he does not have much ready cash. He is expected to contribute more generously at a later date. Arguments and fights sometimes occur, but the damage is rarely serious and murderous behavior generally does not take place in this setting (52). When women are present, as is frequently the case at ceremonials and in the vicinity of bars and trading posts, men may pursue them and fights are likely to break out between spouses.

This form of drinking was recorded early in the reservation period as occurring in railway towns and at Squaw dances on the reservation. Referring to the period between 1871 and 1888 in the area around Kayenta, Dyk's Navajo informant describes how a group of peers could exert pressure on an abstainer:

> My friends would come around with whiskey and would try to make me drink. They would try to pour it down my throat but I would let it run out onto the ground (53).

A number of our younger Navajo friends tell how difficult it is to resist the blandishments of drinking companions at the present time.

Most of the men, in the groups given interviews, drink in this manner part of the time. It is easy to see parallels with the male war or raiding party for which magical power, a sense of solidarity, and fearlessness are prerequisites for success. Early Navajo trading expeditions were also composed almost exclusively of males. One may easily conceive of the peer group as forming the first and most enduring setting for drinking among the Navajo.

Nevertheless, it must be recognized that there are several contemporary conditions that keep the pattern alive. It is still the male who does the most traveling away from home. Groups of men travel together to other states on seasonal wage-work jobs. They run into each other when in off-reservation towns. They form groups while serving together in the armed forces and groups of friends just travel from Squaw dance to Squaw dance together. The continuation of the on-reservation prohibition statutes also appears to foster the practice of drinking in back alleys and other isolated places. The liquor supply must be consumed before returning to the reservation.

Family and Extended Kin Group Parties. Drinking in the home is a practice less easily observed by the white investigator. Nevertheless, many of our traditional informants reported that they started drinking in this context. Although not explicitly reported during the early years of the reservation, it was probably one of the forms of drinking indulged in by the *ricos* and their followers. Our descriptions, obtained from middle-aged traditional informants, date from the beginning of this century. Thus, we think it is an older pattern than published descriptions indicate, and we also believe that it is associated with wealth and the economics of bootlegging prior to the 1930s.

The poor Navajo was unable to pay bootleg prices and was, therefore, dependent on the generosity of others. When away from home, he could expect to be given drinks by groups of friends, or he could contribute his pittance toward the purchase of a common bottle. The *rico,* by contrast, was able to send a relative or retainer off reservation to purchase whiskey and to bring it back to the camp.

One of our middle-aged informants recalled having worked for such a *rico* as a young man. Whiskey was brought in from near Flagstaff, Winslow, or Utah on horseback. The *rico* would then dole it out, a cup at a time, to his workers somewhat in the nature of a reward for services. A "party" might take place later that night in the old man's hogan. Grandchildren of this rich old man recall that even his wives drank heavily on these occasions. The children would experiment with what was left in the jugs after the adults had passed out.

In later years, bootleggers would make regular deliveries to the more wealthy families who could be counted on to purchase with some regularity. This pattern of family drinking persists to the present time. Recently, however, it has become both more widespread and more visible. With the coming of roads and the shift to a cash economy, more married couples are able to travel and drink together in public settings both on and off reservation. Thus, what has been interpreted as a recent growth of drinking by women probably had roots in the late nineteenth century.

Individual Drinkers. Although there are more individual heavy drinkers today then previously, it is doubtful whether there are proportionately more of them. In most instances the chronic drinker, if male, started drinking in the peer group or the family context and only in his later years emerged as a man who was unable to stop drinking. This is considered to be deviant behavior, even though there is little penalty. The chronic female drinker is an even rarer phenomenon, but is far more conspicuous. These individuals are most often social isolates and are labeled as deviants by the community.

Off-Reservation Patterns. The observation of off-reservation drinking behavior is complicated by the difficulty in distinguishing between long-term town dwellers, urban transients, and casual visitors from the reservation. In Gallup, where public drinking is impressive, there is a distinction between the behavior of the educated, steadily employed Navajos and that of the less acculturated Navajo. Education and steady employment, especially of the white-collar variety, are associated with lower middle-class Anglo drinking patterns. Navajos in governmental and tribal employ may be found drinking decorously in cocktail lounges and in the bars of several popular motels. Even less conspicuous, however, are the many Navajos employed in Gallup who may drink a few beers in a bar or take home a six-pack after work to watch television in the evening.

In Flagstaff, with a smaller Navajo population and farther from on-reservation settlements of any size, the Navajos who drink in public places in the Anglo mode are so few that they are unnoticed. The majority of Navajos, who are long-term residents of the city who drink, tend to drink at home. The drinking in public is done by the visitors from the reservation or by persons living in town for short periods of time. Thus, the observable, and hence the commented upon form of Navajo drinking, is the form that we have already described as peer group drinking. Reservation-style drinking is also prominently displayed at the Gallup Indian Ceremonial and the Flagstaff Fourth of July Powwow.

Because public drinking on reservation is dispersed over large areas while that in town is concentrated about the bars or powwow grounds, the Anglo gains the impression that town dwellers are more involved with alcohol than reservation dwellers. The observer, impressed with the magnitude of the urban drinking scene, is inclined to attribute it to the effects of acculturation and town life itself.

Without disputing the fact that many individuals may drink from despair, we have suggested in this chapter that a number of other factors have been involved in shaping the Navajo drinking practices of today. We have noted that the state of intoxication was not incompatible with value orientations of early Navajo culture and that a number of desirable effects of drinking are mentioned by informants at the present time. We also noted that the economics of supply and demand make liquor a prestige item, thus providing a considerable impetus for the average Navajo to drink as soon as the shift to a cash economy and a change in the off-reservation liquor laws made cheap intoxicants available. We have also explored the earlier modes of Anglo drinking, which were prevalent during the periods when Navajos were learning how to drink. We have suggested that Navajos only recently have been exposed to the contemporary "acceptable" forms of drinking of the American middle class. Finally, we have suggested that it is difficult for the anthropological investigator to observe the broad range of drinking behaviors with any degree of accuracy and that it is almost impossible to make quantitative statements based on observations of general public drinking. In the succeeding chapters we shall give the results of research that measures the overall levels of drinking and compares the total drinking patterns of several contrasting Navajo populations.

NOTES

1. H. E. Driver, *Indians of North America* (Chicago: University of Chicago Press, 1961), p. 93.
2. Ibid, p. 97.
3. Ibid, pp. 96–97.
4. J. P. Clum, "The San Carlos Apache Police," *New Mexico Historical Re-*

view, 4 (1929): 203–219. General N. A. Miles, *Personal Recollections and Observations* (Chicago: Werner Co., 1896), pp. 534 and passim.

5.   D. N. Brown, "A Study of Heavy Drinking at Taos Pueblo," mimeographed (Department of Anthropology, University of Arizona, 1965), pp. 2–3.

6.   Ibid, p. 3.

7.   E. H. Spicer, *Cycles of Conquest* (Tucson: University of Arizona Press, 1962), p. 243.

8.   Brown, "Heavy Drinking," p. 4.

9.   F. McNitt, *The Indian Traders* (Norman: University of Oklahoma Press, 1962), p. 8.

10.   R. Underhill, *The Navajos* (Norman: University of Oklahoma Press, 1965), p. 55.

11.   Ibid, p. 56.

12.   McNitt, *Indians Traders,* p. 17.

13.   L. R. Bailey, *The Long Walk: A History of the Navajo Wars, 1846–68* (Los Angeles: Westernlore Press, 1964), pp. 26, 46, 58n. McNitt, *Indian Traders,* p. 53.

14.   McNitt, *Indian Traders,* pp. 13, 22–3, 26.

15.   Ibid, pp. 22–23, 37, 40.

16.   Brown, "Heavy Drinking," p. 5.

17.   J. Gregg, *Commerce of the Prairies,* M. L. Moorehead, ed. (Norman: University of Oklahoma Press, 1954) (first published in 1845), p. 273.

18.   McNitt, *Indian Traders,* p. 227.

19.   Brown, "Heavy Drinking," p. 6; McNitt, *Indian Traders,* p. 52.

20.   McNitt, *Indian Traders,* p. 53.

21.   Ibid, pp. 45, 48, 53.

22.   Ibid, p. 52.

23.   Ibid, pp. 231, 234.

24.   F. Reeve, "The Government and the Navajo, 1878–1883," *The New Mexico Historical Review,* 16 (1941): 278.

25.   W. Dyk, *A Navajo Autobiography,* Viking Fund Publications in Anthropology, n. 8 (1947), pp. 19, 45.

26.   McNitt, *Indian Traders,* p. 54; Franciscan Fathers, *Ethnological Dictionary of the Navajo Language* (St. Michaels, Arizona: The Franciscan Fathers, 1910), p. 217.

27.   W. Y. Adams, *Shonto: A Study of the Role of the Trader in a Modern Navajo Community,* Smithsonian Institution, Bureau of American Ethnol-

ogy, Bulletin No. 188 (1963), p. 76; Franciscan Fathers, *Navajo Dictionary*, p. 217.

28. R. A. Black, personal communication, August, 1969.

29. L. Crane, "Narrative Section of the Annual Report for the Moqui Indian Reservation" (U.S. Department of Interior, Indian Service, 1915).

30. McNitt, *Indian Traders*, p. 54.

31. Phelps Stokes Fund, *The Navajo Indian Problem* (New York: Phelps Stokes Fund, 1939), pp. 79–80.

32. Ibid, pp. 76, 79.

33. C. MacAndrew and R. B. Edgerton, *Drunken Comportment: A Social Explanation* (Chicago: Aldine, 1969).

34. Ibid, pp. 148–149.

35. Ibid, p. 146.

36. McNitt, *Indian Traders*, pp. 22–23.

37. MacAndrew and Edgerton, *Drunken Comportment*, pp. 146–147.

38. McNitt, *Indian Traders*, p. 232. At that time Coolidge had a population of one hundred persons.

39. Ibid, p. 232.

40. Ibid, p. 232.

41. MacAndrew and Edgerton, *Drunken Comportment*, pp. 148–149.

42. R. Benedict, *Patterns of Culture* (New York: Houghton Mifflin, Sentry Edition, 1961), pp. 78–79.

43. B. Kaplan and D. Johnson, "The Social Meaning of Navajo Psychopathology and Psychotherapy," in *Magic, Faith and Healing*, A. Kiev, ed. (New York: The Free Press, 1964), pp. 204–205.

44. Letter from agent Riordan quoted in McNitt, *Indian Traders*, p. 60.

45. Underhill, *The Navajos*, p. 162.

46. Ibid, p. 163.

47. Ibid, p. 162.

48. R. VanValkenburgh quoted in McNitt, *Indian Traders*, p. 203, n. 5. R. VanValkenburgh, "Navajo Naat'aani," *The Kiva*, 13 (1948): 14–23, p. 17.

49. L. Wyman and C. Kluckhohn, *Navajo Classification of Their Song Ceremonials*, American Anthropological Association Memoir 50 (1938), p. 5. VanValkenburgh, "Navajo Naat'aani," p. 14.

50. Franciscan Fathers, *Navajo Dictionary*, pp. 217, 439.

51. R. J. Savard, "Effects of Disulfiram Therapy on Relationships within the Navajo Drinking Group," *Quarterly Journal of Studies on Alcohol, 29*

(1968): 909–916. F. N. Ferguson, "The Peer Group and Navajo Problem Drinking," Abstracts of papers of the American Anthropological Association, 64th Annual Meeting, 1965. F. N. Ferguson, "Navajo Drinking: Some Tentative Hypotheses," *Human Organization, 27* (1968): 159–167.

52. J. E. Levy, S. J. Kunitz and M. Everett, "Navajo Criminal Homicide," *Southwestern Journal of Anthropology, 25* (1969): 124–152. D. B. Heath, "Prohibition and Post-Repeal Drinking Patterns among the Navajo," *Quarterly Journal of Studies on Alcohol, 25* (1964): 119–135. C. Kluckhohn, *Navaho Witchcraft* (Boston: Beacon Press, 1957), p. 94.

53. Dyk, *Navajo Autobiography,* p. 19.

Part Two

THE RESEARCH

Chapter Four

METHODOLOGY

This and succeeding chapters present the research that comprises the major portion of the study. This research is of two types: (1) several record studies, designed to provide epidemiological and historical data for the Navajo, Hopi, and White Mountain Apache tribes, and (2) an investigation of four groups of Navajos that relates varying patterns of drinking to the different levels of acculturation exhibited by the four groups.

The record surveys deal with whole tribal populations and seek to explain the variations in rates of drinking, homicide, and suicide between the three tribes. These studies had three objectives:

1. To test some common notions about the relationship between the major social pathologies and different social types as well as levels of acculturational stress.
2. To place the Navajo tribe in a comparative framework with some other tribes in the Southwest.
3. To provide a background against which the smaller Navajo groups could be viewed in order to determine their representativeness of larger segments of the Navajo population.

The second study involves a series of interviews administered to four groups of Navajos. These populations range from acculturated town dwellers to traditional pastoralists. Drinking histories, descriptions of drinking episodes, medical and social problems due to drinking, and the results of several attitudinal questionnaires are utilized to determine the nature of drinking in these groups and to test the notion that the extent and type of drinking varies with acculturational level.

The results of the comparative record surveys are given in Chapter Five. Those of the interview study are given in Chapters Six and Seven.

-------------------------- METHODOLOGY OF THE --------------------------
RECORD SURVEYS

Three major social pathologies (homicide, suicide, and alcoholic [Laennec's] cirrhosis) were studied by reviewing tribal police records, U.S. Public Health Service records, and state death certificates. We wished to establish mortality rates and the patterning of these pathologies by age, sex, residence, marital status, age of onset, and age at time of death. In the case of homicide and suicide, we were also interested in motive, surrounding circumstances, and the association with alcohol.

There were considerable problems concerning the reliability of reporting and the interpretation of findings that involved low-frequency occurrences in small populations. Since each study has been published elsewhere, we shall not explain in detail how these problems were handled for each tribe. Instead, we shall mention the appropriate publication when necessary. Here we will briefly review the sources of the data.

Public Health Service Records. Indians have received some federal health services since the early years of the nineteenth century when, on occasion, army surgeons undertook to treat them. From 1849, when the Bureau of Indian Affairs was transferred to the Department of the Interior, until 1955 health services were administered by the Bureau. In 1955 health care became the responsibility of the U.S. Public Health Service. Over the past 15 years, the services to Indians have increased through the expansion of existing facilities, the creation of new facilities, and a rise in available manpower. Thus the surveillance and reporting of various diseases have improved, particularly those requiring hospitalization.

Records of hospital admissions and their diagnoses are filed in central Area Offices. Because these health services are free of charge, most Indians (even when admitted to private hospitals) are ultimately transferred to Public Health Service (P.H.S.) hospitals when they suffer from such serious ailments as cirrhosis of the liver. The incidence of, and deaths from, all forms of cirrhosis occurring among the three tribes were reviewed from all P.H.S. hospitals, both on and off reservation, serving the areas in which the people lived. The death rates for the three tribes were computed for a three-year period 1965–1967. Apache and Hopi deaths were checked against state death certificates. A 10-year period, 1956–1965, was added to the Hopi cirrhosis population to gather added demographic data on these patients (1).

Although levels of cirrhosis reveal nothing about drinking patterns, they indicate, to a large degree, the extent of steady excessive drinking in a population. It is one of the few gauges of drinking that is free of social variables always found in such measures as arrests for drinking or "trouble with alcohol."

Police Records. From 1955 to the present, police reporting, especially among the Navajo, has been on a par with that of the surrounding states. Homicide and suicide rates were computed for 10-year periods. For the Navajo (1956–1965), our figures came exclusively from the Navajo Tribal Police Department. For the Hopis (1956–1965), police records of the Hopi police were utilized and augmented by newspaper reports from nearby off-reservation towns. For the White Mountain Apache (1962–1968), police records and death certificates were utilized. For each tribe, the control of off-reservation suicides and homicides was problematic. Homicide was defined as criminal homicide (i.e., first and second-degree murder and nonnegligent manslaughter) following the practice of the Federal Bureau of Investigation, Uniform Crime Reports (2).

Historical Records. During the early reservation period, there was no reporting of suicide or, of course, cirrhosis. Homicides were reported by tribe in the annual report of the Commissioner of Indian Affairs for the decade of the 1880s. In addition, a number of anecdotal accounts are contained in a variety of sources. Navajo tribal police records start in the 1930s. Recognizing the inadequacy of such reporting, this type of material may only be used to indicate gross differences in rates between tribes or the existence of such acts in *minimally* estimated amounts in the past. Anecdotal material may give some information concerning the nature of earlier forms of homicide and suicide and their association with alcohol.

———————————— METHODOLOGY OF THE FIELD ————————————
STUDY AMONG THE NAVAJOS

The field study on which the bulk of our study is based was carried out among four populations of Navajos, each selected in a somewhat different fashion. Three groups were chosen to represent a range from the least to the most acculturated. A fourth group, comprised of "self identified" problem drinkers, was studied to determine whether these drinkers were comparable with heavy drinkers found in the three "average" populations. The interviews collected social and economic data, intended to place the groups more accurately on an acculturational scale, and material concerning the use of alcohol. A brief description of the four groups follows.

(1). **Traditional-Kaibito Plateau.** This group consists of a single extended kin group dependent primarily on pastoralism and migratory wage work, which was considered typical of the traditional populations living in the western Navajo reservation. The group was studied intensively by Levy between 1960 and 1962 and served as a base population for research in medical anthropology undertaken as part of the Navajo Health Education Project of the University of California School of Public Health (Berkeley) located in Tuba City, Arizona.

In 1960, this kin group consisted of 106 people. In 1967, when we reinterviewed them, there were 47 people 21 years of age or older. We are concerned with these adults in the rest of the study.

The kin group consists of two matrilineages related by marriage and bound together by cooperative ties in ceremonial activities, sheep shearing, and lesser, more informal enterprises. These cooperative behaviors had persisted from the mid-1930s to approximately 1965 when a number of economic factors combined to lessen the intensity of the cooperation. The senior males of each matrilineage were well-known ceremonialists, and one was a leading *rico* in the area prior to stock reduction.

Between 1960 and 1967, several members of this group died. Four older people died from natural causes, and two younger males died in accidents. One old lady was interviewed a few months before she died. The next of kin supplied information on the remaining five cases.

(2). **Transitional—South Tuba.** Originally a Mormon settlement, Tuba City became the headquarters of the western Navajo reservation in 1904 and today is the Tuba City Subagency. With offices of the Navajo Tribe, the Bureau of Indian Affairs, a Public Health Service hospital, a public school, and a federal boarding school, it is one of the few places on the reservation where steady wage work is available. Although most of the work is with the schools and various tribal and government agencies, a few jobs are provided by gas stations and trading posts in town.

Over the years, an area known as South Tuba has grown up adjacent to the government compound of Tuba City. In this area live most of the Navajos who have moved out of the hinterlands or from other parts of the reservation to take advantage of local job opportunities. Recent years have seen an increase in the number of substantial trailer homes and cinder block houses. A federally financed, low cost, housing project was built after our research was completed. In many respects, however, the area has the atmosphere of a shanty town.

In 1960, preparatory to installing a water system, the Navajo Health Education Project and the sanitation department of the Public Health Service conducted a complete census of South Tuba. From this census, Levy drew a random sample of households with a total population of 100 individuals. This population was studied over a period of two years as a part of the study that included the Kaibito Plateau population. Clearly the population of South Tuba had changed between the time of Levy's first study and the time that our interviews were done. When interviewed in 1967, all families in the sample had lived in South Tuba for at least eight years. All families studied in 1960 were in the area in 1967 and again when they were interviewed in 1969. Two adult males had died from natural causes between 1962 and 1967. The total number of adults who were 21 years of age and older in 1967 was 39.

(3). Acculturated—Flagstaff. As we have already mentioned, Navajos have been involved in wage work in border towns since the coming of the railway in the 1880s. The proportion of Navajos living in Flagstaff has remained relatively constant, at least since the end of World War II, comprising approximately 3 percent of the city's population.

Job opportunities for Navajos increased markedly in Flagstaff during the war when an army ordnance depot was established at Bellemont, 13 miles west of town. Currently, many of the Navajos employed at the depot live in Flagstaff. At its peak, the depot employed 1300 people, most of them Navajo. There were interpreters for the ones who spoke little or no English, and housing was provided by the army.

Since the war, the work force at the depot has fluctuated but in general it has declined so that, by the summer of 1969, there were 577 employees, 87 of whom were Navajo. This decline has had an influence on the demographic characteristics of the Flagstaff Navajo population because civil service regulations give job preference to veterans. Since veterans generally have better language skills than other Navajos, the overall result has been a sharp decrease in the number of employed Navajos whose English is poor and who are less well educated.

The population we studied lived in Flagstaff itself. The depot and a Bureau of Indian Affairs dormitory account for a good portion of the employment of Indians in town. Since much of the economy is seasonal and geared to the tourist trade, the Navajos' share in the job market tends to be at the unskilled and menial level. Those Navajos who have lived in Flagstaff for a long time are those employed in civil service, which has protected them from the fluctuations of the tourist trade.

The study group was selected from a census of the Navajo population in Flagstaff conducted by Kunitz in 1968. In this census, there were 32 families with household heads who had lived in town for 10 or more years. These families were reinterviewed in 1969. Twenty-eight were still in town. Every adult in each of these families who had lived for 10 or more years in Flagstaff was interviewed. The total number was 48.

(4). Self-Identified Problem Drinkers—Disulfiram Hospital Group. The hospital group studied was comprised of individuals who had voluntarily sought help for their drinking problems from the Disulfiram treatment program of the Tuba City Hospital.

Disulfiram is a drug that interrupts the metabolism of alcohol by blocking one of the enzymes involved in its degradation. This causes toxic products to build up in the blood when the patient drinks alcohol after having taken the drug. The effects are variable but generally they include flushing, lacrimation, often nausea, and sometimes shock.

Because of these effects, Disulfiram has had varying degrees of success in the treatment of alcoholism. The patient is maintained on a dose of one pill each day or every other day. It is hoped that while taking the pill, the patient will refrain from drinking for a long enough time that the "craving" will be lessened or disappear. It has often been remarked, however, that too frequently most patients refrain from taking the Disulfiram and not the alcohol.

In 1964, a large project supported by the National Institutes of Mental Health was begun in Gallup, New Mexico, to study the effects of Disulfiram therapy on a group of Navajo alcoholics. The 121 individuals in the project all had long police records and were referred to the project by judges in the city court (3). A similar project was begun at the Fort Defiance Indian Hospital, even though many patients in this program were not court referred (4). A third program was begun in the winter of 1966 at the Tuba City Indian Hospital.

The patients selected for study in the Tuba City group were the first 35 patients admitted to the hospital, none of whom were court referred. We wished to determine whether self-identified drinkers came from the same segments of the population and drank in the same manner as individuals identified as problem drinkers in the three groups already described. In short, we wanted to know whether patients in these programs were representative of the "average" Navajo problem drinker. It was thus important to get *self-identified* problem drinkers and to avoid court-referred cases who might be taking the drug merely to avoid a jail sentence.

All individuals in this group were 21 years of age or older. By limiting ourselves to a study of adults, we avoided problems involved in getting parental permission for access to medical records and in dealing with juvenile police records. In addition, since many teen-agers spend much of the year in off-reservation boarding schools, their opportunities for drinking and being arrested are different from those of the adults who spend most of the year on reservation or in a nearby town.

The actual success of the treatment program was of secondary interest. The hospital group were first interviewed in the hospital and then reinterviewed in their homes between one and two years after their entry into the program. In this way, an idea could be formed of the long-range effects of the program. However, the Tuba City program, unlike those in Fort Defiance and Gallup, provided virtually no supportive follow-up contact for the patient after his initial evaluation in the hospital and his first drug prescription. We would not, therefore, expect the Tuba City success rate to be nearly so high as those of the other programs.

The hospital group was not chosen for its sociological characteristics, as were the other groups, but for its identification with Navajo problem drinking. About one half came from South Tuba. The others came from more rural areas similar to that of the Kaibito Plateau. We would then expect this group to fall somewhere between the Plateau and South Tuba groups on an acculturational scale.

THE INTERVIEWS

The questionnaires administered to the four groups are reproduced in Appendix I. In general the questions are obvious and need no explanation. The questions dealing with drinking behavior (trouble due to drinking, preoccupation with alcohol, and definition of alcohol) are all taken from the National Health Survey by Mulford and Wilson (5). We discuss this section of the questionnaires in detail in Chapter Seven. Our aim was to gather data in a manner comparable to that used with the general white population.

INTERVIEWING PROCEDURES

Interviews were administered to the four groups at different times. The Kaibito Plateau and South Tuba groups were interviewed in the early spring of 1967. They were contacted again in the summer of 1969 to get added information about service in the armed forces, ceremonial participation, and voting behavior. The Flagstaff group was interviewed in the summer of 1969. The hospital group was interviewed in the hospital upon admission to the treatment program in late 1966 and early 1967 and later in their homes in 1969.

All interviewing on reservation was done by one of two interpreters: a senior interpreter trained by Levy in 1960, who has done medical interpreting for 10 years, and a younger man, formerly employed by the Public Health Service and trained for the project by the senior interpreter. In Flagstaff, where language was less of a problem, the interpreter was a young woman. In this instance, it was found that many women responded more freely to an interpreter of their own sex. In Flagstaff, all interviews were administered by Kunitz. On the reservation, either Levy or Kunitz were present at most of the interviews. Any interviews that the interpreters conducted alone were discussed with us on the same day.

Most of the on-reservation interviews took place through an interpreter but, since our senior interpreter was experienced and had worked with Levy for many years, we felt that language problems were minimal. In Flagstaff, where most informants spoke English, questions were often asked in both languages to ensure adequate understanding. It is our strong impression that the questions were well understood.

COOPERATION AND RAPPORT

The purpose of the project, we told the informants, was to try to increase our understanding of alcohol use among the Navajos and to make findings and recommendations available to the appropriate agencies. The grant was sponsored and administered by the Indian Health Service. Our goals were obviously perceived as legitimate—of all informants contacted, only one refused to participate in the study. Although, generally, we felt that the informants displayed a high degree of cooperation, each group related to the project in a different way—a circumstance that affected the openness of the responses to the interview questions.

Levy and both interpreters were well known to the Plateau group, having worked closely with them since 1960. Hence, the group responded to the questionnaires with great candor and gave a wealth of detail about the history of drinking in the area, personal use of alcohol, and the like. Both Kunitz and Levy were known to individuals in South Tuba. It was our impression, nevertheless, that this group's close proximity to the government agencies made them more guarded in their replies. Although they answered all questions, they elaborated less on their personal involvement with alcohol. The hospital group accepted us more or less as a part of their experience as patients entering a Disulfiram treatment program. They were more candid than many South Tuba informants but less relaxed and confidential than the Plateau informants. In Flagstaff the fact that Kunitz was a medical doctor who, for two years, had been in the Indian Health Service strengthened the medical nature of the study in the informants' minds and made up for the lack of prior personal contact with individuals in the group. The fact that Kunitz had known some of the informants' relatives on reservation was a great help in gaining rapport. His ability to give qualified medical advice and, in some instances, tangible help to some of the families was also an advantage.

In summation we feel that rapport and cooperation were far better than could ordinarily be expected in a formal interview situation because of the legitimate goals of the project and our prior contact both with many of the individuals and with the area. Informant reliability could also be checked in a very general way in that no informant gave information about his police or medical records that was at variance with those records.

SAMPLING AND THE USE OF STATISTICS: A WORD OF CAUTION

It is clear from our descriptions of the four samples that they, in fact, are not random. We repeat briefly here how they were obtained and the problems that this raises for statistical analysis.

The Kaibito Plateau sample is the most problematic. Originally, we had hoped to develop a sampling frame from the Tribal Census. This proved to be impossible because of the inaccuracies in the census, the dispersed nature of the population, some people's use of more than one name, and the limitations of our funds. Consequently, we picked as our sample of rural, traditional Navajos a kin group with whom we had worked in the past. The fact that it was a kin group means that our observations were not independent—that there may have been something about that particular group that made all of its members answer in a consistent fashion that is idiosyncratic when compared to other kin groups. The methodologically rigorous investigator may find this to be an area in which we can legitimately be criticized. In addition to the practical considerations mentioned above, this group was chosen because it was thought to be typical of such traditional groups. Nonetheless, the reader must beware that in applying tests of significance based on the assumption of independence of observations we are engaging in what the pure of heart would consider a questionable, if not immoral, activity. We are making the assumption that: (1) the observations are independent, and (2) the sample thus obtained is a random sample of all such kin groups. Our inferences are to similar populations that differ only in time and space.

The South Tuba sample was actually a true random sample of all households enumerated in that area. Again, however, in making statistical inferences we are generalizing not only to the sampling frame but implicitly to populations in other transitional communities.

The Disulfiram group was not a random sample either, although the observations are independent. We are assuming, however, that they are in effect a random sample of the voluntary entrants into such programs all over the reservation. More than that, we will ultimately suggest that they are typical of many traditional Navajo drinkers.

The Flagstaff respondents were again not a random sample but were all the Navajo long-term residents of the town. In this case, we are treating them as a random sample of all such residents of off-reservation towns.

Given the sampling problems as we have outlined them here, the reader may wonder why we have bothered with tests of significance at all. Some investigators in similar circumstances would merely report the figures without embellishing them with such tests. We have used them, however, because once having accepted the fantasy that these are random samples, we would like to be able to generalize with some degree of certainty to the rest of the population of which we are assuming that our samples are representative.

We have used nonparametric statistical tests to avoid making assumptions about the distribution of variables measured. In general, we have used the 5 percent level to declare statistical significance. The p-value is reported throughout to aid the reader who feels that the 5 percent level is inappropriate.

We have generally presented our data on acculturation, traditionalism, and drinking behavior by sample group. That is, rather than comparing the drinking behavior of individuals of different educational levels, for instance, we have compared the behavior of individuals between the groups already described. By doing this, we have run the risk of committing the ecological fallacy: inferring the characteristics of individuals from the correlations of aggregate data (6). The rationale for this form of presentation is that we are interested in characterizing groups both by the level of acculturation or traditionalism and by the most common form of drinking behavior.

The value of ecological correlations is that they may be regarded as "functions of a common underlying cause inherent not in the individuals as such but in inter-individual differences of relationships" (7). However, because some questions may arise concerning the inferences we are drawing about individuals, we have presented some of our data by parameters other than sample group; for instance, by educational level, income, and religion.

NOTES

---

1. For added detail on the use of these records, see S. J. Kunitz, J. E. Levy and M. Everett, "Alcoholic Cirrhosis among the Navajo," *Quarterly Journal of Studies on Alcohol, 30* (1969): 672–685. S. J. Kunitz, J. E. Levy, C. L. Odoroff, and J. Bollinger, "The Epidemiology of Alcoholic Cirrhosis in Two Southwestern Indian Tribes," *Quarterly Journal of Studies on Alcohol, 32* (1971): 706–720. M. Everett, "Cooperation in Change? Western Apache Evidence" (paper presented at the Annual Meeting, Society for Applied Anthropology, Mexico City, April, 1969).

2. J. E. Levy, "Navajo Suicide," *Human Organization, 24* (1965): 308–318. J. E. Levy, S. J. Kunitz and M. Everett, "Navajo Criminal Homicide," *Southwestern Journal of Anthropology, 25* (1969): 124–52. J. E. Levy and S. J. Kunitz, "Notes on Some White Mountain Apache Social Pathologies," *Plateau, 42* (1969): 11–19. Everett, "Cooperation in Change?"

3. F. N. Ferguson, "Navajo Drinking: Some Tentative Hypotheses," *Human Organization, 27* (1968): 159–167. "Community Treatment Plan for Navajo Problem Drinkers," Final Report for Grant MH-01389, McKinley County Family Consultation Services, Gallup, New Mexico, 1969.

4. R. J. Savard, "Effects of Disulfiram Therapy on Relationships within the Navajo Drinking Group," *Quarterly Journal of Studies on Alcohol, 29* (1968): 909–916. C. F. Szutzer, R. J. Savard, and J. H. Saiki, "The Use of Disulfiram in Treatment of Alcoholic Problems in an American Indian Population" (Fort Defiance, Arizona: U.S. Public Health Service, Forth Defiance Indian Hospital, no date).

5. H. A. Mulford and R. W. Wilson, *Identifying Problem Drinkers in a Household Health Survey,* National Center for Health Statistics, P.H.S. Publication No. 1000, Series 2, No. 16 (Washington, D.C., 1966).

6. W. S. Robinson, "Ecological Correlations and the Behavior of Individuals," *American Sociological Review, 15* (1950): 351–357.

7. H. Menzel, "Comments on Robinson's 'Ecological Correlations and the Behavior of Individuals,'" *American Sociological Review, 15* (1950): 674.

Chapter Five

SOCIAL PATHOLOGIES IN
THREE SOUTHWESTERN TRIBES

The prevalent view of social pathology and particularly drinking among
North American Indians is that levels of social pathology tend to be high
and that the high levels are the direct result of social disintegration produced by conquest and acculturation. Moreover, drinking promotes deviance because it lessens social inhibitions and releases aggression. This explanation was discussed in Chapter One.

As applied to the Navajo and Hopi tribes, the expression of the
prevalent view has been clear. Kluckhohn, the Leightons, and VanValkenburgh have explicitly stated that the Navajos were comparatively free of
homicide before World War II. Outbreaks of violence in general and of
homicide in particular, they report, have increased with levels of tension
generated by social disintegration and the growing use of alcohol (1). Students of the Hopis have asserted not only that there was no homicide
among these people but that its absence was due to lack of alcohol on their
reservation (2). References to the Apaches have been less assertive, although here too the impression is that suicide, homicide, and alcoholism
are on the rise.

In this chapter we present our findings from a series of studies of several
social pathologies among the Navajo, Hopi, and White Mountain Apache
tribes. These findings, in our view, support the alternative explanation of
Indian drinking that we outlined in Chapter One. We have surveyed police
and medical records to determine whether the rates of homicide and suicide

are, in fact, rising and whether the increases are positively associated with alcohol use.

──────── SOCIAL PATHOLOGY AND LEVELS ────────
OF SOCIOCULTURAL INTEGRATION

Following Field's suggestion that the degree of drunkenness, at least in public, is related to the degree of social integration (3) and that of Bacon, Barry, and Child that drunkenness is greater in societies emphasizing individual independence and achievement (4), we have placed our tribes on a scale of sociocultural integration. The Hopis, sedentary, with a lineal descent system, and village and ceremonial corporateness, are at the high end of the scale and should exhibit the lowest levels of social pathology. The Navajos, pastoral herders, part-time agriculturalists with matrilineal clans, are placed next and should display slightly higher pathology levels. The White Mountain Apaches are somewhat more difficult to place because, even though they had developed matrilineal clans, their agriculture was sporadic and they retained more of their band-level organization than did the Navajo who had developed sheepherding and agriculture to a higher degree. Nor, it might be added, had the Apaches had as intimate contact over a long period of time with Pueblo groups as had the Navajos. The Plains tribes might be placed between the band level and the sedentary tribes because of their development of tribal superstructures.

Homicide.   The homicide rates for the period 1883–1889 are given in Table 5.1. No data are available for the Hopis because no agency was established for them during that decade. Nevertheless, if we assume that their rates were not very different from those of the Eastern Pueblos, we see that the homicide rates fall along our scale in the expected manner.

Although reporting accuracy during that period must have been problematic, the magnitude of the differences between Pueblos and Navajos on the one hand and the band-level tribes on the other is such that we can confidently maintain that differences in aboriginal social types were related to the genesis of social deviance. Elsewhere we have used ethnographic accounts to compute a minimal rate of homicide for the Kiowa during the prereservation period 1800–1869, which was approximately the same as that reported in the 1880s (5).

Contemporary rates for the various tribes can still be grouped in a simi-

Table 5.1   Annual Averages of Homicide Rates
(per 100,000 Population) for Selected
Tribes, 1883–1889 *

Tribe	Population	Rate
A. Eastern Pueblo Agency	8,600	1.9
B. Navajo	17,000	5.88
C. South Plains		
Kiowa-Comanche	4,000	14.25
Southern Cheyenne	5,000	13.20
D. North Plains		
Pine Ridge Sioux	6,800	14.7
Yankton Sioux	1,900	22.0
Crow	3,000	19.0
Fort Peck, Assiniboine,		
and Sioux	4,000	50.0
Blackfoot	3,700	51.3
E. Basin Plateau		
Fort Hall Shoshone	1,600	71.25
Western Shoshone	500	86.0
Nevada Paiute	1,000	130.0
F. Apache		
Eastern Apache	1,500	86.6
Western Apache	3,500	165.0

* Compiled from the Annual Reports of the Secretary of
the Department of the Interior and the Reports of the
Commissioner of Indian Affairs, Washington, D.C.,
1883–1889.
Note: The homicide rate for the general U.S. population
in 1900 was approximately 5 per 100,000.

lar manner: Hopis, 6; Navajos, approximately 5.3; and White Mountain
Apaches, 72 per 100,000 population annually (6).

Suicide.   Although there was no consistent reporting of suicides during
the early years of the reservation period, our contemporary data suggest
that here too the band-level societies have the expected higher rates: Hopis,

approximately 10; Navajos, approximately 8; White Mountain Apaches, approximately 20; Eskimos, 41.7; and Shoshone-Bannocks, 98 per 100,000 population annually (7).

Drinking and Drunkenness. The levels of public drunkenness displayed by the three tribes appear to fit the expected pattern, with the Navajos closer to the Apaches than to the Hopis. Public drinking in the villages is virtually unknown among the Hopis. Drunks are being arrested at rodeos, and some informants maintain that young people are drinking in the villages more openly than heretofore. Nevertheless, drinking groups are not seen in the villages by outside observers, and public ceremonies are noticeably decorous and sober. Navajo drinking patterns have already been described. The White Mountain Apaches have institutionalized public drinking parties that are an integral part of their public religious ceremonies.

When we examine the mortality rates from alcoholic cirrhosis, however, a different picture emerges (8). For the Navajos, the death rate from cirrhosis, even when age adjusted for people 20 years old and over, is slightly smaller than the national rate. For the general population, the age-adjusted rate was 19.9 in 1964. For the Navajos, it was approximately 15 during the period 1965–1967. The White Mountain Apaches' age-adjusted rate for the same three-year period was 44 per 100,000 annually. Surprisingly, the Hopi age-adjusted rate came to 104, which exceeded that of San Francisco, the highest reporting area in the nation. Although there are questions concerning the statistical interpretation of these differences that stem from the short periods we were forced to use for these tribes and from the very small populations of the Hopi and Apache tribes, we have concluded, for the present at least, that the Hopi rates are really higher than those for the other tribes (see Table 5.2) (9).

These findings indicate that the level of public intoxication varies independently from the level of steady, excessive drinking. We also suggest that the association between the level of sociocultural integration and such pathologies as homicide, suicide, and public drinking may largely reflect the degree of flamboyance or the "acting out" nature of the deviant acts and not the total levels of deviance generated in each society. The fact that different types of deviance may vary independently of each other is obvious; the identification of cultural factors affecting both incidence and characteristics of each type of deviance, however, is at best a difficult task.

Table 5.2 Expected and Observed Numbers
of Deaths from Cirrhosis

Tribe	Expected per Year	Observed 1965	1966	1967
Navajo (low estimate)	4.9	6	7	—
Navajo (high estimate)	5.6	6	7	—
Apache	0.3	1	1	1
Hopi	0.3	2	2	4

STABILITY OF RATES AND PERSISTENCE OF PATTERNS

To date, we have not found evidence for a steady increase in the rates of either homicide or suicide. Nor have we found clear-cut evidence of periodic increases during particularly stressful crises. Accepting the inadequacy of data from the past we have, nevertheless, concluded that the available evidence points to a general stability in the rates and to a basic persistence of patterns. That changes in the environment or the social structure itself may result in gradual changes in the patterning of these acts remains a distinct possibility.

Rates. The White Mountain Apache suicide and homicide rates have either remained stable since the 1880's or even decreased. In 1908, Hrdlička made a rough estimate of the incidence of suicide, which yields an approximate annual rate of 50 per 100,000 (10). The present rate, based on estimates made by two observers is between 20 and 30. The homicide rate for all western Apaches between 1883 and 1889 was 165, whereas the contemporary rate is between 60 and 70. It is possible that many of the earlier killings were caused by feuds and would have been considered as justified by the Apaches at that time. Everett has suggested that the early years of the San Carlos reservation were particularly traumatic ones. Another possi-

bility is that the long-range trend is to approximate the rates of the surrounding non-Indian populations as Apache social organization changes
(11).

The Hopi data are equally difficult to interpret. There are accounts of
traditional forms of hidden suicide and homicide in the past but no official
reporting until very recently. Elsewhere we have pointed out that with average homicide and suicide rates the numbers of expected suicides occurring
in such a small tribe, especially one that tended to hide deviant acts, would
have been almost impossible for the average anthropologist to detect before
1950 (12).

The Navajo picture is clearer. For the years 1883–1889, the reported
Navajo homicide rate was approximately 5.9. Between 1937 and 1941, the
cases in the files of the Navajo police yield an average annual rate of between 4.4 and 5.8, which suggests that the difficult years of the stock reduction program did not result in obviously increased rates. For the 10 year
period 1956–1965, the rates appear stable and average between 4.5 and
5.3 per 100,000, depending on the population estimate utilized (13).

Navajo suicide rates were computed for the years 1954–1963 and
again between 1964 and 1969. The rates have remained stable with an average annual rate in the neighborhood of 8.28 per 100,000 population.
This is slightly lower than the national averages for the same period (14).

Patterns.   The patterns of both homicide and suicide among the Navajos
have not changed appreciably since the nineteenth century. The dominant
pattern is for a married, active male between 35 and 40 years of age to kill
his wife because of sexual jealousy or other domestic problems. More frequently than expected, the murderer will then commit suicide. Suicides
committed without homicide are done by married males in the same age
group and for the same motives. The suicide most frequently commits the
act in or near the dwelling so that the ghost may contaminate the spouse
and her relatives. Suicide thus appears to be a passive-aggressive act very
closely linked with homicide (15).

Though many of the strains attendant upon contemporary Navajo adjustment to a wage-work economy make the life of males especially difficult, there are specific references to this form of homicide and suicide in the
past. Wyman and Thorne noted it in the 1930s (16). Kneal, writing of the
1920s, called a murder followed by a suicide the "Navajo custom" (17). In
Son of Old Man Hat, one of the Navajo autobiographies recorded by Walter Dyk, Son of Old Man Hat tells of a discussion he had with his mother

when he was a little boy sometime in the 1870s. Her response seems to refer clearly to a period before the captivity in Fort Sumner.

When a man talks as you're talking now, he gets that way. As soon as he gets a woman, as soon as they get acquainted he may start beating his wife, and they'll begin to have a quarrel every once in a while. So you mustn't say you will be that way when you grow up. It's pretty dangerous to have a wife or a husband. Some men, when they have wives, may kill their wives or may get killed by them, and some commit suicide (18).

The descriptions of family conflicts in *Son of Old Man Hat* and those described by Emerson Blackhorse Mitchell in his recent autobiographical work are strikingly similar (19). The emotional lability of Navajo males and the traditional instability of Navajo marriage have been described by Leighton and Kluckhohn (20). Frequent physical conflict between husbands and wives appears to be common (21). It seems that the difficulties of Navajo marriage have not changed appreciably from aboriginal times to the present.

——————— **THE RELATIONSHIP OF ALCOHOL** ———————
INTOXICATION TO VIOLENCE

That Navajos tend to commit acts of aggression while drunk is a common observation (22). That it is the effects of ethanol that cause such acts has been accepted as fact by virtually all students of the Navajo. However, steadily increased use of alcohol does not appear to have appreciably influenced homicide and suicide rates, which has encouraged us to examine the matter further. On the one hand, we note that the proportion of Navajo homicides with alcohol present in the offender (73.2 percent) is significantly higher than has been recorded for urban whites (39.7 percent) or Negroes (60 percent) (23). On the other hand, we note that the causal relationship between the two is often accepted on blind faith as when McNitt, referring to a large number of traders murdered by Navajos between 1901 and 1934, maintains that "the murderers were usually drunk" (24) (From *Indian Traders,* by Frank McNitt. Copyright 1962 by the University of Oklahoma Press). Actually, however, he does not describe one instance in which this was the case. Instead, the murders appear to have been well planned and committed in cold blood with robbery as the motive. Suspects, later proved innocent, are mentioned as having been drinking. That, and the fact that drunkenness was observed at nearby "Squaw dances," is the only evidence given for the presence of alcohol in any of the cases described (25).

Evidence for causal relationship might be demonstrated if one could show that homicide was more frequent in areas where drinking is prevalent. We found that this does not appear to be the case. The incidence of alcoholic cirrhosis varies on the reservation depending on the accessibility of alcohol. Remote areas such as the Kayenta and Chinle Service Units (P.H.S. administrative areas) have a lower than expected prevalence, whereas such areas as Fort Defiance, Winslow, and Gallup-Tohatchi have higher than expected prevalences (26). The incidence of homicide and suicide remains constant in all areas of the reservation, however (27).

Among urban Negroes and whites, the presence of alcohol in the offender tended to increase the violence of the act. Among the Navajos, there appeared to be an inverse relationship between violence and acts of suicide and homicide where alcohol was present. The homicide act was less violent when the offender was drunk than when he was sober. And the proportion of suicides that were preceded by murder was higher before 1945 (when few suicides had been drinking) and much lower after 1956 (when the number of cases involving alcohol had risen to over 47 percent) (28).

Finally, when the arrest records of homicide offenders were compared with those of nonhomicidal controls (the Tuba City and Plateau groups), we could find no difference between the offenders and the controls in the proportion of alcohol-related arrests, the proportion of crimes other than those related to alcohol, or the average number of arrests per year. Most Navajo males, it appeared, had many arrests for possession of alcohol on reservation or drunkenness, and the homicide offenders had not been greater drinkers nor more criminal in other respects than was the average Navajo male. Thus, while the association between intoxication and the act of homicide is there, the causal nature of the relationship seems doubtful.

───────── RELATIONSHIP BETWEEN DRINKING ─────────
AND LEVEL OF ACCULTURATION

In light of these findings, the often asserted association of drinking with acculturation and social disintegration presented several disturbing questions. The level of drinking was on the increase among the Navajo as was the level of acculturation generally. Moreover, alcoholic cirrhosis was more prevalent around Gallup, Fort Defiance, and Winslow, the areas with the largest concentrations of acculturated Navajos. However, taking into account the early Navajo "fondness" for intoxicants one could interpret the high prevalence of cirrhosis around off-reservation towns as a positive correlation between steady drinking and an adequate source of supply.

To test the idea that of the major social pathologies only drinking was clustered in off-reservation areas, we looked at the distribution of such pathologies among the Hopis off reservation, in procouncil (progressive) villages, and in anticouncil (traditional) villages on reservation.

During the 1940s, Thompson administered psychological tests to school-age Hopi youths in a progressive village undergoing "culture crisis" and in the more traditional villages of First Mesa. She found that the greater acculturation in the progressive village of New Oraibi was reflected in the results of the tests. The acculturated boys appeared to be more cautious, restrained, and troubled by a vague anxiety than were the traditional youths of First Mesa who seemed relatively spontaneous and outgoing. The boys of the acculturated village showed a marked tendency toward personality disturbances which, if found among white children, would be called compulsive neurosis. Thompson interpreted these findings as revealing the degree to which Hopi personality suffered in an acculturated village (29).

The children tested by Thompson would be the adults of the 1960s, and the contemporary deviance displayed by Hopi adults would have had its genesis in the culture crisis of the 1930s and 1940s. Today, we would expect to find higher levels of deviance in Oraibi than in the villages of First Mesa. We actually found the social pathologies (suicide, homicide, cirrhosis, all other diagnoses of chronic alcoholism, suicide attempts, and hysteria) to be equally prevalent in Oraibi and other crisis communities and in the Hopi villages of First Mesa. The Tewa village of Hano and all Tewa residents of Polacca were omitted from the comparison. The differences between the two groups as described by Thompson were, then, not reflected in overt forms of social deviance. Nor, in fact, were the rates of prevalence different when the villages most reliant on wage work were compared with those that were least reliant (30).

It was only when villages were classed according to their present political stance that a significant clustering of social pathologies was found. The anticouncil villages were then comparatively free of social pathology. Several observations complicated the interpretation, however. The most outstanding one was that, although cirrhosis was absent from the anticouncil villages, present in procouncil villages, and overrepresented in off-reservation areas, cases of chronic alcoholism were found in expected amounts in all three types of community. Certainly, alcohol per se was not associated with culture crisis and acculturation on a community level.

These findings suggest that deviance was generated equally in traditional and acculturated communities but that the deviant tended to be expelled from the more traditional villages where older forms of social control were still at work. This interpretation was further strengthened after it was found that, when cases of cirrhosis were returned to their village of origin, there was no difference in the distribution of the disease as found in traditional and acculturated communities.

────────────────── DISCUSSION ──────────────────

The weight of the evidence gained from this type of study confirmed our earlier idea that patterns of deviance are largely explainable in terms of social type. The stability of rates and the persistence of patterns of suicide and homicide over long periods indicate that neither increased acculturation nor increased alcohol use have been the major factors influencing these types of social deviance. That the prevalence of homicide, suicide, and public drunkenness scale according to levels of sociocultural integration further strengthens our belief that the basic configurations of culture are important in determining both the form and the amount of social deviance. Disregarding brief flurries or "epidemics" of homicide or suicide, which might be transient reactions and would become apparent largely in small populations, we would look to major shifts in family organization and child-rearing practices as the important acculturational factors affecting the genesis of social deviance. Such major changes do not appear to have taken place among the three tribes studied to a sufficient degree to obliterate aboriginal patterns entirely.

Although the use of alcohol is recent for the Hopis and Navajos, we feel that the patterns of alcohol use may still be explained mainly in terms of persisting cultural configurations. The growing availability of a desired commodity serves more to obscure the patterns of alcohol use than to clarify them. The fact that acculturation has increased while alcohol has become more available indicates a fortuitous association between the two.

The complicated picture presented by the Hopi data suggests that further research must concentrate on more precisely defined levels of acculturation as related to specific types of drinking. Research on Hopi drinking is currently under way. The results of more detailed research among smaller groups of Navajos are presented in succeeding chapters. For the Hopi, it is important to discover whether the high rate of death from cirrhosis is associated with steady hidden drinking and whether this type of drinking is found more among individuals still living in a traditional Hopi context. For the Navajos, we would like to know whether a major shift in drinking patterns has occurred in the move to off-reservation areas, whether this new drinking pattern leads to a higher incidence of cirrhosis than the older pattern of group drinking, and whether, in fact, the off-reservation cirrhotics are the more acculturated Navajos who live permanently off reservation.

NOTES

1. C. Kluckhohn and D. Leighton, *The Navajo* (Cambridge: Harvard University Press, 1946), pp. 104–162; D. Leighton and C. Kluckhohn, *Children of the People* (Cambridge: Harvard University Press, 1947), pp. 96–98; R. VanValkenburgh, "Navajo Common Law II: Navajo Law and Justice," *Museum of Northern Arizona, Museum Notes,* 9 (1937): pp. 51–54.

2. L. Thompson, *Culture in Crisis: A Study of the Hopi Indians* (New York: Harper, 1950), p. 51; L. Thompson and A. Joseph, *The Hopi Way* (Chicago: University of Chicago Press, 1945), p. 47; H. S. Colton, "A Brief Survey of Hopi Common Law," *Museum of Northern Arizona, Museum Notes,* 7 (1934), p. 24.

3. See discussion in Chapter One; P. B. Field, "A New Cross-Cultural Study of Drunkenness," in *Society, Culture and Drinking Patterns,* D. J. Pittman and C. R. Snyder, eds. (New York: Wiley, 1962), p. 52.

4. M. K. Bacon, H. Barry, III, and I. L. Child, "A Cross-Cultural Study of Drinking: II. Relations to other Features of Culture," in *A Cross-Cultural Study of Drinking: Quarterly Journal of Studies on Alcohol, Supplement,* No. 3 (April, 1965), p. 43.

5. J. E. Levy and S. J. Kunitz, "Indian Reservations, Anomie and Social Pathology," *Southwestern Journal of Anthropology,* 27 (1971): 97–128.

6. J. E. Levy, S. J. Kunitz, and M. Everett, "Navajo Criminal Homicide," *Southwestern Journal of Anthropology,* 25 (1969): 124–152; J. E. Levy, S. J. Kunitz, C. L. Odoroff, and J. Bollinger, "Hopi Deviance: An Historical and Epidemiological Survey" (unpublished); J. E. Levy and S. J. Kunitz, "Some Notes on White Mountain Apache Social Pathologies," *Plateau,* 42 (1969): 11–19; M. Everett, "Cooperation in Change? Western

Apache Evidence" (paper presented at the Annual Meeting of the Society for Applied Anthropology, Mexico City, April 9–15, 1969).

7. J. E. Levy, "Navajo Suicide," *Human Organization*, 24 (1965): 308–318; J. E. Levy, S. J. Kunitz, and M. Everett, "Homicide;" J. E. Levy, and S. J. Kunitz, "White Mountain Apache;" A. E. Hippler, "Fusion and Frustration: Dimensions in the Cross-Cultural Ethnopsychology of Suicide," *American Anthropologist*, 71 (1969): 1074–1087, p. 1080; L. H. Dizmang, J. Watson, P. A. May, and J. Bopp, "Adolescent Suicide at Fort Hall Indian Reservation," (paper presented before the Annual Meeting of the American Psychiatric Association, San Francisco, May, 1970).

8. National reporting bases rates in all deaths from cirrhosis of all types. We have done the same but would note that *all* Apache, Hopi, and virtually all Navajo deaths were from alcoholic cirrhosis.

9. Our data on cirrhosis among the three tribes is discussed in more detail in S. J. Kunitz, J. E. Levy, C. L. Odoroff, and J. Bollinger, "The Epidemiology of Alcoholic Cirrhosis in Two Southwestern Indian Tribes," *Quarterly Journal of Studies on Alcohol*, 32 (1971): 706–720; see also, S. J. Kunitz, J. E. Levy and M. Everett, "Alcoholic Cirrhosis among the Navajo," *Quarterly Journal of Studies on Alcohol*, 30 (1969): 672–685; and J. E. Levy, S. J. Kunitz, C. L. Odoroff, and J. Bollinger, "Hopi Deviance."

10. A. Hrdlička, *Physiological and Medical Observations among the Indians of Southwestern United States and Northern Mexico*, Bureau of American Ethnology, Bulletin 30 (1908), p. 171.

11. M. Everett, personal communication; M. Everett, "Co-operation."

12. J. E. Levy, S. J. Kunitz, C. L. Odoroff, and J. Bollinger, "Hopi Deviance."

13. J. E. Levy, S. J. Kunitz, and M. Everett, "Homicide," p. 128.

14. J. E. Levy, "Suicide," p. 309; C. T. Goodluck, "Some Problems Resulting from Acculturative Stress in a Navajo Community" (Senior Paper, Department of Anthropology, Prescott College, Prescott, Arizona, 1970), p. 67.

15. J. E. Levy, "Suicide;" J. E. Levy, S. J. Kunitz and M. Everett, "Homicide."

16. L. C. Wyman and B. Thorne, "Notes on Navajo Suicide," *American Anthropologist*, 47 (1945): 278–288.

17. A. H. Kneal, *Indian Agent* (Caldwell, Idaho: Caxton Press, 1950).

18. W. Dyk, *Son of Old Man Hat, A Navaho Autobiography*, 2nd ed. (Lincoln: University of Nebraska Press, 1966), pp. 47–48.

19. E. B. Mitchell and T. D. Allen, *Miracle Hill, the Story of a Navajo Boy* (Norman: University of Oklahoma Press, 1967).

20. D. C. Leighton and C. Kluckhohn, *Children*, pp. 109–111.

21. D. B. Heath, "Prohibition and Post-Repeal Drinking Patterns among the Navajo," *Quarterly Journal of Studies on Alcohol*, 25 (1964), p. 126.

22. Ibid, p. 126.

23. J. E. Levy, S. J. Kunitz, and M. Everett, "Homicide," p. 132.

24. F. McNitt, *The Indian Traders* (Norman: University of Oklahoma Press, 1962), p. 322.

25. Ibid, pp. 322–338.

26. S. J. Kunitz, J. E. Levy, and M. Everett, "Navajo Cirrhosis," p. 680.

27. J. E. Levy, S. J. Kunitz and M. Everett, "Homicide," p. 131.

28. Ibid, pp. 131–133.

29. L. Thompson, "Attitudes and Acculturation," *American Anthropologist, 50* (1948): 200–215; L. Thompson, *Culture in Crisis,* p. 179.

30. J. E. Levy, S. J. Kunitz, C. L. Odoroff and J. Bollinger, "Hopi Deviance."

—————————————— Chapter Six ——————————————

LEVELS OF ACCULTURATION

Thus far, we have suggested that the variations in prevalence, distribution, and style of three major "social pathologies" displayed by the Navajos, Hopis, and White Mountain Apaches may be best explained in terms of configurations of culture that have survived from aboriginal times. Each society has developed somewhat different ways of dealing with stressful situations, whether generated by the social organization itself or by external factors. Here and in the next chapter we examine the Navajo in greater detail to see how the different levels of acculturation are associated with changes in either the style of drinking or the involvement with alcohol.

First, let us compare our four study groups according to a number of conventional measures of acculturation, especially those of family organization, occupation, and level of education. Attention is given to religious and political behavior and to experiences in the armed forces.

—————————————— AGE AND SEX ——————————————

Table 6.1 gives the age and sex distributions of the four groups. The hospital group is not a "natural" population but is drawn only from a population defined by its drinking behavior. Almost all are male and are younger than the men of Kaibito Plateau and Flagstaff but not of South Tuba. The men of the two former groups are younger than the other men because South Tuba is a wage-work community that has attracted young men and because many of the hospital group are from South Tuba. In addition, as we see later, the hospital group tends to be young because it is young men who drink.

Table 6.1 Age Distribution of Men and Women

Age Group	Hospital		Plateau		South Tuba		Flagstaff	
	M	W	M	W	M	W	M	W
20–24	4	0	3	3	4	0	1	1
25–29	7	1	1	4	6	3	1	2
30–34	9	2	2	8	3	4	1	6
35–39	4	0	3 *	0	1	1	4	3
40–44	3	1	1	3	2	2	0	3
45–49	2	1	2	3	2	2	3	6
50–54	1	0	3 *	0	2	2	3	4
55–59	0	0	1	1	1	1	3	2
60–65	0	0	0	1	0	0	0	2
>65	0	0	5 **	3 *	2	1	1	0
Unknown	0	0	0	0	0	0	1	1
Totals	30	5	21	26	23	16	18	30
Median	32.2	31.2	47.5	33.8	32.5	40	43.3	44

* Each asterisk represents one individual who died before the 1967 survey. Proxy interviews were obtained from next of kin in each case. The age listed in the table refers to age at time of death. All of these individuals were well known to one of the investigators (J.E.L.) for several years before they died.

The remaining three groups exhibit few differences. The Flagstaff group, however, has twelve more women than men because virtually all of the Flagstaff residents live in nuclear family groups. A widowed or divorced woman tends to remain alone or with children in town. In addition, three Navajo women in Flagstaff were married to non-Navajo men who are not included in the tabulations.

————————— SIZE OF FAMILY AND —————————
TYPE OF FAMILY UNIT

Table 6.2 demonstrates the results we expect. Kaibito Plateau people live predominantly in the traditional Navajo matrilocal extended family. The division is about equal in the South Tuba group, indicating that even in this sort of wage-work community, patterns of cooperation and living are not radically different from the more usual Navajo arrangement. In Flagstaff, essentially all of the families are nuclear in type, containing only the biological family. Even the so-called extended family—when the father's or mother's relatives live in the household—tends to be a small group, perhaps one or two outside of the biological family.

The hospital group also tended to live in neolocal families, reflecting primarily the fact that many of them came from South Tuba.

Again, household or camp size varied in the same direction—decreasing from the rural to the urban group, although the Navajos in

Table 6.2 Type and Size of Family Unit

Type of Unit	Hospital		Plateau		South Tuba		Flagstaff	
	Number	Per-cent	Number	Per-cent	Number	Per-cent	Number	Per-cent
Matrilocal extended	6	17.1	38	81.0	17	43.5	3	6.2
Patrilocal extended	2	5.7	0	0	0	0	2	4.1
Neolocal	20	57.0	5	10.6	22	56.5	43	89.9
Other	2	5.7	4	8.5	0	0	0	0
Unknown	5	14.3	0	0	0	0	0	0
Totals	35	99.8	47	100.0	39	100.0	48	100.2
Mean number of individuals per family unit	7.6		13.9		6.5		4.7	

Flagstaff still have larger families (4.7) than the average Flagstaff family (3.6) (1).

───────────────── MARITAL STATUS ─────────────────

The traditional Navajo marriage was a serial monogamy or a polygyny. The preferred forms of the latter were sororal polygyny—the union of a man to two or more parallel cousins—and the marriage of a man to a woman and one or more of her daughters by a previous marriage. The instability of Navajo marriage has often been commented upon (2). Marriages tended to become permanent only after the partners had reached middle age. Only two polygynous marriages were found in the traditional Plateau group. The persistent marital instability is reflected in Tables 6.3 and 6.4. Single, widowed, or divorced people are rare in all groups, especially in the case of males. Acculturative change is shown by the fact that wage-earning males in South Tuba and Flagstaff have had fewer prior marriages than the men in the more traditional group. The marital history of women does not vary between groups.

A high rate of divorce is characteristic of traditional Navajo society

Table 6.3   Marital Status

	Hospital		Plateau		South Tuba		Flagstaff	
	M	W	M	W	M	W	M	W
Single	3	0	2	1	2	0	1	3
Married	25	1	19	15	17	13	17	19*
Divorced	1	1	0	1	1	1	0	3
Separated	1	0	0	4	2	1	0	0
Widowed	0	3	0	5	0	0	0	4
Unknown	0	0	0	0	1	1	0	1
Totals	30	5	21	26	23	16	18	30

* Includes three women married to non-Navajos.

Table 6.4   Number of Previous Marriages

	Hospital		Plateau		South Tuba		Flagstaff	
	M	W	M	W	M	W	M	W
None	20	0	8	15	14	10	14	16
One or more	6	4	8	8	4	5	1	9
Unknown	1	1	3	2	3	1	2	2
Not applicable	3	0	2	1	2	0	1	3
Totals	30	5	21	26	23	16	18	30

Comparison (Plateau vs. South Tuba vs. Flagstaff by none vs. one or more prior marriages)	Sex	df	Chi-square	p Value
	Women	2	.0396	.05
	Men	2	7.7293	.05

where it is a normal phenomenon rather than a sign of social disintegration. The effects of acculturation are seen in the males of the Flagstaff group whose marriages had become more stable. Their successful adaptation to town life appears to involve the adoption of white modes of monogamy.

———————————— EARNING A LIVING ————————————

The independent nuclear family is adaptive to a wage-work economy in an urban setting. It is not surprising, then, to find the Flagstaff group not only living in nuclear family groups but also to be the most involved with wage work (Table 6.5). The difference in the type of economy is also reflected in the average per capita income in each of the four groups. In this instance we find the Flagstaff per capita income to be more than three times as great as that found in the Plateau group.

The high proportion of welfare recipients, the retired, and the unem-

Table 6.5 Occupational Distribution

Occupation	Hospital		Plateau		South Tuba		Flagstaff	
	Number	Per-cent	Number	Per-cent	Number	Per-cent	Number	Per-cent
Seasonal wage	5	14.2	2	4.2	5	12.8	7	14.8
Steady wage	5	14.2	6	12.7	13	33.3	28	58.3
Sheepherder	4	11.4	27	57.4	3	7.7	0	0
Seasonal wage and sheep	3	8.5	5	10.6	1	2.5	0	0
Social welfare and retired with social security and unemployed	15	42.8	5	10.6	14	35.9	6	12.5
Medicine man and sheep	1	2.8	2	4.2	0	0	0	0
Housewife and/or students	0	0	0	0	0	0	7	14.6
Unknown	2	5.7	0	0	3	7.7	0	0
Totals	35	99.6 *	47	99.7 *	39	99.9 *	48	100.2 *
Average annual per capita income		$370		$363		$675		$1,418

* Does not equal 100 percent because of rounding.

ployed in both the hospital and Tuba City groups is caused by such individuals' concentrating in a settlement, like Tuba City, where they are near the post office to receive welfare and pension checks as well as near the social welfare agency and the hospital. Furthermore, the cost of living is low on the reservation when compared to that in a town. Thus it is difficult to envision such communities as Tuba City producing anomic or dependent people so much as attracting them from the surrounding rural areas.

Similar problems arise in interpreting the rather large differences in per capita income among the various groups. On the surface the traditional Plateau group seems to be deprived in relation to wage-work populations, especially that in Flagstaff. There are, however, a number of other factors that make per capita income an unsatisfactory gauge of economic deprivation.

The higher per capita incomes earned in Flagstaff are spent in a high cost of living area. Off-reservation residents have high rents or mortgage payments. They also pay state and federal income taxes, whereas only federal income taxes are levied on salaries earned by reservation dwellers. Reservation produce in the form of livestock, wool, or arts and crafts is not taxed. Medical care is free on the reservation. Flagstaff residents must travel 50 to 75 miles to the nearest Public Health Service hospital. It is often more economical for the urban wage worker to seek private medical care. Wage earners in Flagstaff and South Tuba send their children to public schools. Children from rural areas on the reservation are sent to federal boarding schools where they are fed, clothed, and housed at no expense to the parents for nine months of the year. Although in many respects Kaibito Plateau is still a subsistence economy, the bottom is kept from falling out by federal and tribal programs as well as the unique land holding and tax status of Indian reservations.

Finally, one must consider that Navajos living in Flagstaff may be deprived by the standards of the town rather than those of the reservation. One must ask: By what yardstick do Flagstaff Navajos measure themselves —other Navajos living on reservation or the people with whom they have daily contact in town?

By off-reservation standards, the Flagstaff group appears to be deprived (3). They are less well educated, have lower status jobs, and live in poorer areas of town than the majority of Flagstaff residents (Table 6.6). In addition, as many of them remarked, they are exposed daily to various subtle and not-so-subtle rebuffs and discriminatory practices from which on-reservation Navajos are more sheltered. They have nothing to return to on the reservation. Virtually none of them have sheep permits (Table 6.7), and jobs are scarce on reservation.

When the 28 households in the Flagstaff group were ranked according to social class by using Hollingshead's "Two-Factor Index of Social Position" (4), 4 were in class III, 7 in class IV, and 17 in class V. Clearly, the range of class positions, even for the Navajos who have lived in town for more than 10 years, is narrow and concentrated primarily at the bottom of the social pyramid.

Table 6.6   Comparison of Occupational Groups
of Navajo Residents of Flagstaff and a Random
Sample of the General Population

Occupational Status	General Flagstaff Population (Percent) *	Navajo Residents	
		Number	Percent
Professional, technical, and managerial plus clerical and sales	53.2	4	11.4
Service	15.0	18	51.4
Farming, processing, machine trades, bench work, and miscellaneous	14.2	3	8.5
Structural	9.1	10	28.6
No answer	8.2	0	0
Totals	99.7 †	35	99.9 †
Unemployed (welfare, housewives, students)		13	

* Arizona State Employment Service, *An Arizona Resource Study: Flagstaff, 1969*. Research and Information Series, No. ECO-3-19, (Phoenix: May 1969).
† Does not equal 100 percent because of rounding.

This, of course, is not surprising. Studies of urban Indians in other areas have consistently found the same patterns (5). Indeed, it is the usual explanation of the excessive drinking so frequently seen among Indian migrants to urban areas. To anticipate our discussion of drinking patterns in the four groups, however, we shall use these same findings to question whether, in fact, it is deprivation that explains the patterns that emerge. Although urban migrants may appear less "deprived" than their reservation kinsmen, in terms of their contacts with the dominant society they may be more deprived.

In Chapter Three we pointed out that one factor that forced people into the raiding complex in the prereservation period and forces them into the migrant labor pool at present is the stratification system on reservation. It

Table 6.7   Ownership of Sheep Permits
in the Four Groups

Permits	Hospital Number	Hospital Per-cent	Plateau Number	Plateau Per-cent	South Tuba Number	South Tuba Per-cent	Flagstaff Number	Flagstaff Per-cent
Those with permits	14	40.0	18	37.5	5	12.8	5	10.4
Those without permits	18	51.4	24	50.0	28	71.8	41	85.4
Unknown	3	8.6	5	12.5	6	15.4	2	4.2
Totals	35	100.0	47	100.0	39	100.0	48	100.0
Mean number of units for those with permits		97.8		107.4		143.7		64.4
Mean number of units (less unknowns)		41.5		45.8		21.6		6.9

is obvious that the class of *pobres*—persons without much stock—is getting relatively and absolutely larger (6). The land base and carrying capacity of the range are fixed, but the population is exploding. This accounts for the large proportion of the Plateau and hospital groups who do seasonal (i.e., migrant) wage work. It also accounts for permanent moves off reservation.

We have also shown that few individuals in the Flagstaff sample have sheep permits. It was not possible to gather adequate data on how many sheep permits their parents owned, but we attempted to determine the family source of income when our respondents were growing up (Table 6.8). Although the categories are not precisely the same as in Table 6.5, it is striking that about 41 percent of our off-reservation informants came from families where steady wage work was the primary source of income. Also, only 31 percent of the families of origin of the Flagstaff group depended completely on livestock. Thus, a generation ago these families were less in-

Table 6.8 Source of Income of Flagstaff
Informants' Families of Origin

Source of Income	Frequency	Percent
Agriculture (farming)	0	0
Livestock	15	31.2
Steady wage work	13	27.0
Occasional wage work (including migrant)	0	0
Steady wage work supplemented by livestock	7	14.5
Livestock and occasional wage work	5	10.4
Agriculture and livestock	2	4.2
Agriculture and wage work	2	4.2
Medicine man and livestock	1	2.1
Unknown	3	6.2
Totals	48	99.8 *

* Does not equal 100 percent because of rounding.

volved in the traditional economy and more involved in the wage economy than the present generation of Kaibito Plateau informants.

Clearly, the fact that these families were poorer in traditional terms and were being forced into the wage economy on a full-time basis accounts largely for the stability of the Flagstaff group's residence off reservation. Furthermore, it is our contention that these factors originate in the stratification system of traditional Navajo society, although obviously intensified by the effects of white contact, particularly stock reduction, which may have increased the number of *pobres.*

The fact that individuals in our Flagstaff group grew up in families that were poor in traditional terms and were also exposed to parental figures who did wage work had the effect of providing models different from the traditional ones. This was reinforced, as we point out below, by their educational experience.

—————————— EDUCATIONAL BACKGROUND ——————————

Indian education has been the subject of numerous studies over the past years (7). In general, it has been found wanting. Especially since the Civil War, more and more Indians have been placed in boarding schools where strict regimentation, denigration of the Indian students' tribal heritage, poor teaching, and inappropriate training have combined to create disastrous effects.

Although the period of the administration of Indian affairs under John Collier was marked by an attempt at the creation of community schools, there are still many children in Bureau of Indian Affairs boarding schools. "Of the 152,000 American Indian school children, 36,000 attend boarding schools. Of these boarding school students, 21,000 are Navajo" (8). A generation ago when most of the people in our four groups were attending school, the proportion of boarding school children was probably even higher.

It seems fair to characterize the Indian boarding schools as total institutions.

> In total institutions there is a basic split between a large managed group, conveniently called inmates, and a small supervisory staff. Inmates typically live in the institution and have restricted contact with the world outside the walls; staff often operate on an eight-hour day and are socially integrated into the outside world. Each grouping tends to conceive of the other in terms of narrow hostile stereotypes, staff often seeing inmates as bitter, secretive, and untrustworthy, while inmates often see staff as condescending, high-handed, and mean. Staff tends to feel superior and righteous, inmates tend, in some ways at least, to feel inferior, weak, blameworthy, and guilty.
>
> Social mobility between the two strata is grossly restricted; social distance is typically great and often formally prescribed (9).

In addition, Indian boarding schools have typical degradation ceremonies —washing and cutting of hair, bathing, new clothes, and, more subtly, a denigration of the society from which the child comes.

Many observers have pointed out that the society in which the Indian child usually spends the first five years of his life makes a start in teaching him how to live as an Indian—be he a Sioux, Navajo, Hopi, or a member of any other tribe (10). When he enters school, an attempt is made to teach him how to be an Anglo-American. The disjunction between the two worlds is frightening and upsetting for many children.

As a result of the school experience, many Indians are said to be aimless, to lack self-confidence, and to indulge in such deviant behavior as glue and gasoline sniffing and the drinking of alcoholic beverages.

Because the educational experience is often a traumatic one, said to result in excessive drinking, and because educational achievement is one gauge of acculturation, it is important to compare the kind and amount of exposure

Table 6.9   Years of Schooling of Individuals
in the Four Study Groups

Years of Schooling	Hospital	Plateau	South Tuba	Flagstaff
0	13	25	9	3
1	3	1	0	1
2	0	0	2	1
3	3	3	0	1
4	3	1	0	0
5	1	6	2	0
6	0	2	3	6
7	1	2	2	1
8	2	3	2	6
9	2	0	2	1
10	1	0	4	2
11	0	1	3	6
12	4	3	6	11
13	0	0	1	5
14	0	0	0	0
15	0	0	0	2
16	0	0	2	0
Unknown	2	0	1	2
Totals	35	47	39	48
Mean years of education	3.9	3.0	7.1	9.1

to various educational systems that members of our four groups have had. Table 6.9 indicates the amount of schooling, in years, of the various groups. Table 6.10 lists the types of school last attended by each informant.

These tables reveal a number of interesting comparisons. Not surprisingly, of the persons who attended school in each group, the largest number is made up of those who attended Bureau of Indian Affairs boarding schools. Nor is it surprising that more of the Flagstaff group attended off-

Table 6.10 Type of School Last Attended
by Individuals in Each Group

Type of School	Hospital	Plateau	South Tuba	Flagstaff
Bureau of Indian Affairs off-reservation boarding school	11	11	17	12
BIA on-reservation boarding school	5	10	2	15
BIA day school on reservation	0	0	0	0
BIA border-town dormitory	0	0	0	0
On-reservation public school	1	0	4	0
Off-reservation public school	1	0	0	4
On-reservation mission school	0	0	1	1
Off-reservation mission school	0	1	0	2
Other (including college)	0	0	4	8
None	13	25	9	3
Unknown	4	0	2	3
Totals	35	47	39	48

reservation public schools, mission schools, or college. Notice that many people did not attend school at all (Table 6.11). In fact, the pattern is as follows: the hospital and Plateau groups are not significantly different; they both differ significantly from the South Tuba group, which differs from the Flagstaff group. Not unexpectedly, therefore, the mean years of education for the hospital and Kaibito Plateau groups are essentially the same, and they differ from the other two groups, which differ from each other.

Table 6.11   Comparison of Those With and Without Schooling in the Four Groups *

Schooling	Hospital		Plateau		South Tuba		Flagstaff	
	Number	Per-cent	Number	Per-cent	Number	Per-cent	Number	Per-cent
None	13	42	25	53	9	24	3	7
Some	18	58	22	47	28	76	43	93
Totals	31	100	47	100	37	100	46	100

Chi-square $= 25.7$

$df = 3$

p is less than .001

* Unknowns excluded.

In each case, the increasingly urbanized group has more education than the more rural groups. This is not surprising. However, it is unexpected that the Plateau and hospital groups do not differ from one another. This pattern follows that shown earlier in regard to the possession of sheep permits.

The Flagstaff informants come from families that, a generation ago, were poorer in traditional terms than the Plateau group is at present. This exposed them to parental wage workers as models. It also increased the likelihood that they would attend school. There were no livestock for them to tend at home, and their families had every reason to encourage them to acquire new skills. At boarding schools they were exposed for long periods to teachers and guidance personnel who also provided alternate models to the traditional ones—in this case, White-middle- or lower-middle-class ones.

The fact that such alternate models are necessary for successfully learning new patterns of behavior is a cliché of the social sciences, and we point out in the following chapter that it not only includes attitudes toward work appropriate to the wage economy but also attitudes concerning the use of alcoholic beverages.

———————————— MILITARY EXPERIENCE ————————————

Service in the armed forces is often said to be a major cause of Indian drinking. As in the case of education, it is often said to be a markedly acculturating experience. Many Hopi informants, for instance, have pointed to military service as the major cause of increased drinking in that tribe.

In a passage quoted earlier, however, Downs remarked that military experience, in itself, was not the force for change that many people have said it was (11). Rather, it was the changes on reservation due to stock reduction that forced many veterans to leave the reservation for good after they returned from the army in the late 1940s.

Vogt, in a study of Navajo veterans, pointed to a somewhat similar phenomenon. Depending on his prearmy background and the kind of unit he was in, the military experience may or may not have had an impact on the Navajo serviceman. In general, the veterans who were "not effectively socialized to conservative Navajo values" (12), and who had many contacts with white society prior to their military service—that is, were more acculturated to begin with—were more affected by their experience than those who were less acculturated.

In the light of these observations, our findings are not surprising (Table 6.12). The Plateau, South Tuba, and hospital groups are similar in the proportion of men from each who were in military service, and the entire on-reservation group differs significantly from the off-reservation people in Flagstaff.

It also appears that their respective experiences in the service were different. In the Flagstaff group were all of the men in our entire study who had served in the well-known Navajo code-talker outfit. This group had been specially trained during World War II to use Navajo as a code. They served with marine units throughout the South Pacific and were able to communicate from one unit to another in the only code never to be broken by the Japanese.

Two requirements for being in this unit were a good command of En-

Table 6.12   Military Experience of Men in Each Group

Military Experience	Hospital		Plateau		South Tuba		Flagstaff	
	Number	Per-cent	Number	Per-cent	Number	Per-cent	Number	Per-cent
In service	4	19	6	29	4	17	11	61
Not in service	19	63	14	67	17	74	6	33
Unknown	7	23	1	5	2	9	1	6
Totals	30	99 *	21	101 *	23	100	18	100

Chi-square $= 12.5$

$df = 3$

p less than .001

* Does not equal 100 percent because of rounding.

glish and a knowledge of Navajo. Clearly, those in the Flagstaff group, who had more education than our other informants, were better able to qualify for this special unit. Therefore, although quite a number of men from all of our groups were in the service, the kind of experience they had and the subsequent recognition that they received were largely determined by how well educated they were to begin with. It was, moreover, the Flagstaff men who were best qualified as a group precisely because of their better education.

Of all our informants who were in the army, the vast majority had begun drinking before they entered. What they did learn about drinking in the army was, chiefly, what we would expect. The men who were in units without other Indians did their drinking with Anglos. When there were other Indians in the unit, they tended to drink together. As a number of our informants remarked: when they were with white men, they drank like white men; when they were with Indians, they drank like Indians.

Here as elsewhere it became clear that there was a style of drinking that many of our informants, both white and Indian, regarded as Indian. This included such things as drinking in a group in which the bottle was passed around, and drinking to the point of intoxication or unconsciousness.

Drinking like a white man meant drinking one's own drink more slowly, perhaps getting a bit high but not grossly drunk or passing out; in essence, being moderate rather than extreme in one's behavior. There was no one, however, of either those in Flagstaff or those on the reservation, who felt that his present pattern of drinking had been learned in the army.

────────────────── VOTING BEHAVIOR ──────────────────

Voting behavior has interested sociologists for many years but, for obvious reasons, has not concerned the anthropologists studying various American Indian tribes. As Indians become more politically active, however, an analysis of their voting pattern may offer helpful insights into changing levels of acculturation—as measured by the extent of political participation and by changes in self-image as reflected by party preference in national and state elections.

During the summer of 1969 we gathered data on the voting behavior of the Plateau, South Tuba, and Flagstaff groups in the national elections of 1968 and the tribal elections of 1966. We have published our results elsewhere; here, we give only a brief summary and discussion of our findings (13).

Degree of Participation.   Although more of our on-reservation informants voted in the tribal elections of 1966 than did the Flagstaff Navajo, a total of 72 percent voted (unknowns were counted as not voting). This compares favorably with the 39 percent of eligible voters participating in the national, state, and county elections of 1968 in Coconino County, Arizona, where all of our Navajo informants resided. Flagstaff residents participated in the 1968 national election in the same proportion as the general population of the county. A much smaller percentage of on-reservation Navajos voted in the national elections (19 percent).

Navajo participation in their own as well as in national elections has increased rapidly during recent years. In 1953, Aberle found that no one had voted in national elections in the remote Aneth area although 66 percent had voted in Mexican Springs (14). By 1961, Moore found that 27 percent of his Aneth informants had voted in the presidential elections of 1960 (15). Shepardson has pointed out that the form of government now taking shape on the Navajo reservation is becoming institutionalized because there is a "consensus on the value of accepting and participating in the new system" (16).

It appears that Navajos participate in the elections that most concern them at levels equal to and greater than those of the general population in the same county. Thus, although increasing levels of participation over a period of time may be an indication of change and acculturation, the measure does not satisfactorily distinguish between traditional and acculturated groups at the present time. One might also question the use of this gauge as a measure of the degree of Navajo alienation.

Party Preferences. It has been said that 95 percent of the Indians of this country are Democrats (17). It was of considerable interest to find that only the Flagstaff informants voted Democrat in 1968 while those living on reservation voted Republican. This, we believe, reflects the image of the self as an Indian vis à vis the white society.

After the stock reduction program of the 1930s, on-reservation Navajos became disillusioned with the Democratic party. This changed in 1960 when, in reaction to the Republican policy of termination, the on-reservation vote switched to Kennedy and the Democrats. In 1968, Coconino County predictably went almost two to one for Nixon and Goldwater (Senate). The general on-reservation vote in Tuba City, which included non-Indian residents, was also predominantly Republican. Eighty-three percent of our on-reservation informants voted Republican. It appears that on-reservation Navajos vote conservative along with the rest of the surrounding areas except when federal Indian policy takes precedence as an issue. The on-reservation voter, then, does not identify with the urban ethnic minorities but concerns himself with relationships between the federal government and the reservation, and remains aware of the general conservative cast of the surrounding states.

The Flagstaff Navajos present a sharp contrast. Approximately 70 percent of those voting went for Humphrey and Elson (Senate). In Flagstaff only the precincts in which Mexicans and Negroes live went Democratic. Since almost all of the long-term Flagstaff Navajos live in the precincts that voted Republican, this cannot be viewed as a result of influence from the neighborhood and certainly not from the general population of the state. Instead, it appears that Flagstaff Navajos consider their political and economic position as paralleling that of other nonwhite ethnic minorities. As one Flagstaff informant remarked, "I was talking to some Negroes and Mexicans, and they treat them the same way they treat us."

Thus, the major difference between on- and off-reservation Navajos is not in the degree of their participation in political life but in a shift in self-perception. The successful town dweller comes to identify his situation with that of other citizens at the same economic level and minority position. The on-reservation Navajo is still primarily concerned with his special reservation status and how it is affected by federal Indian policy. Not only is he isolated from daily contact with other minorities but political realities dictate that he should not identify with them.

—————————— RELIGIOUS LIFE ——————————

During the past 100 years, the Navajos have been exposed to a variety of new religions: first, various forms of Christianity and, more recently, peyotism. The religious affiliation of individuals in the four study groups is shown in Table 6.13. Not surprisingly, the proportion of traditionalists is by far the greatest in the Plateau group (including those who combine peyotism with traditionalism) and the least in Flagstaff. The distribution of

Table 6.13 Religious Preference

	Hospital		Plateau		South Tuba		Flagstaff	
Religion	Number	Per-cent	Number	Per-cent	Number	Per-cent	Number	Per-cent
Traditional	8	23.5	11	23.6	6	15.3	2	4.2
Traditional NNAC*	1	2.9	12	25.5	0	0	0	0
NNAC	0	0	13	27.6	0	0	9	18.8
Catholic	4	11.7	2	4.2	1	2.5	4	8.3
LDS ‡	4	11.7	1	2.1	4	10.2	5	10.4
Protestant	10	29.3	4	8.4	20	51.1	21	43.8
None	6	17.6	3	6.3	2	5.0	4	8.3
Unknown	2	2.9	1	2.1	6	15.3	3	6.3
Totals	35	99.6 †	47	99.8 †	39	99.4 †	48	100.1 †

* NNAC, Navajo Native American Church.   ‡LDS, Latter Day Saints (Mormon)
† Does not equal 100 percent because of rounding.

peyotism both on and off reservation is unexpected in light of Aberle's assertion that: "A high level of acculturation predicts a low level of peyotism. This finding is tentatively interpreted by reference to acculturation as a process that provides solutions to problems for contemporary Navajos" (18).

Traditional Religion. Over 75 percent of Plateau residents think of themselves as traditionalists, even though many also attend peyote meetings. A major factor influencing the degree of traditional ceremonialism in the Plateau area and among Tuba City traditionalists is economic. Traditional Navajo healing ceremonies are costly; they involve the cooperation of large numbers of kin and take several days to perform.

In 1960, Levy collected data on the ceremonials conducted over a five-year period (1956–1960) among the Plateau and South Tuba groups. In 1969, comparable data were collected by Kunitz for the five-year period 1965–1969.

Between 1956 and 1960, 80 ceremonies were performed for adult patients in the Plateau group. For the years 1965–1969, the total number of ceremonies remained the same, but 62 were peyote meetings. For the vast majority of adults, this did not represent a religious conversion so much as a shift to a cheaper and shorter (one-night) healing ceremony that required little cooperation from kinsmen.

The traditionalists in South Tuba had 20 ceremonies performed between 1956 and 1960 and 19 between 1965 and 1969. Again, the level of ceremonial activity has not declined. On the other hand, ceremonies in South Tuba are of the shorter one- or three-night forms rather than the full five- and nine-night ceremonies performed among the Plateau people. The shorter forms are adaptive to the wage-work economy in South Tuba and to the general difficulty in obtaining help from distant kinsmen. The use of the cheaper forms of ceremony was observed during the first five-year interval among the South Tuba group. It appears that the economic pressures were felt much later by the Plateau group.

The few traditionalists in Flagstaff had participated in ceremonies during the brief returns they had made to the reservation over a five-year period.

Peyotism. It is not surprising that peyotism spread rapidly among traditionals in the Plateau area. Its lack of popularity in South Tuba and its relative popularity in Flagstaff require discussion.

The Native North American Church (peyote) has been called one of the "religions of the oppressed" (19). It was only in the late 1930s that the peyote religion entered Navajo country, although it had been used extensively by Plains tribes since 1878. Its adoption by the Navajos coincided with the stock-reduction program, and Aberle has suggested that those who lost the most were the most likely to become members of the Native North American Church.

Peyotism did not spread to the Tuba City area until 1959. Before that time, the Plateau people had only heard rumors about the church and were definitely opposed to it. By 1964, however, over one half of the adults were attending peyote meetings. Older adults accepted peyote as an economically feasible alternative to the traditional healing ceremonies. The extended-kin group was suffering from a manpower shortage as many of the younger males sought government employment or spent increasing amounts of time away from home engaged in migratory wage work. Those who converted completely to peyote were the young married couples who found it compatible with their seasonal wage-work pattern. For these younger Navajos, peyotism provided access to supernatural power as well as to leadership roles that had become difficult to achieve in the traditional manner since the days of stock reduction. All males who considered themselves converts to the peyote church mentioned that peyote was a means to combat drinking.

Peyotism found no foothold in South Tuba or in other settlements near trading posts such as Coppermine. Although the reasons for this are not clear, our guess is that the South Tuba group had already made adjustments to the steady wage-work economy of Tuba City.

The nine peyotists living in Flagstaff are four married couples and one divorced woman living with three of her children. Four of these individuals are second-generation peyotists. Thus, for approximately half of the peyotist population in Flagstaff, the conversion had taken place a generation before in a reservation setting. The first-generation peyotists had also converted while still on the reservation, and all of them were less acculturated and less well employed than the second-generation members of the church.

Christianity.   Membership in a Christian church is characteristic of more than half of the informants in all groups except the Plateau group. Christianity appears to be an appropriate alternative to traditional ceremonialism.

The most striking theme running through our discussions with off-reservation Navajos was that of loneliness. The move into an off-reservation town broke kin ties and lessened the number of contacts with other Navajos. The Navajo churchgoers serve as surrogate families and provide a new network of friendships in the city. Christianity also parallels some of the functions of the Native North American Church and provides a morality appropriate for living in white society. Both churches condemn drinking and provide justification for giving up the old ways. Both religions protect specifically against witchcraft which, among Christians, is equated with the Satanic power of the traditional medicine men. For people freed of the traditional mechanisms of social control—fear of gossip and accusations of witchcraft, for example—it provides a new code of behavior and set of social sanctions.

None of the people whom we interviewed in Flagstaff and South Tuba were from families with as much livestock as the Plateau group now owns. For these people, wage work and Christianity have offered alternatives to a difficult life which the traditional society had not been able to provide. By contrast, the persons who owned stock had a stake in the old way of life and have adapted to change within a traditional framework. Peyote is used in conjunction with traditional religion rather than as an alternative, and seasonal wage work is sought instead of out migration.

SUMMARY

We have presented data comparing the four study groups along several parameters. Although we have not been able to devise a single index of acculturation combining all of the various factors, the general trend is quite clear. The Plateau group is the least acculturated and the closest to traditional patterns. The Flagstaff group is the most acculturated. The South Tuba group occupies an intermediate position on most of the scales. The hospital group falls somewhere between the South Tuba and Plateau groups reflecting the fact that approximately half of them live in South Tuba while the rest come from areas similar to the Kaibito Plateau.

In addition to the differing levels of acculturation that have been measured, a picture of differentiated out migration and adaptation has emerged. Within the overall trend to better education and a shift to a cash economy, we find that change has not taken place in an identical manner in all segments of Navajo society. The earlier Navajo system of stratification has provided the bases for divergent lines of adaptation. The *pobres*, with little access to economic or religious power in the traditional society, used education, Christianity, and wage work as alternatives to an already difficult life.

The *ricos* and those who could reasonably aspire to upward mobility in the traditional system have maintained their religion and pastoralism in a protected reservation environment and have adapted to the generalized pressures for change by combining pastoralism with seasonal wage work and peyotism with traditional ceremonialism in a manner that attempts to preserve the core of traditional Navajo pursuits.

Viewed in these terms, we do not perceive all change as reflecting social disintegration and personal disorientation or anomie. Nor, at this level of analysis, do we see evidence for generally increasing social deviance in the more acculturated groups. If, as we believe, these differing modes of adaptation are adequate for different segments of the population, we would expect to find patterns of drinking varying in a similar manner, that is, adaptive to white norms off reservation and to Navajo norms on reservation.

--------------------------- NOTES ---------------------------

1. Arizona State Employment Service, *An Arizona Resource Study: Flagstaff 1969.* Research and Information Series, No. ECO-3-19 (Phoenix: May, 1969), p. 18.

2. J. E. Levy, "Navajo Suicide," *Human Organization,* 25 (1965), p. 315; D. C. Leighton and C. Kluckhohn, *Children of the People* (Cambridge: Harvard University Press, 1948), p. 96; C. Kluckhohn, *Navajo Witchcraft,* 2nd ed. (Boston: Beacon Press, 1962), p. 100.

3. S. J. Kunitz, J. E. Levy, P. Bellet and T. Collins, "A Census of Flagstaff Navajos," *Plateau,* 41 (1969): 156–163. S. J. Kunitz, J. E. Levy and C. L. Odoroff, "A One Year Follow-Up of Navajo Migrants to Flagstaff, Arizona," *Plateau,* 42 (1970): 92–106.

4. A. B. Hollingshead, *Two-Factor Index of Social Position* (New Haven: Department of Sociology, Yale University, 1957).

5. R. Jessor, T. D. Graves, R. C. Hanson and S. L. Jessor, *Society, Personality and Deviant Behavior* (New York: Holt, Rinehart and Winston, 1968); W. H. Hodge, *The Albuquerque Navajos,* Anthropological Papers of the University of Arizona, No. 11 (Tucson: University of Arizona Press, 1969); C. W. Tyler, Jr. and A. L. Saeger, Jr., "Maternal Health and Socioeconomic Status of Non-reservation Indians," *Public Health Reports, 83* (1968): 465–473; T. D. Graves, "The Personal Adjustment of Navajo Indian Migrants to Denver, Colorado," *American Anthropologist, 72* (1970): 35–54; J. A. Price, "The Migration and Adaptation of Ameri-

can Indians to Los Angeles," *Human Organization*, 27 (1968): 168–175.

6. R. W. Young, *The Navajo Yearbook* (Window Rock, Arizona: The Navajo Agency, 1961), p. 212.

7. See, for instance, the bibliography in B. Berry, *The Education of American Indians, A Survey of the Literature* (a report prepared for the Special Subcommittee on Indian Education of the Committee on Labor and Public Welfare, U.S. Senate, U.S. Government Printing Office, Washington, D.C., 1969).

8. R. L. Bergman, "Boarding Schools and the Psychological Problems of Indian Children" (umpublished report to the Committee on Indian Health of the American Academy of Pediatrics, 1967), p. 1.

9. E. Goffman, *Asylums, Essays on the Social Situation of Mental Patients and other Inmates* (Garden City, N.Y.: Doubleday Anchor Books, Inc., 1961), p. 7.

10. E. H. Erikson, *Childhood and Society* (New York: W. W. Norton, 1963); H. L. Saslow and M. H. Harrover, "Research on Psychosocial Adjustment of Indian Youth," *American Journal of Psychiatry*, 125 (1968): 224–231.

11. J. F. Downs, *Animal Husbandry in Navajo Society and Culture*, University of California Publications in Anthropology, Vol. 1 (Berkeley and Los Angeles: University of California Press, 1964), p. 21.

12. E. Z. Vogt, *Navaho Veterans, A Study of Changing Values*, Papers of the Peabody Museum of American Archaeology and Ethnology, Vol. XLI, No. 1, Reports of the Rimrock Project Values Series, No. 1 (Cambridge: Harvard University Press, 1951), p. 117.

13. S. J. Kunitz and J. E. Levy, "Navajo Voting Patterns," *Plateau*, 43 (1970): 1–8.

14. D. F. Aberle, *The Peyote Religion among the Navajo* (Chicago: Aldine, 1966), p. 99.

15. H. C. Moore, "Culture Change in a Navajo Community, *American Historical Anthropology, Essays in Honor of Leslie Spier*, C. L. Riley and W. W. Taylor, eds. (Carbondale: Southern Illinois University Press, 1967).

16. M. Shepardson, *Navajo Ways in Government*, American Anthropological Association Memoir, 96 (1963).

17. "Editorial," *Navajo Times* (Window Rock, Arizona, July 17, 1969).

18. D. F. Aberle, *Peyote*, pp. 193–194.

19. V. Lanternari, *The Religions of the Oppressed* (New York: Alfred A. Knopf, 1963).

Chapter Seven

DRINKING PATTERNS AND
THE SEQUELAE OF DRINKING

Let us examine the relationships between drinking behavior and level of acculturation. The questionnaire results and police records obtained from individuals in the study groups provide data that permit us to measure involvement with alcohol as well as the sequelae of alcohol use, both physiological and social, in a manner comparable with studies of drinking in non-Indian societies.

The importance of maintaining the comparability of our data took precedence over the need to describe Navajo drinking in its own terms. The dangers involved in the use of questions and scales developed in one society for research conducted in a very different one are numerous. Two of our measures did not appear to yield reliable results. Others appeared to perform their task more adequately. Most important, however, the results of the different tests, even the most unreliable, were never contradictory. Throughout our discussion we explain the reliability of each measure.

————————— **THE EXTENT OF DRINKING** —————————

In our discussion of drinking in the Southwest we suggested that more and more Navajos were drinking larger and larger amounts of alcohol. The only evidence we could find on this question was descriptive and impressionistic; that is, observers thought they saw more drunkenness each year,

134

and the percentage of arrests for drunkenness and possession of alcohol on reservation had been increasing steadily for some years. While it is probably true that more alcohol is being consumed by more Navajos now than in the late nineteenth century, this type of evidence does not help us to decide whether there are proportionately more Navajo alcoholics now than there were before World War II, for instance. Nor does it tell us whether Navajos drink more or less than do Anglos. The answers to these questions are crucial, however, and it was with this objective that we utilized questions and methods employed among the general white population.

The Prevalence of Drinking.   Over the years, a number of studies have attempted to gauge the prevalence of drinking throughout the nation and to relate drinking behavior to other variables. One of the earliest studies was undertaken by Riley and Marden (1). This was followed, some years later, by the work of Mulford (2) and of Cahalan and Cisin (3).

These investigators agree that, generally, more men than women drink, that drinking is more common in younger age groups, and that it increases along a spectrum from rural farm to urban areas of over 1 million population. Nationally, 71 percent of the adult population drinks, 8 percent used to drink but quit, and the remainder (21 percent) are lifelong abstainers. These proportions vary from region to region throughout the country as well as by age, sex, occupation, income, religion, and other factors (4). One of the striking findings in Mulford's survey was that the percentage of those who have quit drinking increases as one moves down the socioeconomic scale.

Cahalan and Cisin, in their later nationwide study, found comparable data on the prevalence of drinking: "Seventy-seven percent of the men and sixty percent of the women qualified as nonabstainers (said they drank at least once a year)" (5).

In striking contrast, we find that the level of drinking does not exceed 42 percent among the Navajo groups. There are, in fact, fewer people drinking at a given time among the Navajo groups than Mulford found in any region or type of community (6). This low proportion of drinkers is due less to any large number of lifelong abstainers than it is to the presence of many individuals in each Navajo group who were once drinkers but who stopped. In Flagstaff, however, we found over 45 percent, mostly women, who were total abstainers, a proportion unmatched by the national samples or the other Navajo groups.

Table 7.1 shows our data by sex for the three nonalcoholic groups. The

Table 7.1 Drinking Status of Men and Women in Three Groups

Drinking Status *	Plateau		South Tuba		Flagstaff	
	M	W	M	W	M	W
Lifelong abstainer	1	9	0	9	2	20
Total stopped, due to:	12	14	6	4	7	3
Peyote	(6)	(6)	(0)	(0)	(1)	(0)
Christianity	(0)	(0)	(1)	(2)	(2)	(1)
Other reasons	(6)	(8)	(5)	(2)	(4)	(2)
Currently drinking	7	1	13	1	9	7
Totals	20	24	19	14	18	30

Comparisons	Chi-square	df	p Value
Women between groups	16.24	4	less than .01
Men vs. women within groups:			
Kaibito Plateau	10.77	2	less than .01
South Tuba	19.37	2	less than .001
Flagstaff	10.90	2	less than .01
Men between groups (abstainers omitted):			
Plateau vs. South Tuba plus Flagstaff	3.11	1	approx. .07
South Tuba vs. Plateau vs. Flagstaff	4.05	2	approx. .13

* Unknowns not shown.

chi-square analysis indicates that there are significant differences between men and women within each group—far more men than women drink. Notice the differences between women in the three groups. A higher proportion of women in the more acculturated groups are total abstainers, although more Flagstaff women are currently drinking than women in the other groups.

There are almost no male abstainers in any of the three groups. There is also a tendency for Plateau males to have stopped drinking more often than did males in the other groups. Aging itself causes a cutting down on drinking and the median age of Plateau males is somewhat higher than that of the South Tuba men, but not of the Flagstaff men. It is also possible, however, that the group binge-drinking pattern of the Plateau male involves early acquaintance with some of the more terrifying features of drinking. Deaths from exposure, freezing, or auto accidents are frequent consequences of massive binges in open country. Becoming aware with this type of mishap early in life may help to develop an incentive to quit, which other types of drinkers do not have. In any event, the high proportion of Navajo males who have quit after years of heavy drinking leads us to question the chronic addictive nature of "Indian alcoholism."

The Quantity and Frequency of Drinking. The Quantity-Frequency Index was first developed by Straus and Bacon to measure the extent of drinking (7). It has subsequently been used by a number of other investigators in various modified forms (8). It has been criticized and expanded by Knupfer and Cahalan and Cisin (9). The criticism has generally been that the Quantity-Frequency Index does not distinguish clearly enough between types of drinkers. For example, 14 drinks in a week represent different styles of drinking if they are taken either in one sitting on Saturday night or at the rate of 2 drinks every evening. The Quantity-Frequency Index we used was taken from Mulford's study (10) and is subject to the same criticisms.

The question was asked, "How much do you usually drink at one sitting?" The replies were categorized as follows.

Small amount: 1–5 glasses of beer
                  1–3 bottles of beer
                  1–2 drinks of liquor
                  1–3 glasses of wine

Medium amount: 6–9 glasses of beer
                 4–6 bottles of beer
                 3–4 drinks of liquor
                 4–5 glasses of wine

Large amount: 10 or more glasses of beer
                 7 or more bottles of beer
                 5 or more drinks of liquor
                 6 or more glasses of wine

Regarding these divisions, Mulford has written:

> This trichotomy was arrived at after converting standard "bottles,"
> "glasses," and "drinks" to amounts of absolute alcohol. It seems rea-
> sonable to assume that at least among drinkers there is a considerable
> consensus concerning the meaning of a "bottle" or a "glass" of beer, a
> "glass" of wine, and a "drink" of liquor (11).

This assumption did not prove so reasonable for the people with whom we
were working, and one of the major difficulties with our data is the question of measuring how much is actually drunk. We deal with this point
below.

After determining how much an informant drinks at a sitting, one also
finds out how often he or she drinks. The two factors are then combined
into the following scale.

Type 1. Drinks infrequently (once a month at most) and consumes small
         amounts (not more than approximately 1.6 ounces of absolute alco-
         hol).

Type 2. Drinks infrequently (once a month at most) and consumes medium
         amounts (1.6 to 2.88 ounces of absolute alcohol) or large amounts
         (more than 2.88 ounces of absolute alcohol).

Type 3. Drinks more than once a month but consumes small amounts.

Type 4. Drinks two to four times a month and consumes medium or large
         amounts.

Type 5. Drinks more than once a week and consumes medium or large
         amounts.

> A major shortcoming of the index is that it does not gather all alco-
> holics into one category. That is, one might suppose that all alcoholics
> would fall into the heavy drinking category. However, since types 2
> and 4 as well as 5 have no upper limit on quantity (but frequency is
> limited) we are likely to find the infrequent binge drinker either a

type 2 or type 4. For this reason, in the present study Q-F types 2,4 and 5 are considered one category (12).

In Table 7.2 we show our data in the form used by Mulford. For men, it is clear that gross distinctions are possible; that is, hospital men are not represented in Types I and III ("nonalcoholic" types) and, in this, they differ from the other three groups of men. A similar distinction holds for the women.

Table 7.2 Quantity-Frequency Index of Men and Women in Four Groups *

Type	Hospital		Plateau		South Tuba		Flagstaff	
	M	W	M	W	M	W	M	W
I	0	0	1	3	1	2	2	2
II	7	1	3	3	3	0	0	1
III	0	0	2	4	2	2	2	3
IV	11	2	2	4	7	1	6	0
V	11	1	9	0	4	0	3	1
Totals	29	4	17	14	17	5	13	7

* Does not include unknowns and not-applicables but does include ex-drinkers.

We have not given statistical analyses of these data because, as we pointed out above, the assumptions on which the index rests are questionable for our purposes. First, the assumption of consensus among drinkers is misleading. The style of drinking, especially on reservation, involves passing a bottle around a group, making quantification of how much any individual actually imbibes almost impossible. Second, the wine that is drunk on reservation is most often the cheap, fortified variety. The alcohol content is 20 percent rather than the usual 12 percent found in most table wines. Therefore, estimating the amount of absolute alcohol an individual ingests is also highly problematical.

It was our impression that the style of drinking and the amount drunk vary significantly between the on- and off-reservation groups, but not significantly between on-reservation groups, particularly the hospital and Plateau groups. Indeed, our off-reservation informants often made the distinction themselves. The on-reservation pattern is one of peer group drinking as we have pointed out in Chapter Three. The usual drink is cheap, fortified wine that is passed around from person to person until the bottle is emptied. The off-reservation pattern is more like the one we associate with lower or lower middle class, blue collar workers: "I pick up a sixpack on my way home and drink it while I'm watching television." One off-reservation informant, when discussing the difference between his style of drinking and the style on reservation, volunteered the observation that the reason the latter group gets so drunk is because of passing the bottle around. He himself only drank from a can of beer which he would not share with others. He thought that perhaps germs got into the wine as it was passed around, and it was this that caused the drunkenness to reach epidemic proportions in such groups.

The scale was, however, useful in obtaining information on the kinds of beverages drunk by the different groups. It is clear, from the data presented in Table 7.3, that our impressions tend to agree with information given by respondents with a few interesting differences. The hospital and Plateau people drink primarily wine; South Tuba people drink primarily beer and liquor; and Flagstaff people drink primarily beer. This pattern is interesting because it indicates a similarity in the beverage of choice between the two least-acculturated groups. Fortified wines are probably the cheapest way to consume the largest amounts of alcohol. The fact that the Plateau and hospital groups are so similar reflects not only economic considerations but also notions of the best (i.e., fastest) way to get drunk. Equally important is the fact that the South Tuba and Flagstaff groups do not prefer wine. On the one hand, this indicates that, as a group, they have more cash but, on the other hand, we note that it is the two more acculturated groups that tend to use the same beverages as does the general population.

Thus, although by the usual Quantity-Frequency Scale we cannot distinguish between the three "normal" groups, taking into account the beverage of choice enables us to make distinctions. Not only can we distinguish between Kaibito Plateau and the other groups, but also between South Tuba and Flagstaff. That is, more people in South Tuba drink liquor than in Flagstaff. Again, this indicates what might be an important difference in that liquor too can lead to rapid intoxication, and its use may imply a willingness to get drunk and the availability of needed cash to do so with a more expensive beverage. In contrast, the preference for beer in Flagstaff

Table 7.3 Beverage of Choice in Each Group *

Beverage	Hospital Number	Hospital Percent	Plateau Number	Plateau Percent	South Tuba Number	South Tuba Percent	Flagstaff Number	Flagstaff Percent
Beer	9	27.3	6	19.4	9	40.9	12	60
Wine	23	69.7	17	54.8	4	18.2	3	15
Liquor	1	3.0	8	25.8	9	40.9	1	5
All Three	0	0	0	0	0	0	4	20
Totals	33	100	31	100	22	100	20	100

* Does not include unknowns and not-applicables but does include ex-drinkers.

indicates a close similarity to a more usual working-class pattern of drinking.

At this juncture it is difficult to compare Navajo drinking with white drinking. We can say, based on our observations and some of the findings in this section, that Navajos do not drink in the same way as whites, although the most acculturated group has several characteristics that are closer to white styles. We cannot, however, get any idea of whether Navajos really drink more per capita than do whites or whether they are more alcoholic.

——— PERSONAL INVOLVEMENT WITH ALCOHOL ———

If gross measures of quantity and frequency of alcoholic intake could not distinguish between different styles of drinking, we wondered whether questions designed to elicit attitudes and personal drinking habits could. Two sets of scaled questions developed by Mulford and Miller—the Definition of Alcohol and the Preoccupation with Alcohol scales—were modified for use with the Navajos.

Definition of Alcohol and Reasons for Drinking. The Definition of Alcohol Scale was designed to determine the personal effects and personal involvement that drinkers felt with alcohol. It was made up of statements taken from answers to the open-ended questions, "What do alcoholic beverages mean to you? How do you define liquor?" The full list of questions is given in references (13) and (22). In Mulford's analysis, they formed a Guttman scale that increased from the social-effects aspect of drinking ("liquor makes a social gathering more enjoyable") to the personal effects aspect ("liquor helps me forget I am not the kind of person I really want to be"). The more questions an individual answered positively, the higher on the scale he fell and the more he tended to be a "personal effects" drinker rather than a social drinker.

These types were then cross-tabulated with other scales, such as the Quantity-Frequency Index, Trouble Due to Drinking, and the Preoccupation Scale (discussed below), and were found to correlate. The higher a person scored on the personal effects or definition scale, the more likely he was to drink heavily and to have social difficulties related to his drinking. As Mulford and Miller explained their findings:

> From a symbolic-interaction point of view we might suppose that the personal-effects drinker, especially the extreme personal-effects drinker, is using alcohol as a means of securing a redefinition of himself and his relationship to others and perhaps of achieving an even more general reconceptualization of his symbolic environment. This may include complete oblivion. Examining the content of the scale items, proceeding from the bottom, it appears that the self and an increasingly "unfavorable" or "deficient" self becomes progressively more involved (14).

> The meaning of the scale items and the greater extent of drinking by those who define alcohol for its personal effects was interpreted as follows:

> (1) The personal-effects drinkers seek a greater number of goals through the use of alcohol; (2) they have a greater number of situational opportunities to drink; and (3) they drink in situations where there is a relative absence of restrictive group norms (15).

Jessor and associates used a similar scale derived from Mulford's work in their triethnic study. They found that high scores on their version of the scale correlated with high rates of deviant behavior (as measured by number of times the individual reported that he had gotten drunk, police records, and so on) as well as high scores on their Quantity-Frequency Index. In addition, they found that the Indians in their sample scored higher on all of these scales that did either the Spanish or Anglo informants. They regarded this as substantiating their hypothesis that deprivation caused both high drinking rates and high rates of deviance. Regarding the personal-effects reasons for drinking they write:

> Such reasons can be considered indirectly to reflect the degree of pressure on a person toward the use of illegitimate means; and personal-effects drinking, involving the frequent and heavy use of alcohol, is more likely to be associated with the socially disapproved consequences of drinking, such as frequent drunkenness (16).

In our study we used eight of the questions first used by Mulford and Miller (17). All were not used because of the difficulty of interpreting a number of them into Navajo. Proceeding from social effects to personal effects, the questions are:

1. Alcoholic beverages make a social gathering more enjoyable.
2. A drink sometimes makes me feel better.
3. Alcoholic beverages give me pleasure.
4. Alcoholic beverages make me more carefree.
5. Alcoholic beverages help me overcome shyness.
6. Alcoholic beverages make me less self-conscious.
7. Alcoholic beverages make me feel more satisfied with myself.
8. Alcoholic beverages help me get along better with other people.

In our analysis, these did not form a Guttman Scale and so they were scored as either zero (for a positive response) or one (for a negative response). The lower scores represented more positive answers.

Table 1 of Appendix III presents the differences for men and women within groups. The number of women in the hospital group was too small to make a statistical test meaningful, but the scores did not differ from the men's scores. In the Kaibito Plateau group, the difference in scores was significant, with men giving more "personal-effects" answers than women. The differences within the South Tuba and Flagstaff groups were not significant.

We compared men between groups and women between groups by using the Kruskal-Wallis one-way analysis of variance (18). In light of the findings given below, this is significant. In the style of drinking that Navajos report, there are striking differences. However, in the reasons given for drinking, that is, in the personal effects, there is no difference between the groups. There are two possibilities: either the questions are irrelevant and do not get at the reasons people drink; or there really is no difference.

It is conceivable that, although the scores for the entire scale might be the same, the pattern of responses within the scale might differ from group to group. Since we were not using a Guttman scale, the total score would not reflect these variations in the pattern of responses. This did not appear to be the case, that is, the same questions tended to be answered similarly from group to group.

It was our impression that many of our respondents had difficulty answering these questions because, by and large, they were not very introspective and psychologically minded. Several of the questions are not easily distinguished from one another, and it may be that to answer one either positively or negatively means that the respondent will answer several of the others the same way just because they appear to be essentially the same question.

Despite these reservations, the fact that there is no difference between groups is noteworthy in that the questions do appear to be able to distinguish between white alcoholics and nonalcoholics. We think that the Navajo informants tended to answer more of the questions affirmatively than nonalcoholic Anglos interviewed by Mulford. Although they were not designed with this in mind, many of the questions not only deal with redefining one's self and one's environment but also with the related issue of assertiveness. Indeed, questions 4–7 deal with this issue exclusively. Recalling what we said in Chapter One, that there is evidence to indicate that people drink in order to be assertive, we suggest that the higher proportion of positive responses on the part of our Navajo informants could be explained by saying that, for Navajos more than for most Anglos, drinking facilitates assertiveness.

If this scale is, in fact, getting at the issue of facilitation of assertiveness, it is suggestive that such motives do not appear to differ from group to group. What does differ is overt behavior as measured both by contacts with the police and self-reported drinking behavior. That is, although we cannot distinguish between the groups by their responses to these psychologically oriented questions, we can distinguish between them in terms of actual behavior.

People who score high on the "personal effects" reasons for drinking but who do not drink as much as we would expect, are "deviant" cases in terms of Mulford and Miller's theory. They suggest that:

> It may be that the "deviant" cases who define alcohol for its personal effects but who are light drinkers are being restrained by negative

definitions of alcohol and by definitions of self, such as "I am a good father and husband," which are incompatible with heavy drinking (19).

This is also a reasonable explanation of our findings. The Flagstaff group especially is in a position where, no matter what they might *like* to achieve with liquor, excessive drinking would be threatening to their positions as struggling members of a minority group in an Anglo-American town and incompatible with their self-images as steady wage workers, respectable home owners, and the people who are different from the on-reservation Navajos.

We do not insist on this as an explanation because of our reservations about the use of this index. As we said above, it seems to require more introspection and psychological-mindedness to answer this battery of questions than most of our other questions. Furthermore, several of the questions require rather fine distinctions, and we do not have complete confidence that our respondents were uniformly able to make these distinctions because of the problems of translating from English to Navajo.

When we asked people why they drank, the great majority said such things as, "to have a good time," "to be sociable," "to relax." One man said that when he drank, he was not afraid of witches. Another person said the people in her family used to drink to get one of the old men high in order to get him to sing his songs—something he wouldn't have done when sober. One woman said she drank because she was lonely.

Savard found that among the group of Navajo drinkers with whom he worked, alcohol was used to facilitate social participation rather "than as a means of escape" (20). Ferguson, in her study of Navajo drinkers in Gallup, distinguished between those who were "recreational" and those who were "anxiety" drinkers (21). Recreational drinkers were indulging in some of the new-found pleasures of town and undergoing little in the way of value conflict or acculturational stress. The former group responded to Disulfiram therapy, the latter did not.

The point is that people drink for a variety of reasons, most of them having to do with facilitating social interaction, overcoming inhibitions, and being more assertive. Rarely is oblivion or escape the reason given for drinking, although it clearly is an important one in some cases. Given these reasons for drinking, the way that one goes about it depends on what he has learned about the state of drunkenness, and how the surrounding society reacts to different types of drunken behavior. Unacculturated Navajos define the state of drunkenness as something good and the response of those around them to drunkenness is supportive of such behavior. Increasingly, acculturated Navajos have competing definitions of drunkenness and are more subject to external constraints that punish such behavior.

Index of Preoccupation with Alcohol. The Preoccupation Scale devised by Mulford was based on a series of questions first used by Jellinek in 1945 when he questioned a group of members of Alcoholics Anonymous on their drinking habits (22). Subsequently, a revised questionnaire was used with a larger group of Alcoholics Anonymous members and hospitalized alcoholics. In his 1958 survey, Mulford used a number of these questions in a survey of a random sample of Iowa residents. The scale was found to be cumulative; that is, it could be used to form a satisfactory Guttman Scale. As Mulford summarized the results:

1. The Preoccupation Scale repeatedly identifies a small (approximately 3 to 6 per cent, depending on whether scale type III, as well as types I and II, is considered "alcoholic") segment of the population with similar sociocultural characteristics.
2. The scale has the logically expected association with other indicators of extreme deviant drinking.
3. The segment of the general population identified by the scale approximates Jellinek's formula estimates in size and sociocultural distribution, and
4. Up to 90 per cent of hospitalized alcoholics met the scale criteria (23).

The scale was more successful, however, in identifying known alcoholics of lower socioeconomic status than in identifying those of higher status. In addition:

Of the four measures (Definition, Trouble Due to Drinking, Quantity-Frequency, and Preoccupation Scales), the one most predictive of each of the other three was the Preoccupation Scale. It is concluded that the Preoccupation Scale may be a useful index for identifying "alcoholics" in the general population of Iowa (24).

The Preoccupation Scale differs from the Definition of Alcohol Scale in that it deals primarily with the social or behavioral manifestations of drinking rather than the personal reasons given for drinking. Mulford had used 12 items that, in his analysis, were cumulative and that proceeded from the least to the most severe manifestations of excessive alcohol use. We used 11 of these 12 items. The one item omitted ("I take a few quick ones before going to a party to make sure I have enough") was not felt to be applicable to the Navajo situation. All of the other items were the same as in Mulford's various studies. Proceeding from roughly the least to the most extreme forms of alcohol use, the scale we used was as follows.

1. I don't nurse my drinks. I toss them down pretty fast.
2. I drink for the effect of alcohol (with little attention to the type of beverage or brand name).
3. Liquor has less effect on me than it used to.
4. I awaken the next day not being able to remember some of the things I had done while I was drinking.
5. I neglect my regular meals when I am drinking.
6. I take a drink the first thing when I get up in the morning.
7. I get intoxicated on work days.
8. Once I start drinking it is difficult for me to stop before I get completely intoxicated.
9. I sneak drinks when no one is looking.
10. I worry about not being able to get a drink when I need one.
11. I stay intoxicated for several days at a time.

The responses to these questions (either agree or disagree) did not form a Guttman Scale in our analysis. Instead, as with the Definition Scale, we scored the responses as zero for positive and one for negative. Lower scores, therefore, indicated more positive responses.

Table I of Appendix IV compares the scores of men and women within each group. We have not included the hospital group in this analysis because of the small number of women. Of the other three groups, only on Kaibito Plateau do the men differ from the women by having significantly more positive responses. This is similar to the pattern described previously in the responses to the Definition scale.

In Tables 2 and 3 of Appendix IV we compare men and women across groups as we did in the Definition Scale. The responses of the women do not differ significantly from one group to the other. The responses of the men, on the other hand, do differ: the Plateau and hospital men have scores that are considerably lower than the Flagstaff and South Tuba men.

Although, as we suggested previously, we cannot determine any differences in the attitudes of men drinkers using the Definition Scale, it is clear that the results of the Preoccupation Scale do distinguish between the more acculturated and traditional groups. We consider this scale considerably more valid than the Definition Scale because it does not call for reports of subjective states but deals with actual behavior that can more reliably be described.

It is interesting that the same questions found to be the most reliable in identifying white alcoholics also pick up a group of Navajo self-referred alcoholics but fail to distinguish between them and a group of men not regarded as alcoholic. This is important because, although we cannot distinguish between our various samples by the social-psychological indicators that have been successful in comparable studies among whites, the behavioral indicators do allow us to make distinctions. We maintain that it is on the basis of this behavior, which is diagnostic of deviant drinking in white society, that Indians tend to become labeled as alcoholics, and not on the basis of psychological variables. Moreover, it is on the basis of such behavior that the police make arrests, that social workers and physicians diagnose psychopathology and, ultimately, that many Indians themselves come to believe that they are alcoholics. The question that needs to be asked, however, is this: Does this behavior truly represent alcoholism as we are used to diagnosing it in white chronic alcoholics? We would answer negatively.

One of the remarkable things that we found was the ease with which men who would have been labeled as alcoholics (and, in many cases, were so labeled) gave up drinking entirely at some point in their lives. They experienced none of the anxiety or difficulty that we are used to seeing among Anglo alcoholics. The Plateau group included more men who had currently stopped drinking than did the South Tuba and Flagstaff groups, and we would suggest that many of them drank an extraordinary amount when young and then gave it up with little difficulty when they saw the social and physical costs that it entailed. The very ease with which it was given up seems to indicate that it did not play as central a role in their lives as it does in the lives of white alcoholics.

We can also contrast our results with Mulford's survey of white drinking practices, although not as precisely as we would like. It will be recalled that he categorized drinkers into five types by using a Guttman Scale. His 12 questions were broken down into four categories of 3 questions each. Type V drinkers were those people who drank but who answered none of the questions affirmatively. They were said not to be preoccupied with alcohol. Type IV drinkers answered two or three of the three most benign questions affirmatively. Type III drinkers answered not only the most benign questions but two or three of the next category as well, and so on for each of the succeeding categories.

We dropped one of Mulford's questions and our remaining questions did not form a Guttman Scale. Nevertheless, it was possible to make an approximate comparison by calculating what the possible scores would have to be for an individual in Mulford's typology to be scored in the same fashion as the Navajo informants. In Table 7.4 we have presented these data contrasting Mulford's respondents with ours (25).

Table 7.4 Type Drinker Derived from Preoccupation with Alcohol Score in Percent

Types	Alcoholics	General Sample	Hospital	Plateau	South Tuba	Flag-staff
I–III (0–8)	50.9	4.5	85.7	12.7	20.5	4.2
IV (9–10)	10.9	7.4	8.6	2.1	7.7	12.5
V (11)	38.2	60.4	—	2.1	2.6	12.5
Abstainers	—	—	—	(21.3)	(23.1)	(45.8)
Ex-drinkers	—	—	—	(55.3)	(25.6)	(20.8)
Total nondrinkers	—	26.8	—	76.6	48.7	66.6
Unknown †	—	0.9	5.7	6.4	20.5	4.1
Totals	100.0	100.0	100.0	99.9 *	100.0	99.9 *
			(n=35)	(n=47)	(n=39)	(n=48)

* Does not equal 100 percent because of rounding.
† Current status and/or score unknown.

The most striking contrast between Anglos and Navajos is provided by the general profile of the different groups when classed by Type of Drinker derived from the Preoccupation with Alcohol score. In the general sample of whites, only 4.5 percent are Types I–III, the alcoholics and incipient alcoholics. Type IV, the moderate drinkers, comprised only 7.4 percent, while the vast majority, 60.4 percent, are Type V drinkers who are not preoccupied with alcohol and are generally light or occasional social drinkers.

The profiles of each of the nonalcoholic Navajo groups is considerably different. In the two on-reservation groups, Plateau and South Tuba, 12.7

percent and 20.5 percent, respectively, have scores equivalent to Types I–III. In South Tuba, there were a few equivalents of Type IV and V drinkers; in the Plateau group there were almost none. Over half of the Plateau group and 48.7 percent of the South Tuba group are currently not drinking. Among whites, it appears that the majority occupy middle ground: nonpreoccupied, light or occasional drinkers. By contrast, reservation drinkers are equally divided at the extremes. Either they do not drink at all or they drink heavily (see also Appendix IV, Tables 4 and 5).

The Flagstaff group is intermediate between the on-reservation and white patterns. About an equal percentage of Flagstaff Navajos and whites are in the category equivalent to Types I–III (4.2 percent and 4.5 percent). There are relatively fewer moderate (Type IV) and unpreoccupied (Type V) Navajo than Anglo drinkers, but many more who are nondrinkers (66.6 percent versus 16.8 percent).

Mulford's typology failed to identify 38.2 percent of all whites being treated for alcoholism. Instead of scoring as Types I–III they gave Type IV or V responses. The scale was far more successful in identifying Navajo hospitalized alcoholics. This raises an important question: If over one third of white alcoholics did not score at the alcoholic end of the scale while 85 percent of the Navajo alcoholics did score, then *on what basis is alcoholism being diagnosed in the different populations?*

We have already mentioned that the psychologically oriented questions of the Definition of Alcohol Scale did not distinguish between the four groups of Navajos but that the questions of the Preoccupation with Alcohol Scale, which deal with overt behavior, did distinguish between them. Moreover, the distinctions measured by the Preoccupation Scale correspond largely to the behavior observed by us on the reservation over a period of years: the on-reservation style of drinking includes many of those behaviors that whites have come to associate with chronic alcoholism.

It is our belief that Navajos are diagnosed as alcoholics more by their overt behavior than by their psychological problems. If the typical Navajo pattern of drinking embraces behaviors labeled "alcoholic" in the white population, then it is obvious that many Navajos may be diagnosed as alcoholics with little reference to the internal processes thought to be associated with this state of being.

Whether these Navajos are really alcoholic is still open to question if, by alcoholic, we are referring to some psychopathology of which the observed behavior is only a symptom. This same question has been raised more obliquely by Savard and Ferguson, although they accept the behavioral diagnosis of alcoholism (26). Although we do not deny that the pattern of drinking causes serious problems such as automobile accidents and death from exposure or freezing, we question whether the behavioral pattern is the result, or symptom, of a psychopathology as has so often been suggested.

A number of unexpected responses to question 3 give a further intimation that many individuals who scored in the alcoholic range, that is, Types I–III, were not addicted to alcohol but used it as a trigger for an experience that was valued in itself. Usually, the longer a person drinks, the less effect alcohol has on him and the more he must drink to become inebriated. Many of the on-reservation respondents, who answered the majority of the questions in the affirmative, denied that this was true. On the contrary, they maintained that the opposite was the more common experience of the long-term heavy drinker; the more they drank, the less it took them to get drunk. One respondent maintained that he knew long-term drinkers who only needed to smell an open bottle of wine to get drunk. The same phenomenon has, of course, been noted from time to time among non-Indians as well.

Throughout the preceding discussion we have presented comparisons between sample groups, not between individual respondents regardless of sample group. We gave our rationale for this method of analysis in Chapter Four. In Appendix V, however, we have displayed our data in a different manner, comparing individuals with different characteristics, regardless of sample group. Not surprisingly, we find that the men who consider themselves traditionalists, traditionalist-peyotist, or simply peyotist give significantly more affirmative responses to the preoccupation-with-alcohol questions than the men who consider themselves Christians (including Mormons). Likewise, those with little education give more affirmative responses than those with more than eight years of schooling, and those with the lowest incomes give more affirmative responses than those with relatively higher incomes.

THE CONSEQUENCES OF DRINKING

The previous discussion has focused on two questions: the degree to which drinking tends to increase with acculturation and the degree to which "alcoholism" has been diagnosed among, or generally attributed to, the Navajo on the basis of similarities of overt behavior rather than by criteria of psychological states.

In the first instance we noted that while more of the acculturated, town-dwelling Navajo drank, this appeared to be an adjustment to white norms rather than representing any increase in the levels of problem drinking. It was the on-reservation drinker who displayed the "alcoholic-like" behavior and who appeared to be more involved with alcohol than the town-dwelling Navajo. By these gauges the level of problem drinking appeared to decrease as the acculturational level increased. But several considerations led us to question whether these heavy-binge drinkers were, in fact, alcoholics, although they may label themselves as such and doctors may concur in the judgment and accept them in alcohol-treatment programs. We noted the ease with which unexpectedly large numbers of traditional Navajos, many with long histories of heavy drinking, could give up the "habit" entirely. We noted also that heavy drinkers on reservation did not appear to have developed a tolerance for alcohol but the opposite, a decreased tolerance. We have therefore suggested that the diagnosis of alcoholism has been made on the basis of behavior alone with the presence of a pathological process assumed but not demonstrated.

By turning our attention to the sequelae of drinking we may investigate these questions further. The various physiological sequelae of heavy drinking, alcoholic cirrhosis, tremulousness, and alcoholic hallucinosis, are all thought to be good indicators of excessive "alcoholic" drinking. The social consequences of drinking, trouble with family, difficulty holding a job, and high arrest rates may either be the results of truly heavy drinking or of a number of social factors not directly linked to the alcoholic nature of the drinking behavior.

The Medical Sequelae of Drinking.   A number of medically oriented questions were included in the questionnaires. Questions 1 to 6 dealt with such symptoms and signs as hematemesis, melena, jaundice, and neuropathies. We found that these questions did not distinguish between our on-reservation alcoholic, nonalcoholic, and abstemious informants. This was probably due to the relatively frequent occurrence of hepatitis and other pathologies causing these symptoms in the Navajo population, which would not be found as often in the average white population. Consequently these questions were not administered to the Flagstaff informants. The questions dealing with the symptoms of withdrawal, tremulousness, and hallucinosis were administered to all four groups.

Liver Disease.   One of the sequelae of excessive alcohol consumption is liver damage. Although the precise mechanism of how this damage is pro-

duced is still not well known, it is quite certain that there is a causal relationship. Previously, in this study and elsewhere, we have discussed the epidemiology of alcoholic cirrhosis among the Navajo (27). We have pointed
out that the prevalence of the disease increases as one moves from remote
areas on the Navajo Reservation to areas adjacent to border towns. However, the proportion of those who die of the disease within the population
contracting the disease remains constant in all areas.

All three of our on-reservation groups lived in the Tuba City Service
Unit, an area administered by the U.S. Public Health Service staff in Tuba
City. This is one of the areas with a comparatively low prevalence of cirrhosis. We reviewed the hospital records of all individuals in the three on-
reservation groups and found evidence of liver disease in three of the hospital group. In addition, we had liver function studies done on 13 members
of the other two reservation groups who had given histories of heavy drinking. None of these individuals had evidence of liver disease (28). Liver
function tests were not done in Flagstaff.

The fact that none of the heavy drinkers tested in the Plateau and South
Tuba groups had abnormal liver function is not surprising, but it is consistent with our earlier findings. It appears that reservation drinkers may
drink heavily but that the intermittent style of their drinking does not predispose to liver damage.

Hallucinatory Experiences.   One of the indicators of physical dependence on alcohol is the withdrawal syndrome. For some reason, after prolonged ingestion of a number of substances, including alcohol, opiates, and
barbiturates, the body's metabolic functioning comes to depend on the drug
in question to such a degree that when it is not available various symptoms
occur. The symptoms of alcohol withdrawal are of two types. The minor
phase, which occurs from six to eight hours after the last drink and may
last up to 48 hours, may include tremors, hallucinations, convulsions, and
minimal disorientation. The onset of the major phase occurs between 36
and 48 hours after cessation of drinking and includes, in addition to tremulousness and hallucinations, delirium tremens, psychomotor activity, autonomic activity with much sweating, and profound disorientation.

We asked our informants if they had ever been tremulous and nervous
after drinking and if they had ever heard or seen things that were not there
or that they could not understand. The responses of the drinkers are given
in Tables 7.5 and 7.6. In Table 7.7 we present the numbers of informants
reporting delirium tremens as opposed to those reporting other hallucina-

tory experiences. Finally, Table 7.8 shows the percentage of those reporting tremulousness who had accompanying hallucinations including the micro-hallucinations of delirium tremens.

By calculating the prevalence of hallucinatory experiences on the basis of those having tremulousness, we gain a rough control over the extent of drinking done by the different populations we wish to compare. Because alcoholism is diagnosed differently in different ethnic groups, it is possible that some of those called alcoholic in one group would not drink to nearly the same extent as people diagnosed as alcoholic in another group. If we used these diagnosed cases in each group as the denominator for calculating the prevalence of hallucinatory experiences, the results would not be comparable. Because tremulousness is the most common symptom of both the minor and major phases of the withdrawal syndrome, we have some assurance that all those who experience it do drink in about the same range.

Table 7.5 indicates that the proportion of those reporting tremulousness after drinking is highest in the hospital group followed by the Plateau, South Tuba, and Flagstaff groups in that order. A similar pattern emerged

Table 7.5   Alcoholic Tremulousness in Four Groups

Group	Drinkers Reporting Tremulousness †		Drinkers Denying Tremulousness †		Totals	
	Number	Percent	Number	Percent	Number	Percent
Hospital	25	75.7	8	24.2	33	99.9 *
Plateau	21	67.7	10	32.2	31	99.9 *
South Tuba	14	51.8	13	48.1	27	99.9 *
Flagstaff	6	26.0	17	73.9	23	99.9 *
Totals	66	57.9	48	42.1	114	100.0

Chi-square $=15.5$

$C=.34$

$df=3$

$p=$ less than .01

* Does not equal 100 percent because of rounding.
† Includes ex-drinkers.

Table 7.6 Alcohol-Related Hallucinatory Experiences in Four Groups

Group	Drinkers Reporting Hallucinations *		Drinkers Denying Hallucinations *		Totals	
	Number	Percent	Number	Percent	Number	Percent
Hospital	20	60.9	13	39.4	33	100
Plateau	12	38.7	19	61.3	31	100
South Tuba	8	29.6	19	70.4	27	100
Flagstaff	5	21.7	18	78.3	23	100
Totals	45	39.5	69	60.5	114	100

Chi-square $=10.29$

$C=.28$

$df=3$

$p=$ less than .02

* Includes ex-drinkers.

Table 7.7 Presence of Delirium Tremens in Four Groups *

Groups	Delirium Tremens	Other Hallucinatory Experiences
Hospital	6	14
Plateau	3	9
South Tuba	2	6
Flagstaff	4	1

* None of these differences is significant by Fisher's Exact Test.

Table 7.8   The Presence of Hallucinatory
Experiences in those Reporting Alcoholic
Tremulousness

	Hallucinations		Total Reporting Tremulousness
Group	Number	Percent	Percent
Hospital	20	80	25
Plateau	12	57	21
South Tuba	8	57	14
Flagstaff	5	83	6
Totals	45	68	66

for those reporting hallucinations (Table 7.6). There is, then, a strong indication that the more traditional the group, the heavier the drinking. This finding agrees with the results of the Preoccupation with Alcohol Scale scores.

Delirium tremens is one of the most startling symptoms of the major phase of the withdrawal syndrome. Classically, delirium tremens are micro-hallucinations consisting of insects, small animals, and other bizarre forms of flora and fauna. The other types of hallucinations have been described by Kessel and Walton:

> Things around him may appear distorted in shape; shadows seem to be real and to move. Shouting or snatches of music may be heard, and he may also misinterpret innocent remarks by bystanders whether they are addressed to him or not (29).

Table 7.7 indicates that the numbers in each group who describe classical delirium tremens, although not differing significantly, do show an interesting pattern. Fewer individuals on reservation reported classical delerium tremens than other kinds of hallucinatory experiences. In Flagstaff, however, the most commonly reported experience was the classical delirium tremens. There is some indication here that the heavy drinker off reservation may be more like the white alcoholic if, as is generally believed, the presence of delirium tremens is the result of a longer period of steady excessive drinking than is required to produce the other types of hallucinations or tremulousness alone.

Kessel and Walton report that about 25 percent of the alcoholics who experienced tremulousness also experienced accompanying hallucinations, a finding supported by a number of other sources (30). Robins and her associates report that of a group of young Negro males who experienced tremulousness, approximately 30 percent experienced alcoholic psychoses. Morgan reports that 25 percent of hospitalized alcoholics suffering from tremulousness had accompanying visual hallucinations (31).

The proportion of Navajo drinkers reporting hallucinations is considerably higher than the 25–30 percent found elsewhere (see Table 7.8). Sixty-eight percent of all respondents reporting tremulousness had accompaning hallucinations of some sort. Isbell and his associates (32) and Adams (33), among others, have clearly demonstrated that tremulousness, delirium tremens, and alcoholic hallucinosis are not related to nutritional factors. Moreover, as Adams has pointed out, few of the patients he observed with these symptoms had abnormal liver function studies. Indeed, many of them had good or adequate diets (34). This is consistent with our suggestion, reported elsewhere (35), that the Navajo style of binge drinking predisposes less to cirrhosis than to the other sequelae.

In their study of auditory hallucinations in the acute alcoholic psychoses, Gross and associates suggested that a possible cultural difference might be one of the contributing factors in determining who had and who did not have auditory hallucinations (36). Of 103 white patients, 66 percent had auditory hallucinations; of 44 Negro patients, 100 percent had auditory hallucinations. Although they did not pursue the matter further, it turns out that the difference is significant (p less than .001). A similar finding was reported by Mott and associates in a study of three groups comprised of 50 individuals each; one a group of schizophrenics, another of alcoholics, and a third of general medical patients, all of whom had been admitted to the same hospital. They found that hallucinatory experiences had occurred in each group. Mental patients appeared to experience hallucinations irrespective of social and cultural variables. Normal patients, on the other hand, were more likely to hallucinate if they believed in the reality of religious visions, were Negro or were female (37).

It should be noted that we are not here discussing the content of hallucinations but their prevalence. We thought it possible that the high prevalence of hallucinations found among Navajo drinkers might be accounted for by a cultural predilection to value hallucinatory or "vision" experiences. Through sheer lack of foresight we neglected to ask questions concerning hallucinatory experiences of total abstainers. In any event, there were so few of these that finding enough to make an adequate control group was beyond our means.

To the extent that Navajos still value the vision experience, they may be more prone to experience hallucinations than, for instance, whites. Boyer's work with the Mescalero Apache would seem to indicate such a possibility: "The great majority of Apaches have experienced hallucinations at some time or other during the courses of their lives" (38). Miller has reported many experiments in which the autonomic nervous system can be taught to react in particular ways to various types of stimuli (39). A similar kind of learning may be involved in the present situation. Our respondents reported decreased tolerance for alcohol. If drunkenness and hallucinatory experiences are positively valued, these responses and the rapid sobering-up experiences reported for some Indians (40) might best be attributed to a learned (i.e., cultural) predisposition. Lemert has documented the same phenomenon among three Northwest Coast Indian tribes. He had some home brew tested for its alcoholic content at various intervals after preparation. The peak was 3.6 percent alcohol by volume reached after 24 hours. Often the brew was consumed before it had fermented even that long. He also reports stories of Indians getting drunk on soft drinks given to them in liquor bottles (41). Two considerations lead us to hold this interpretation in abeyance, however.

In the first instance, if hallucinatory experiences were highly valued we would expect to find a high degree of culturally determined content of the hallucinations parallel to the types of experiences reported by Navajo peyote users. This, in fact, does not appear to be the case. All of the cases of delirium tremens involved the expected microhallucinations of insects, rats, spiders, lizards, and other small animals. One case consisted of "tiny men, the color of wine, who danced in a circle around me." This was bizarre, perhaps, but not specifically Navajo.

The hallucinatory experiences of the minor type, occurring six to eight hours after the last drink, also conform to descriptions obtained from white subjects. Auditory hallucinations consisted mostly of people singing or talking in the background, sometimes the sounds of familiar animals such as horses or sheep moving about or making characteristic noises. The singing was of Navajo social songs, which is, of course, cultural content but not on a level different from that of hearing popular dance music in our own culture. In only two instances were culturally "charged" symbols reported. In one case, bears and snakes, both ceremonially important and dangerous animals, were heard "screaming." In another instance the voice heard was identified as that of a ghost, or spirit of the dead, also an important and dangerous aspect of Navajo belief.

Visual hallucinations were invariably vague, dark, fleeting shapes seen "out of the corner of my eye." These have been identified as "dark shapes," people, horses, sheep, lizards, or cats. Of 20 informants who gave descriptions of their visual hallucinations, only 4 described any with significant cultural symbolism. These were snakes, dogs (manifestations of witches or of the coyote, a supernatural agent of evil), big lizards, and ghosts ("I saw people, they must have been ghosts"). It would seem that even when the subject has the opportunity to "project" a desired content into the hallucinatory experience, Navajos tended not to do so more often than we might expect to find among a white population.

The second and, perhaps, more important consideration was that the prevalence of hallucinatory experiences reported by Hopi subjects was as high as that among the Navajos. The Hopis are definitely not a vision-oriented people. On the contrary, they tend to abhor the intoxicated state and to value sobriety in all things. We expected the proportion of hallucinatory experiences not to exceed that found among whites. Of 10 Hopis reporting tremulousness, 8 also reported having hallucinations (42). If the expected figure of 25–30 percent had been observed, the number should have been in the neighborhood of 3. Using the binomial distribution and a probability of .25, the likelihood of the observed outcome occurring by chance is about 4 in 10,000.

Without closing the door completely on the idea that cultural factors have an influence on Navajo hallucinations, it nevertheless appears more likely that the explanation lies elsewhere. According to Wolfe and Victor, withdrawal symptoms are less frequent and less severe among alcoholics who can control the "tapering off" process. Those who cannot stop their drinking gradually but who pass out, get sick, or suddenly run out of liquor suffer a far higher incidence of withdrawal symptoms (43). The major precipitating factor is the suddenness of the withdrawal. Likewise, Marjot has noted the onset of alcohol withdrawal states within two weeks of the start of a drinking bout among British seamen and beginning when they return to shipboard and are without a continuing source of supply (44). In other words, it seems to take about two weeks for a group of whites to develop a physical addiction to alcohol sufficient to result in delirium tremens upon abrupt cessation of drinking. Navajo informants tell us of withdrawal symptoms after drinking bouts lasting somewhat less than two weeks. It is possible that this is related to some racial differences in the metabolism of alcohol, (45) but it is clear that much of the explanation involves the characteristic style of drinking that takes place in Indian communities.

The reservation style of drinking among the Navajo fosters sudden withdrawal. Navajos, after ingesting large amounts of alcohol at one time, most frequently pass out or find their supply exhausted. Especially on reservation, there are no easily available supplies to help taper off. In border towns, Navajos get arrested or wake up after drinking with no money. Although Hopis tend to have a different style of drinking, they share a similar social environment in several important respects. The Hopi who goes off reservation to drink is in much the same position as the Navajo. When drinking on reservation, the Hopi tends to drink alone and in secret. His supply is hidden at some distance from the home and he must return to the village without being detected. Here, too, there is no local bar to help in the tapering off process. Thus, despite different drinking styles, social and legal prohibitions against drinking, the absence of a ready supply and the position of the Indian public and bar drinker in border towns all foster sudden withdrawal and, in consequence, a high incidence of hallucinatory experiences among Hopis and Navajos alike. It appears that some of the most characteristic signs of "addictive" alcoholism are themselves influenced by the social environment and cannot be taken as true gauges of what whites think of as alcoholism.

The Social Consequences of Drinking.   The troubles that a drinker encounters as a direct result of his drinking are most often included in operational definitions of alcoholism (46). Although they obviously do not measure the amounts consumed or the existence of addictive drinking, they are thought to be indicators of excessive drinking if only because the drinker would not risk such social consequences if "he could help himself." In order to examine the extent of these troubles experienced by Navajos, we utilized several questions employed by Mulford and Wilson and surveyed the arrest records of all respondents. Our principal concerns here were (1) to determine whether the troubles due to drinking increased with the level of acculturation, and (2) whether such troubles were the result of excessive drinking according to the Navajo point of view or whether they were a product of the disjunction between white and Navajo norms.

Trouble Due to Drinking. Mulford has used a scale of "Trouble Due to Drinking," which appears to include items that describe most of the common problems that alcoholics have (47). Nationwide, about 10 percent of the population reported having one or more of these troubles although, as Mulford points out, there may be many false positives here (48). Our data are especially bedeviled by these false positives. The following five items were used.

1. Has any employer fired you or threatened to fire you if you did not cut down or quit drinking?
2. Has your husband (wife) ever left you or threatened to leave you if you did not do something about your drinking?
3. Has your husband (wife) or other family member ever complained that you spend too much money for alcoholic beverages?
4. Have you ever been picked up or arrested by the police for intoxication or other charges involving alcoholic beverages?
5. Has a physician ever told you that drinking was injuring your health?

There are problems in using these questions with Indians for a number of reasons. Many employers complain, for instance, that Indians drink too much and that, although they are good workers much of the time, many have a tendency to be irresponsible in their job obligations. Observers have also pointed out that, apart from the drinking issue, there is the question of how seriously many Navajos take their employment obligations as opposed to conflicting obligations at home that may require their presence during working hours. Many Navajos have not committed themselves wholeheartedly to the job and may be less inclined to place it before everything else. Graves has pointed out that those Navajo migrants to Denver who have exclusively Navajo friends and who persist in the pattern of peer-group drinking tend to be the least economically successful (49). It is clear that the Navajo style of drinking is maladaptive for succeeding in the Anglo wage-work world.

There is also a tendency for white employers to be prejudicial in their behavior toward Navajos. Navajos, like black Americans, tend to be the "last hired and the first fired" and to be fired for behavior that would only result in a reprimand for an Anglo. Because of both these factors, then, it is hard to be sure that trouble on the job is a gauge of "alcoholism" rather than a result of a nonwhite style of drinking and/or prejudice on the part of the employer.

Many of the same problems exist when using trouble with the police as a gauge of "troubles due to drinking." Since alcohol is prohibited on reservation and since prohibition for Indians was repealed off reservation in 1953, it is entirely possible that an individual will have had contact with the police quite apart from whether he is an "alcoholic" in the true sense of the word.

Despite these drawbacks, we have compared the drinkers in each of our four groups along these lines, using Mulford's dichotomy of no troubles versus one or more troubles due to drinking. The results for men and women are given in Table 7.9.

The men and women within each group do not differ except on Kaibito Plateau where men have significantly more troubles than women. Likewise,

Table 7.9 Trouble Due to Drinking *

| | No Troubles | | One or More Troubles | |
Group	Men	Women	Men	Women
Hospital	0	1	29	3
Plateau	2	8	15	6
South Tuba	0	2	17	4
Flagstaff	7	6	8	1

Comparison	Chi-square	df	p Value
Men between groups	24.13	3	less than .001
Men and women within groups:			
Hospital	1.33	1	more than .05
Plateau	5.3	1	less than .05
South Tuba	2.6	1	more than .05
Flagstaff	1.54	1	more than .05

* Does not include unknowns and not-applicables.

the differences between the four groups of women are not significant. The differences between the four groups of men, however, are significant and are accounted for by the fact that fewer Flagstaff men have multiple troubles than do men in the other groups.

The latter finding parallels what our police record survey reveals and is noteworthy because Flagstaff males not only have greater exposure to the police but also a greater potential for trouble on the job (50). Problems on the job and with the police do not necessarily relate to troubles within the family as a result of drinking (items 2 and 3). For each of these items, the responses paralleled what we found in the comparison of no troubles versus one or more. That is, the Flagstaff men differed significantly from the other men in having fewer positive responses. The women did not differ across the groups.

These responses (to items 2 and 3) are confounded as are the questions having to do with police and jobs. The fact that families complain that the informant spends too much money on liquor is biased by the appreciable difference in available cash between on- and off-reservation groups. Clearly, complaints about excessive spending may be indicative of lack of cash rather than alcoholism.

Although threats of divorce or separation may indicate social disintegration, we have maintained that it also may indicate nothing more than the fact that in traditional Navajo society divorce was relatively common and marriages were frequently unstable (51). As we pointed out in the section on marital status and number of prior marriages, the fact that many Plateau men had been married prior to their present marriage was felt to be a reflection of this traditional Navajo pattern. The fact that off-reservation men have fewer prior marriages and that there are fewer reported threats from the wife to dissolve the marriage seems to indicate that there is a change in the man's status as one moves from on reservation to off reservation. This change reflects the fact that to succeed in the male-dominated Anglo world the Navajo man's situation changes so that he becomes more dominant within the family as the breadwinner and head of the house.

In summary, then, it appears that several of these questions are confounded by the legal and social differences between the groups and, in themselves, may not reveal true alcoholism. However, it is significant that the Flagstaff men report fewer troubles than the other groups even allowing for these confounding variables, especially in view of their greater exposure to potential trouble on the job or with the police. On the domestic side, the fact that they report fewer troubles is seen as a reflection of their larger cash income and the change in the role of the male from on-reservation to off-reservation families.

Problems with the Police. Police records for all respondents were reviewed in Flagstaff (in the summer of 1969) and at the headquarters of the Navajo Police Department in Window Rock, Arizona (in the summers of 1967 and 1969). Some of these data have been presented in slightly different form in our study of Navajo homicide (52).

There are many problems in the area of Indian law that we do not propose to deal with here (53). They stem primarily from the special status of Indians as wards of the federal government, sovereign nations, and a disadvantaged, colored, ethnic minority. In general, on-reservation problems of law and order are handled by tribal police. In the case of the Navajos, the police are administered and largely financed by the tribe itself. Other tribes, for instance the Hopis, have an Indian police force that is administered by the federal government. In addition, the on-reservation courts are also run by the tribe with tribal judges and a tribal code of law. Thirteen so-called major crimes, however, are not handled by the tribal courts but rather by federal courts.

Hagan has written a detailed history of Indian police and courts (54). Suffice it to say here that they appear to have been established on a number of reservations, starting in the 1870s, by various civilian Indian agents as a way of controlling the Indians while, at the same time, freeing themselves from control by the army. Until the past 10 or 15 years the Navajo Police Department was very understaffed for the area it had to patrol. Crime reporting was therefore not really comparable to surrounding nonreservation areas until about the middle or late 1950s. Although some of our on-reservation data go back to the 1930s, it is only for the more recent period that we can have more confidence that our figures are comparable for on- and off-reservation areas.

Off reservation, the situation changed in 1953 at the time when federal prohibition for Indians was repealed. Both Heath and Leubben have remarked that this change does not seem to have altered the style of Navajo drinking (55). It may, however, have diminished the proportion of alcohol-related arrests off reservation. This is open to question because, although possession by itself is no longer a crime, it appears that Indians are more likely than others to be picked up for alcohol-related offenses where others, primarily Anglos, are not. In large part, as one white informant, a police officer, remarked, this is because of the Navajo style of drinking: "If you drank in a park, you'd have a police record also."

The Navajo tribe continues to prohibit liquor on reservation, although there is a continuing debate on the advisability of legalizing it and opening tribally owned package stores. If nothing else, this would greatly increase the revenue of the tribe, even though what the human results would be is hard to predict. The effect of prohibition on reservation is to greatly inflate the proportion of offenses related to alcohol, since mere possession is grounds for arrest.

Stewart first pointed out that the crime rate prevailing among American Indians is much higher than among other ethnic groups in the United States (56). About 71 percent of the arrests were for drunkenness alone. These figures came from the Uniform Crime Reports of the Federal Bureau of Investigation and presumably did not include reporting from tribal police departments. However, when he analyzed data from various tribes, it appeared that between 60 and 90 percent of all arrests (depending on the tribe) were alcohol related. The vast majority of these arrests were for drunkenness and disorderly conduct.

These high arrest rates are often explained in terms of socioeconomic deprivation. It has also been suggested that the high arrest rates off reservation offer confirmation for Kluckhohn and Leighton's suggestion that it is the more maladjusted people who migrate (57). Table 7.10 indicates that there are, indeed, differences between our four groups in terms of who does and who does not have an arrest record.

Table 7.10 indicates that for both men and women there are significant differences in the proportion in each group that have had contact with the police. For women, those in Flagstaff and Kaibito Plateau have similar patterns whereas somewhat more in South Tuba have police records, as do all the women in the hospital group. For men, the Flagstaff group has fewer with police records than do the other groups.

There are also significant differences between the sexes for those having arrests versus those with no arrests in the Kaibito Plateau, South Tuba, and Flagstaff groups. In each group, men have had significantly more contact with the police than have the women. In the hospital group, there is no such difference. However, this is not surprising.

The distinctions between the women are not remarkable and need not detain us. The distinctions between the men are important because (1) Flagstaff men are older than all but the Kaibito Plateau group, and (2) they live as an ethnic minority in an Anglo-American town with regular

Table 7.10   Comparison by   Group and Sex of Those
with versus Those without Police Records *

Group	Men		Women	
	Arrest Record	No Arrest Record	Arrest Record	No Arrest Record
Hospital	28	2	5	0
Plateau	16	5	8	18
South Tuba	21	2	7	9
Flagstaff	11	7	8	22
Totals	76	16	28	49

Comparison	Chi-square	df	p Value
Men between groups	10.00	3	less than .05
Women between groups	12.18	3	less than .01
Men vs. women within groups:			
Hospital	.97	1	more than .05
Plateau	5.81	1	less than .02
South Tuba	6.41	1	less than .02
Flagstaff	4.07	1	less than .05

* Includes Flagstaff and Navajo tribal police departments.

police patrols. Both factors would seem to lead to an increased risk of arrest over a lifetime.

On the other hand, since liquor possession is not illegal off reservation as it is on reservation, mere possession is not grounds for arrest in Flagstaff. This is reflected in Tables 7.11 and 7.12 where liquor violations—that is, possession—are common on reservation but are not a factor in the Flagstaff group. Most commonly, however, a liquor violation is only one among several charges in a single arrest episode. It was uncommon to find

Table 7.11   Type of Offense by Study Group: Men

Offense	Hospital	Plateau	South Tuba	Flagstaff
Public intoxication	297	97	147	118
Liquor violation	57	29	34	1
Serving liquor to a minor	6	1	3	1
Drunken driving	24	9	22	3
Total alcohol-related	384	136	106	123
Assault	12	7	7	4
Theft	5	3	3	0
Adultery	9	0	2	0
Failure to support dependents	7	5	0	0
Other (primarily traffic violations)	38	20	40	4
Peyote violation	0	3	1	0
Total nonalcohol related	71	38	53	8
Number of men with police records	28	16	21	11
Mean for those with and without records (all men)	15.1	8	11.6	7.2
Mean for those with records minus liquor violations	12.1	9.1	10.7	11.8
Mean for those with records of nonalcohol-related offenses	2.5	2.4	2.5	.7
Mean for those with records of alcohol-related offenses	13.7	8.5	9.8	11.2
Mean for those with records	16.2	10.9	11.6	11.9

Table 7.12 Type of Offense by Study Group: Women

Offense	Hospital	Plateau	South Tuba	Flagstaff
Public intoxication	99 *	2	30 †	78 *
Liquor violation	3	4	0	3
Serving liquor to a minor	0	0	1	0
Drunken driving	0	1	2	0
Total alcohol-related	102	7	33	81
Assault	1	0	1	1
Theft	2	0	0	2
Adultery	3	3	3	0
Peyote violation	0	2	0	0
Other (primarily traffic violations)	2	2	5	5
Total nonalcohol-related	8	7	9	8
Number of women with police records	5	8	7	8
Mean for those with and without records (all women)	22	.54	2.6	2.9
Mean for those with records of nonalcohol-related offenses	1.6	.87	1.3	1.0
Mean for those with records of alcohol-related offenses	20.4	.87	4.7	10.1
Mean for those with records	22	1.75	6	11.1

* Includes one individual with 65 arrests.
† Includes one individual with 22 arrests.

168

a record in which an individual's only contact with the police resulted from the mere possession of liquor. Usually other charges, such as public intoxication, were involved. Without having made a comparative study of the two police departments, it is our impression that they are both likely to arrest someone on this latter charge, with the Navajo police department perhaps being somewhat more lenient. Thus, although possession of liquor is a crime on reservation and inflates the number of offenses for which an individual is charged when arrested, it does not in itself account for the fact that on-reservation men have a higher proportion of police records than off-reservation men.

The fact that fewer Flagstaff men than on-reservation men have had any contact with the police is, therefore, of interest because it is directly related to their style of drinking. We have found that the more urbanized Navajos have a higher prevalence of drinking than the more traditional groups, but they have fewer medical sequelae and less trouble as a result of their drinking. They less often come to the attention of the police because of their style of drinking. This is all the more noteworthy because they are much closer to possible police surveillance than, for instance, the Kaibito Plateau men who live from 30 to 50 miles from routine police patrols. In South Tuba, where about half the hospital group lives, police patrols are much more like those in Flagstaff, since the Navajo Police Department maintains a station there. Thus, although the different legal systems make direct comparisons difficult, we think it is possible to have some confidence in the findings and the suggestion that the differences between the on- and off-reservation men are real and meaningful.

We have already noted that Stewart found that 71 percent of Indian arrests were for alcohol-related offenses (58). In our study of Navajo criminal homicide, we pointed out that homicide and suicide vary independently of accessibility to alcohol and that alcohol-related offenses may vary independently of other kinds of offenses (59). Tables 7.11 and 7.12 and Appendix II give additional supporting data for this suggestion.

Appendix II presents figures taken from the Flagstaff Police Department's report to the Federal Bureau of Investigation Uniform Crime Reports for the year 1967 (the only year for which they were available). It is clear that Indians are overrepresented in the categories of alcohol-related offenses but are not overrepresented in the other categories. These figures are difficult to evaluate because the denominator is not known: that is, we do not know how many individuals are involved, although it is clear that most of the Indian arrests are accounted for by on-reservation dwellers in

town for a short time rather than migrants to Flagstaff. In addition, the denominator for whites and Negroes is also not clear, since Flagstaff, being on
two major highways, has many transients passing through, many of whom
get picked up by the police.

Difficulties of interpretation notwithstanding, it is clear that the vast majority of Indian arrests are for alcohol-related offenses and not for crimes
against persons or property. Indian arrest rates for the latter types of crime
are not at all unusual (60).

This is made even clearer in Tables 7.11 and 7.12. In these tables we
have listed the number of different types of offenses for which members of
each group have been arrested. We also have calculated the mean number
of offenses, both alcohol-related and nonalcohol-related, for all those who
have police records. It is evident from these figures that the mean number
of nonalcohol-related offenses is remarkably constant from group to group,
with the exception of Flagstaff men. With respect to the others, there is a
variance in the number of alcohol-related offenses. We explain the relatively higher proportion of alcohol-related offenses among Flagstaff men by
the fact that they are Indians living year round in an Anglo-American
town and are therefore more subject to arrest for behavior that the police
associate with Indians. That is, their high proportion of alcohol-related offenses may be viewed largely as a reflection of prejudicial arrests as well as
their own drinking behavior, and their lower number of arrests for nonalcohol-related offenses indicate that in other areas they are as law-abiding
as any other group living in Flagstaff.

In addition to the mean number of arrests for all persons with records in
each group, we have also calculated the mean number of arrests for *all* people in each group, both those with and those without records. Clearly, there
is a marked difference between groups. The pattern is interesting because
the Plateau and Flagstaff men have about the same mean number of arrests. In view of the fact that their situations vis-à-vis the police are so different, this similarity represents what we consider to be a significant difference. That is, even though the Flagstaff men are more subject to police
scrutiny than the Plateau men who live very far from police patrols, their
mean number of arrests are very similar. Plateau men, with less opportunity for police contact than the Flagstaff men, still manage to have about
the same number of arrests, and this indicates that they do a great deal
more drinking than the Flagstaff men.

The Effect of Disulfiram on Arrest Records.   In the treatment program
for Navajo problem drinkers in Gallup, one of the criteria for successful

treatment was a reduction in arrest records from the 18 months before treatment to the 18 months after treatment had begun (61). As the patients were all referred from the court on the basis that they had long police records, and since treatment was in lieu of jail, it is not surprising that the rate should have gone down after treatment was begun.

It was possible to analyze our figures in a similar manner. Our study was different because the people with whom we dealt were not court-referred cases who had the option of treatment or a jail sentence. In addition, there was essentially no follow-up care. Only the persons who cared enough to return to the hospital or to someone designated as a "helping person," who would dispense the pills according to the required schedule, got anything that could conceivably be called follow-up care.

In view of this situation, the results shown in Table 7.13 are of consider-

Table 7.13 Mean Number of Arrests Eighteen Months before and Eighteen Months after Interview

	Hospital	Plateau	South Tuba
Mean number, 18 months before *	3.9	1.25	1.5
Mean number, 18 months after	2.46	1.25	1.5
Number of individuals with police records during the three-year period	28	8	20
p Value †	.05	.44	.29

* Informant number 114, in the hospital group, was not included, since psychiatric consultant advised not to give him the drug.

† By Mann-Whitney U-test.

Note: For hospital patients, the time of interview was the time they were begun on the drug. For Kaibito Plateau and South Tuba, the midpoint of the three-year period, September 1, 1965 to August 30 1968, was chosen (March 1, 1967), since all of the interviews were done in a three-week period surrounding this date.

able interest. The table shows the mean number of arrests for the hospital, Plateau, and South Tuba groups during the three-year period that includes 18 months before interview and the 18 months after interview (the means are calculated only for the individuals who were arrested during this three-year period). Clearly, the Plateau and South Tuba groups do not change, whereas the hospital group shows a marked drop in the mean number of arrests, although it keeps a higher rate than the other two groups.

When we reviewed the medical records of the individuals in the hospital group at intervals after they had been started on medication, we found that, within 11 months, 24 of the 35 patients had been dropped by the hospital from the list of persons considered still active in the program. Six were still taking their medication, and five were of questionable status; that is, they had not been dropped because they had been out of the hospital too short a time, but they had not been back for pills for several months.

On follow-up eight months later, none of the five individuals of questionable status were being carried on the list of active participators in the treatment program. Of the six who had been active at 11 months, five were still considered active, and two, who had been dropped earlier, had resumed taking pills.

The first two follow-ups were record interviews done at the end of January 1968, and again in August 1968. A third follow-up was undertaken in September 1969, when as many of the original group as could be found were interviewed personally. By September 1969, all informants had stopped taking medication. The police records, moreover, indicated that almost all of them continued to drink, at least intermittently, after starting the Disulfiram therapy. Interestingly, a number of informants remarked that of those who had managed to markedly decrease their drinking, most had become successful bootleggers since they no longer tended to drink up their own profits. Whether this was actually true or whether it was gossip was impossible to determine.

Clearly, the Disulfiram treatment program did not keep the self-identified alcoholics from drinking, nor was continued participation in the program predictive of a decrease in troubles with the police. Presumably, then, the decline in the mean number of arrests reflects a change in drinking behavior rather than a decrease in the number of drinkers. This change of drinking pattern and the comparative ease with which individuals in the other groups were able to stop their drinking indicate that problem drinking among the Navajos is not the same as what we are used to calling problem drinking in white populations.

SUMMARY

In this chapter we presented a number of indicators of drinking behavior and its sequelae. We discussed the ways in which Navajo drinking differs from white drinking; the degree to which drinking behavior is correlated with levels of acculturation; and the degree to which measures and indicators developed among white populations may be utilized in studies of populations with different cultures.

Our historical and general ethnographic observations indicated that the prevalent style of Navajo drinking differs considerably from that displayed by white Americans both in regard to overt behavior and in the nature of the involvement with alcohol. Our interview results confirm this impression. On-reservation drinkers generally, and traditional Navajos especially, score more toward the "alcoholic" end of the Preoccupation Scale than do even the known white alcoholics; they suffer more from the withdrawal symptoms we measured but less from liver disease; they also encounter more of the social problems associated with alcoholism than do whites. By these measures we would be justified in concluding not only that Navajos drank differently but also that the difference was of a quantitive rather than a qualitative nature; that, in effect, the level of alcoholism is higher among Navajos than among the general white population. In the balance, however, we have concluded that this is not the case.

The social sequelae of drinking appear to be the direct consequences of (1) overt behavior that is deviant in the eyes of the law and of white society in general, and (2) of prejudicial behavior on the part of whites and the low economic status of Navajos, which makes it difficult for them to support their drinking without doing damage to the family economy. The fact that Navajos have a lower incidence of cirrhosis than would be predicted from their scores on the Preoccupation Scale and the fact that a large proportion of them stop drinking entirely even after years of heavy drinking supports our belief that scores at the "alcoholic" end of the scale denote a different type of overt behavior and not the presence of addictive alcoholism as we know it. In light of this, we are disposed to interpret the high prevalence of hallucinatory experiences among the Navajo drinkers as the result of their style of drinking, which predisposes to sudden withdrawal and not to the existence of untoward amounts of chronic, addictive alcoholism.

The interview results show that the Flagstaff group differs appreciably from the others, especially from the more traditional drinkers. Generally, their scores and, by inference as well as observation, their style of drinking approximate what is reported for the white populations studied. Like lower-class whites, they prefer beer to wine or liquor. The prevalence of drinking in this group is closest to that found among white groups. They have more people identified as nonalcoholic-type drinkers by the Quantity-Frequency Index and as light and moderate drinkers by the Preoccupation Scale. They also suffer less from the physiological and social consequences of drinking than do the other groups. As measured by these scales, then, the level of acculturation stands in an inverse relationship to the level of involvement with alcohol. This and the nature of the difference between Navajo and white patterns of drinking raise questions concerning the definition of alcoholism as a pathology and the notion that problem drinking is the result of strains attendant upon the acculturative process. These questions will be discussed in detail in the final chapter.

Two of our measures of drinking—the Quantity-Frequency Index and the Definition of Alcohol Scale—did not produce reliable results. All measures involved difficulties of interpretation deriving from the differences between social, economic, and legal conditions prevailing among Indian and white populations. Despite these differences, however, the discriminations made between the groups by our measures conformed to our general observations and revealed unexpected differences that the utilization of observational techniques alone could not have shown. By providing, no matter how roughly, a basis for comparison, we feel that these procedures have proved their worth. They cannot be utilized and their results interpreted, however, with any degree of confidence in the absence of detailed observational data.

─────────────────── NOTES ───────────────────

1. J. W. Riley, Jr., and C. F. Marden, "The Social Pattern of Alcoholic Drinking," *Quarterly Journal of Studies on Alcohol*, 8 (1947): 265–273.

2. H. A. Mulford, "Drinking and Deviant Drinking, U.S.A., 1963," *Quarterly Journal of Studies on Alcohol, 25* (1964): 634–650.

3. D. Cahalan and I. H. Cisin, "American Drinking Practices: Summary of Findings from a National Probability Sample, I. Extent of Drinking by Population Subgroups," *Quarterly Journal of Studies on Alcohol, 29* (1968): 130–151.

4. Mulford, "Deviant Drinking," pp. 640–641.

5. Cahalan and Cisin, "American Drinking Practices," p. 137.

6. Mulford, "Deviant Drinking," pp. 640–641.

7. R. Straus and S. D. Bacon, *Drinking in College* (New Haven: Yale University Press, 1953).

8. M. A. Maxwell, "Drinking Behaviour in the State of Washington," *Quarterly Journal of Studies on Alcohol, 13* (1952): 219–239; H. A. Mulford and R. W. Wilson, *Identifying Problem Drinkers in a Household Health Survey,* National Center for Health Statistics (US, DHEW), PHS Publication No. 1000, Series 2, No. 16 (Washington, D.C., 1966).

9. G. Knupfer, "The Epidemiology of Problem Drinking," *American Journal of Public Health, 57* (1967): 973–986; D. Cahalan and I. H. Cisin, "American Drinking Practices: Summary of Findings from a National Probability Sample, II. Measurement of Massed versus Spaced Drinking," *Quarterly Journal of Studies on Alcohol, 29* (1968): 642–656.

10. Mulford and Wilson, "Identifying Drinkers."

11. Ibid, p. 35.

12. Ibid, p. 35.

13. Ibid, p. 36; see also H. A. Mulford and D. E. Miller, "Drinking in Iowa, III. A Scale of Definitions of Alcohol Related to Drinking Behaviour," *Quarterly Journal of Studies on Alcohol, 21* (1960): 267–278.

14. Mulford and Miller, "III. A Scale of Definitions," p. 276.

15. Ibid, pp. 277–278.

16. R. Jessor, T. D. Graves, R. C. Hanson, and S. L. Jessor, *Society, Personality, and Deviant Behaviour* (New York: Holt, Rinehart and Winston, 1968), p. 172.

17. Mulford and Miller, "III. A Scale of Definitions."

18. S. Siegel, *Nonparametric Statistics for the Behavioural Sciences* (New York: McGraw-Hill, 1956), p. 184.

19. Mulford and Miller, "III. A Scale of Definitions," p. 275.

20. R. J. Savard, "Effects of Disulfiram Therapy on Relationships within the Navajo Drinking Group," *Quarterly Journal of Studies on Alcohol, 29* (1968): 909–916.

21. F. N. Ferguson, "Navaho Drinking: Some Tentative Hypotheses," *Human Organization, 27* (1968): 159–167; F. N. Ferguson, *Community Treatment Plan for Navajo Problem Drinkers,* Final Report for Grant MH-01389 (McKinley County Family Consultation Service, Gallup, New Mexico, 1969).

22. H. A. Mulford and D. E. Miller, "Drinking in Iowa, IV. Preoccupation with Alcohol and Definitions of Alcohol, Heavy Drinking and Trouble

Due to Drinking," *Quarterly Journal of Studies on Alcohol, 21* (1960): 279–291.

23. Mulford and Wilson, "Identifying Drinkers," p. 34.

24. Mulford and Miller, "IV. Preoccupation," p. 291.

25. Mulford and Wilson, "Identifying Drinkers," p. 34.

26. Savard, "Effects of Disulfiram Therapy"; Ferguson, "Navaho Drinking."

27. S. J. Kunitz, J. E. Levy and M. Everett, "Alcoholic Cirrhosis among the Navajo," *Quarterly Journal of Studies of Alcohol, 30* (1969): 672–685.

28. The three tests done—serum bilirubin, serum glutamic oxalotransaminase, and serum alkaline phosphatase—were not the most sensitive indicators of liver function. The most useful indicator, the brome sulphathalien test, requires injecting a dye into the patient, the amount dependent on his weight, and the withdrawal of a blood sample forty-five minutes later. This was not practical under field conditions.

29. N. Kessel and H. Walton, *Alcoholism* (Baltimore: Penguin Books, 1965), p. 34.

30. Ibid, p. 34; L. N. Robins, G. E. Murphy and M. B. Breckenridge, "Drinking Behaviour of Young Urban Negro Men," *Quarterly Journal of Studies on Alcohol, 29* (1968): 657–684.

31. H. G. Morgan, "Acute Neuropsychiatric Complications of Chronic Alcoholism," *British Journal of Psychiatry, 114* (1968): 85–91.

32. H. Isbell, H. F. Fraser, R. E. Belleville, and A. J. Eisenman, "An Experimental Study of the Etiology of 'Rum Fits' and Delirium Tremens," *Quarterly Journal of Studies on Alcohol, 16* (1955): 1–33.

33. R. D. Adams, "Nutritional Diseases of the Nervous System in the Alcoholic Patient," *Transactions of the American Clinical and Climatologic Association, 71* (1959): 59–94.

34. Ibid, pp. 67–68.

35. Kunitz, Levy and Everett, "Cirrhosis," p. 682.

36. M. M. Gross, E. Halpert, L. Sabot, and P. Polizons, "Hearing Disturbances and Auditory Hallucinations in the Acute Alcoholic Psychoses, I: Incidence and Significance," *Journal of Nervous and Mental Diseases, 137* (1963): 455–465.

37. R. H. Mott, I. F. Small, and J. M. Anderson, "Comparative Study of Hallucinations," *Archives of General Psychiatry, 12* (1965): 599.

38. L. B. Boyer, "Remarks on the Personality of Shamans: With Special Reference to the Apache of the Mescalero Indian Reservation," in The *Psychoanalytic Study of Society,* Vol. II, W. Muensterberger and S. Axelrad, eds. (New York: International Universities Press, 1962), p. 246.

39. N. E. Miller, "Learning of Visceral and Glandular Responses," *Science, 163* (1969): 434–445.

40. C. MacAndrew and R. B. Edgerton, *Drunken Comportment* (Chicago: Aldine, 1969).

41. E. M. Lemert, "The Use of Alcohol in Three Salish Indian Tribes," *Quarterly Journal of Studies on Alcohol, 19* (1958): 90–107.

42. J. E. Levy and S. J. Kunitz, "Field Notes" (summer, 1969). Two groups of Hopis were interviewed with questionnaires similar to those administered to the Navajos; all known cirrhotics of whom 10 gave reliable information concerning tremulousness and hallucinations; and controls matched for age, sex, and area of residence of whom 18 gave reliable information. Fifteen of the controls were drinkers. Three of these reported tremulousness, two of these also had experienced hallucinations. Seven of the cirrhotics reported tremulousness, and six of the seven also had experienced hallucinations. The Hopi controls resemble the Flagstaff group of Navajos in respect to the proportion of drinkers reporting the medical sequelae of drinking.

43. S. Wolfe, personal communication; S. Wolfe and M. Victor, "The Physiological Basis of the Alcohol Withdrawal Syndrome" (paper presented at the Symposium on Recent Advances in Studies on Alcoholism, sponsored by the National Center for Prevention and Control of Alcoholism, National Institute of Mental Health, Washington, D.C., June 25–27, 1970. To be published in the proceedings of the symposium).

44. D. H. Marjot, "The Length of the Drinking Bout Preceding Alcohol Withdrawal States," *British Journal of Addiction, 64* (1970): 307–314.

45. D. Fenna, L. Mix, O. Schaefer, and J. A. L. Gilbert, "Ethanol Metabolism in Various Racial Groups," *Canadian Medical Association Journal, 105* (1971): 472–475. See also C. Lieber, "Metabolism of Ethanol and Alcoholism: Racial and Acquired Factors," *Annals of Internal Medicine, 76* (1972): 326–327, and E. Rubin and C. Lieber, "Alcoholism, Alcohol and Drugs," *Science, 172* (1971): 1097–1102.

46. M. Keller, "Definition of Alcoholism," *Quarterly Journal of Studies on Alcohol, 21* (1960): 125–134.

47. Mulford, "Deviant Drinking"; Mulford and Wilson, "Identifying Drinkers."

48. Mulford and Wilson, "Identifying Drinkers."

49. T. D. Graves, "The Personal Adjustment of Navajo Indian Migrants to Denver, Colorado," *American Anthropologist, 72* (1970): 35–54.

50. The reason there are fewer men reported in the present discussion from the Flagstaff group as having police records is that not all the police contacts were related to alcohol.

51. See discussion in Chapter VI, also D. C. Leighton and C. Kluckhohn, *Children of the People* (Cambridge: Harvard University Press, 1948), p. 96.

52. J. E. Levy, S. J. Kunitz and M. Everett, "Navajo Criminal Homicide," *Southwestern Journal of Anthropology, 25* (1969): 124–152.

53. "Symposium on Indian Law," *Arizona Law Review, 10,* No. 3 (winter, 1968); W. A. Brophy and S. D. Aberle, *The Indian, America's Unfinished Business* (Norman: University of Oklahoma Press, 1966), especially Chapter II.

54. W. T. Hagan, *Indian Police and Judges* (New Haven: Yale University Press, 1966).

55. D. B. Heath, "Prohibition and Post-Repeal Drinking Patterns among the Navajo," *Quarterly Journal of Studies on Alcohol, 25* (1964): 119–135. R. A. Luebben, "Anglo Law and Navaho Behavior," *Kiva, 29* (1964): 60–75.

56. O. C. Stewart, "Questions Regarding American Indian Criminality," *Human Organization, 23* (1964): 61–66.

57. Luebben, "Anglo Law"; C. Kluckhohn and D. C. Leighton, *The Navaho* (Cambridge: Harvard University Press, 1946), p. 111.

58. Stewart, "Questions."

59. Levy, Kunitz and Everett, "Homicide."

60. T. D. Graves, "The Personal Adjustment of Navajo Migrants to Denver, Colorado."

61. Ferguson, "Navajo Drinking"; Ferguson, "Community Treatment."

Chapter Eight

CONCLUSIONS

The unifying argument about which our discourse has been organized is one that questions a prevalent view of the nature of Indian drinking. According to this view, the use of alcohol to the point of intoxication invariably releases aggression, lessens inhibitions, and alleviates anxiety. It follows, then, that anyone who drinks to the point of intoxication must do so because of an impelling need to escape from the bonds of a reality so unpleasant that anxiety levels are high and the individual is generally constrained. These ideas about the nature and function of alcohol fit well with the anomie concept of deviance leading to the view that alcohol is one of the retreatist responses to social frustration. Noting that American Indians (1) frequently drink to the point of intoxication, and (2) lead difficult lives characterized by rapid social change and social disintegration, for instance, it is reasonable to view Indian drinking as a symptom of anomie.

Our data, it appeared to us, pointed in other directions leading us to formulate several hypotheses as alternatives. These emphasize the many different reasons for drinking and the cultural factors that influence drinking patterns. Our findings, then, will be presented as they support or deny our hypotheses. Subsequently, larger implications and problems inherent in research on this topic may be discussed at greater length.

1. *Highly visible group drinking is socially acceptable in loosely organized rather than tightly integrated tribes, and the patterns of resulting pathologies can be accounted for by these differences.*

After classing the Hopis as highly organized and the White Mountain Apaches as loosely organized we found that:

(a) As expected, the Hopis valued sobriety and were sober in public while the White Mountain Apaches had institutionalized public drinking and intoxication. The Navajos, whom we had placed somewhere between the Apaches and the Hopis, also indulged in group drinking in public. It could be argued that Navajo public drinking was somewhat less institutionalized than that of the Apaches.

(b) As expected, the White Mountain Apaches had the highest rates of homicide, suicide, and acts of individual aggression. The Navajos had considerably lower rates as did the Hopis.

(c) Quite unexpectedly, the White Mountain Apaches had higher death rates from alcoholic cirrhosis than had the Navajos, while the Hopis had a death rate considerably higher than that of the Apaches or any other tribe recorded to date.

The lack of correlation between levels of public intoxication and death rates from alcoholic cirrhosis appears to be important and to demand some discussion. Periodic public drinking that is socially acceptable does not, of itself, predispose to cirrhosis. Between drinking bouts the individual is likely to be integrated into his family, thus maintaining a normal diet. This appears to be the case among the Navajo and we would expect to find correspondingly low rates for the Apache. The fact that we do not, however, may be explained by differences in the accessibility of alcohol. Prohibition laws have been repealed on the Fort Apache Reservation but continue in effect on the larger and more isolated Navajo Reservation. Thus, it is not clear that this form of drinking protects against cirrhosis when the alcohol supply is cheap, abundant, and close at hand.

The remarkably high death rate from alcoholic cirrhosis, found among the Hopi who disvalue drunkenness and do not permit public drinking, indicates that Field's hypothesis holds true only for levels of public intoxication and not for levels of alcohol consumption. Our data indicate that the Hopi who drink do so covertly and steadily. Their drinking pattern is quite unlike the pattern of the Navajo and Apache.

Thus we may conclude that styles of drinking and the patterns of resulting pathologies may be accounted for largely by social and cultural factors. This argues against the notion that Indian drinking is the same phenomenon regardless of tribe and, by implication, against the inference that all Indians drink for the same reasons.

Another point must be discussed. It is argued that, although different types of societies may be predisposed to react to rapid social change and disintegration in different ways, the underlying reasons for drinking are symptomatic of this reaction and are essentially retreatist in nature. The evidence against the retreatist nature of the drinking pertains to our second hypothesis. We point out that as contact with whites has increased rather than diminished over time we would expect to see rising rates of the pathologies that are said to be symptomatic of anomie. In this regard, our data give little reason to believe that the rates of homicide or suicide have increased during the past century. The quantity of alcohol available appears to be the major factor influencing the levels of drinking within each tribe studied. Moreover, the patterns of drinking, homicide, and suicide have shown considerable stability. There is, then, evidence for the persistence of culturally determined patterns.

2. *In a tribe with a positive value placed on individual prowess and magical power, the mind-altering effects of alcohol will neither be rejected nor denied.*

The positive association found between loose social organization and high prevalence of public intoxication, although it indicates the importance of social and cultural factors in determining the forms that drinking might take, does not explicate the causal connections. Throughout this book we have referred, even though vaguely, to a Navajo "cultural predisposition" to drink in a certain manner. At times we have referred to this predisposition in terms of personality, at times in terms of persisting value orientations, and at other times in terms of the cultural level of belief systems and attendant activities. Now, let us be more explicit about our ideas of "cultural predisposition" before we assess the evidence.

(a) We have suggested that different societies develop different types of personality. Hunting-and-gathering societies depend for their survival on individual prowess, competitiveness, and aggressiveness. Social controls of individual aggressiveness and self-assertion are relatively weak, with the result that individuals tend to seek immediate gratification and to become emotionally labile. To the extent that insobriety facilitates aggression and promotes feelings of personal strength and omnipotence, we would expect such peoples to be fond of drinking because the experience would strengthen the image of the self rather than weaken it. The lack of social controls upon excessive acting-out behavior would allow drinking despite the recognition of many untoward effects.

(b) The hunting-and-gathering societies of North America supported the development of this type of personality by believing that an individual could become virtually invincible by obtaining supernatural power. This power was obtained through dreams and visions. The positive value placed on these ecstatic states would be extended to the state of insobriety by virtue of the fact that all share the property of an altered state of consciousness. The experience of drunkenness would be positively valued and would not give cause for concern or anxiety.

(c) Finally, there is the possibility that if the above-described perceptions of alcoholic intoxication exist, drinking may function as a means of achieving power in a modern world where older forms of the power quest for war and raiding are no longer functioning.

The investigation of personality traits has been beyond the scope of this study. Nevertheless, the findings of Havighurst and Neugarten support the idea that the Hopis are more self-controlled and group oriented than are the Navajos who tend to be less self-controlled, emotionally labile and more intent upon self-gratification (1). These findings are not conclusive, however. We do not have direct evidence that Navajo personality was like this in the prereservation periods. Nor is there evidence to suggest that wherever we find such personality traits we will also find flamboyant drinking or, for that matter, hunting-and-gathering societies.

Whether the Navajos place a positive valuation on individual prowess and assertiveness or on the ecstatic state of the vision is another question that we have been unable to approach directly. In our discussion we have followed Kaplan and Johnson who maintain that this individualistic orientation has persisted despite considerable adoption of Pueblo values (2). Their description of what they call "crazy drunken violence" includes a personal recklessness, which these authors believe "expresses a willingness to die and be hurt. This willingness seems to be the dynamic force that dissipates fear and turns one into a superman (3)." The Dionysian character of this behavior is manifested by the fact that the individual who is "crazy violent" is "attacking normal social arrangements (4)." But the Navajos developed agriculture, matrilineality and other Pueblo-like traits, and the stated ideals of the Navajos are quite Puebloan in character. In consequence, there is considerable conflict between what persists of the older Apachean pattern and the newer Puebloan overlay. This conflict, or ambiguity, is expressed in a number of ways. The person who is "crazy violent" is most often thought to be ill. At the same time, however, the behavior itself is rather admired.

Unfortunately, this interpretation is not based on direct evidence for the existence of a covert, Apachean, individualistic orientation. Instead, it should be phrased as a hypothesis itself. If there is a persisting set of Apachean values, it would be consistent with what is known about contemporary Navajo behavior and might explain some of the contradictions and ambiguities of that behavior. Alternative explanations of the observed behaviors are not difficult to formulate, however. What does emerge from the data is that Navajos place a number of positive valuations on drinking and drunkenness which argues against the retreatist nature of their use of alcohol.

It is tempting to suggest that drunkenness is the equivalent of a power vision and is, therefore, an alternative route to power. The connection is made because the dream and the vision share several properties with the state of drunkenness. One would have to demonstrate not only that the Navajos did, in fact, rely on and actively seek supernatural power through dreams and visions but also that they continue to do so today by using alcohol alone or in conjunction with other methods.

The evidence for the existence of individually owned power among the Navajos in the Southwest is as tenuous as the evidence for the persistence of Apachean individualism. Haile discusses the ambiguity with which visionaries are regarded and concludes:

> The lesson is that dreams and visions may have been a source of healing power for legendary heroes. The ordinary Navajo, however, should not presume to obtain such powers by dreams and visions. It spells certain death (5).

Thus, while the existence of such powers is recognized and dealt with in great detail in Navajo myths, individual Navajos do not or ought not to seek or value individual power. Nevertheless, as Aberle has noted, the Navajos have accepted the peyote religion while the Hopis have not, and the visionary experiences obtained through the use of peyote are valued rather than deprecated (6). Our informants recognized the similarity between peyote and alcohol but felt that the benefits of alcohol were illusory. The reasons for this feeling were not obtained by us. Basso notes a similar attitude toward alcohol among the Western Apaches (7). Basso's informants maintain that they have used alcohol to attain power but that the benefits were illusory not because alcohol failed to provide power but because the power obtained failed to transform their lives. The hangover and depression that followed drinking are the antithesis of what power is supposed to do: to maintain a euphoria for long periods of time and help restructure the individual's life. The Navajos' view of peyote approximates the Apaches' view of power today. It produces a state of euphoria that persists over time. We also have noted that some Navajo ceremonialists feel that drinking during ceremonies helps to make the chanting more effective.

Thus we are of the opinion that, while the hypothesis has not been validated, neither has it been rejected. We are convinced that there is sufficient evidence to conclude that much of Navajo drinking is not retreatist in nature. The evidence pertaining to Navajo personality, values, and notions of supernatural power, although meager, is consistent with the hypothesis as stated. However, we should maintain a skeptical attitude for two reasons. The fact that the sober, Apollonian Hopis drink heavily, if covertly, casts doubt on the explanatory value of Field's hypothesis. What is needed is a proposed relationship between various personality traits and different drinking styles. In addition, as Jorgensen has pointed out, the use of an assumed prior state to predict present behavior is too often based on circular reasoning because, in the event that the behavior does not occur, one tends to use the finding to prove that the state did not exist in the first place or that other behaviors serve the same function (8). In short, the dangers of postdicting are great, and research strategies specifically designed to test this appealing idea are called for.

3. *The pattern of alcohol use differs, depending on degree of acculturation. To be like a white man means, in part, drinking like one.*

The prevalent view that drinking increases in association with the level of rapid change and social disintegration gives the impression that drinking is more prevalent among migrants to cities, among the more educated and, generally, among the Indians who are no longer able to lead a traditional life. In addition to the historical evidence for the argument that it was the most successful high-status Navajo who was able to drink in the early years of the reservation, our interview data show that the style of drinking most often considered pathological (i.e., public intoxication) was found among traditional Navajos. Conversely, it was found that Navajos living in town for 10 or more years had adopted white drinking patterns and were not thought to be deviant.

Although these findings certainly argue against the simplistic manner in which we have phrased the position which equates alcohol use with an-omie, the fact that Jessor and his associates were able to explain similar findings by using a modified version of Merton's theory of anomie demands further discussion. Jessor, as we have mentioned earlier, felt that all accul-turated Indians in his study had adopted the general goals of white society. The Indians who were better educated were able to achieve these goals. Thus, there was no goals-means disjunction; they did not feel deprived and did not drink. The less well educated, with the same aspirations, were less well equipped to attain their goals; they felt deprived; and they tended to drink heavily. Similarly, all unacculturated Indians, both successful and un-successful in material terms, held traditional Indian goals *but,* since the tra-ditional life was gone forever, all were doomed to disappointment. There-fore, goals-means disjunction applied to successful and unsuccessful traditionals alike, and all tended to drink (9).

Certainly, the precontact way of life has disappeared for the Navajos. But it is not clear that this is the way of life that contemporary traditionals pine for. Rather, the postcontact ideals of the pastoralist appear to have been maintained to a considerable extent. We have argued that the reserva-tion system has preserved much of the traditional pastoralism despite the traumatic experience of stock reduction. If this is true, we would expect to find the more successful traditionalists drinking less than the unsuccessful ones. Instead, we have found that drinking is prevalent among traditional-ists of all economic levels and that prosperous traditionals, who suffered the most during stock reduction, were the ones who were wealthy enough to drink the most, prior to the 1930s. As one of our Kaibito Plateau infor-mants, a middle aged woman, said, "We used to drink at home with (my) brother and his wife and my mother to enjoy ourselves. At this time we had plenty of money." The variables affecting drinking were found to be the accessibility of alcohol and the age of the individual. Navajo males tend to drink heavily in their younger years and to either stop completely or to decrease their intake considerably after middle age. Drinking may be viewed, then, as having been incorporated into the traditional social order, and it was associated with wealth and high status.

There remains the question of how much deprivation the people in Flagstaff feel. Although we were not able to obtain uniform data for all groups on this issue, it is our distinct impression that the people who have made Flagstaff their home are much more aware of their deprivation in re-gard to the standard they have set for themselves—Anglo society—

than are the reservation dwellers. Many Flagstaff Navajos discussed with us their feelings of anger at the discrimination they suffered both on their jobs and in other social encounters.

Our more traditional informants, like those interviewed by Shepardson and Hammond on Rainbow Plateau, ". . . do not wish to be White men, therefore they do not see themselves as deprived (10)." The least acculturated drink the most, although they may be subjectively less deprived than the acculturated town dwellers. We maintain that the reasons for this distribution of drinking patterns are found in what the various groups have learned about alcohol. The traditional Navajo learns a pattern of alcohol use developed over time with a set of norms and values consonant with traditional values generally. The more acculturated Navajos have learned a pattern that is adaptive to the Anglo world in which they are attempting to make their way. To succeed in the Anglo world means that one cannot behave like a Navajo if such behavior includes binge drinking, getting arrested, losing time from work, and the like. Not learning such behavior is a necessary (although clearly not a sufficient) cause for succeeding in the Anglo world.

4. *Who does and who does not become acculturated depends in large part on where they are located in the traditional Navajo stratification system. Poorer people in Navajo terms have more incentive to adopt white ways than those who are wealthier.*

The persistence of pastoralism on a large reservation has, until now, allowed Navajos not only to maintain many aspects of their traditional life but also to adopt new ways at differential rates. In Chapter Six we pointed out that the Flagstaff informants came from families with less livestock and more exposure to wage work a generation or two ago than the Kaibito Plateau people have been exposed to until, possibly, the past few years. It seems that the parents of our Flagstaff informants had little benefit from the traditional way of life and viewed the Anglo world as a viable alternative. For them, Christianity and wage work were adaptive, and acculturation was an opportunity. Thus, the Flagstaff group was exposed early in life to parental wage-work models at home and to lower-class or lower-middle-class Anglo models in school. With little for them to do on the reservation, they were sent to school and usually went on to some vocational training or even a few years in college.

The Flagstaff group is noteworthy not because they forsook a Navajo way of life but because they were never really exposed to it during their formative years. They never learned the patterns of drinking that are prevalent among traditional families. Instead, they learned the patterns of the wage-work world in which they later made their way. Quite possibly, younger generations of Navajos are having very different experiences as education becomes more commonplace on the Navajo Reservation and as population pressures force young people onto the job market now that the reservation land base has ceased to expand. It is also probable that the experiences of the Navajos and, we think, of the White Mountain Apaches and the Hopis, have been considerably different from those of tribes whose ways of life and land base were destroyed more rapidly in areas of intensive white settlement. Nevertheless, as the findings do exist, we are cautioned against accepting a simple picture that invariably equates acculturation with disintegration both social and personal.

DISCUSSION

Alcohol, Aggression and Family Disintegration. It has been frequently observed that when Navajos get drunk, fights between family members break out. This phenomenon is readily explained by asserting that alcohol, through its drug effect as a superego solvent, releases aggression with the result that otherwise normal family relationships are destroyed. Both Kluckhohn (11) and Heath (12) have observed that these outbreaks of drunken aggression are patterned rather than random. The majority of antagonists in these conflicts are husbands and wives followed by other dyadic relationships such as fathers and sons and uncles and nephews. The question arises whether alcohol causes marital strife or merely facilitates the expression of preexisting hostilities in a socially acceptable setting. That is, by fostering the notion that a man is not himself when in his cups, it follows that he is not responsible for his actions when drinking.

The studies of suicide and homicide led us to doubt the assumption that alcohol created the violence. Neither suicide nor homicide rates varied with level of alcohol use. Murder of a spouse preceding suicide occurred in a larger proportion of instances in the early years when few suicides were committed while drunk than during recent years when most suicides occurred in association with alcohol. Murderers did not have a higher arrest rate for alcohol-related offenses or other crimes than did a group of controls. Nor, finally, were suicide or homicide rates higher in the areas close to the source of supply where the incidence of cirrhosis was highest.

A very strong pattern of both suicide and homicide emerged. Both acts were committed by married men in the prime of life and were associated with marital discord, especially sexual jealousy. This pattern could be traced to the prereservation period and leads us to advance the notion that Navajo society had its own characteristic societal strains, which continue to the present time but also antedate the periods of widespread alcohol use. Violence occurred both then and now but, perhaps, there were greater social sanctions in the past when drinking could not be offered as an excuse. Possibly the use of alcohol to facilitate aggression between family members allows more individuals to vent their hostility without proceeding to "the end of the road" where one might as well murder and then kill one's self. In sum, what we suggest, not entirely facetiously, is that Navajo men do not beat up their wives because they are drunk but that they get drunk so that they may beat up their wives. Drunken violence may represent an attempt to assert one's self in a situation where self-assertion is valued covertly but sanctioned overtly. Hostility, then, may be expressed upon repeated occasions in the form of fights and beatings rather than being repressed and, for the unfortunate few, finally exploding in a seriously damaging form such as murder.

Persistence and Change.   The degree to which we found Navajo drinking explainable in terms of persisting Navajo values and institutions, if only because the findings were so unexpected, has implications both for further research and for the theories of deviance currently used to explain Indian drinking. Merton's theory of anomie, because it assumes that a given set of values is shared by the whole society, is based on a view of American society as essentially homogeneous rather than pluralistic. This view, although it may be based on accurate observation or political ideology or both, may also be based partly on a belief that processes of change and assimilation tend to predominate over cultural persistence and separatism in modern industrialized societies.

We have implicitly assumed that ours is a pluralistic society, at least in respect to the tribes we have studied. While in the broader context of the entire national scene, this may not be the case, the existence of Indian reservations supported by the federal government and recognized as ethnic enclaves allows us to view cultural differences among Indians as both real and continuing. Furthermore, the existence of reservations as both exploited colonies and the recipients of a variety of welfare programs has led to the persistence of many features of traditional social organization as adaptive to the contemporary situation. We do not wish to assert that change has not or is not occurring but, rather, that we have been impressed by the persistence of older traditions and forms of social organization and life styles alongside this continuing change. Indeed, it has been our position that there have been changing attitudes toward drinking behavior but that these have not proceeded uniformly within the Navajo population. Instead, some elements within the population have, due to their originally low status, moved into the Anglo wage-work world where they have assumed many of the values and aspirations adaptive to that world.

In contrast with the situation that prevailed up to a few years ago when most acculturated Navajos could only find work off reservation, many acculturated individuals have been able to find employment in a number of programs on the reservation, especially since the creation of the office of Navajo Economic Opportunity in the mid-1960s. Although still largely a residual population of the unemployed and/or unemployable, the reservation increasingly is attracting back or retaining the acculturated individuals who, in the past, would have had to have found work elsewhere. A variety of positions have been created for paraprofessionals in human service occupations such as social welfare, mental health, and alcoholism treatment. By inclination and training, these paraprofessionals tend to accept the dominant society's view of mental illness and alcoholism. This view usually includes the idea of adaptive and maladaptive behavior as the defining criterion of sickness (13).

The assumption of these new definitions, learned from Anglo professionals, becomes a means to both "scientifically" legitimatize these new roles and to discredit older forms of behavior that are deemed inappropriate for the wage-work world that Navajos are entering in ever-increasing numbers. Indeed, the emergence of these new groups is symptomatic, we believe, of the profound changes that Navajo society is undergoing. As new groups of "moral entrepreneurs" emerge who have the power to label some behaviors as "sick" and others as "healthy," a variety of behaviors soon come to be labeled as beyond the bounds of acceptable conduct, thus giving added impetus to the shift toward a society more like the dominant one.

In our view, then, no single explanation of drinking fits the variety of patterns identified among the three tribes or within Navajo society itself at the present time. As a result, our explanations lack both the elegance and the parsimony of the retreatist or anomie explanation. Nevertheless, since our interpretations appear to fit the observations more adequately, we have opted to pursue their implications further.

At the outset, our selection of tribes for study predisposed toward finding more evidence of persistence than change and to highlighting differences between traditional styles of drinking. The Navajo, Hopi and White Mountain Apache tribes have all been relatively free from intense face-to-face interaction with whites, and all have maintained rather large, semi-isolated reservations that foster the continuation of subsistence economies. Thus it is not surprising to find so little evidence of social disintegration. While it may be possible to investigate the relationship between social change and drinking on these reservations, to do so would involve the selection of much larger samples of individuals living both on and off reservation than can be conveniently handled by the average field project.

Rather than holding the nature of Indian-white contact constant and comparing tribes of different levels of sociocultural integration as we have done, it would be profitable to compare tribes of a similar cultural type but with varying degrees of exposure to white society. These comparisons ought to reveal the process of change more readily.

Another line of inquiry is suggested by the work Bacon, Barry, and Child who, as we pointed out in Chapter Five, note that drunkenness is greater in societies that emphasize individual independence and achievement and that societies with a high level of alcohol consumption tend to train for responsibility (14). Such studies relate drinking styles more directly to personality factors than to the types of social organization thought to foster the creation of particular types of personality.

It has been noted that child-rearing practices tend to change more slowly than many other areas of behavior and that the most rapidly acculturated Indians are frequently those who were raised with a white model in the home (15). A study of child-rearing practices in both on- and off-reservation populations might give a more accurate gauge of acculturation for a variety of populations than would the less precisely measured "degree of integration with whites," for instance. Heavy drinking that occurred in groups whose child-rearing practices approximated those of the neighboring whites or that had changed radically when compared with the aboriginal practices could then be clearly related to processes of change.

Any research among small Indian communities living in constant interaction with members of the dominant society will have to take the phenomenon of secondary deviance into account (16). Our own research has dealt mainly with primary deviance, in this instance the genesis of drinking itself. Partly because two thirds of our interviewees were living in the most isolated portion of the Navajo Reservation and partly because we worked only with adults most of whom had learned their drinking behaviors many years ago, we were not able to examine what happens to Indians who live and act as Indians while, at the same time, living in close proximity to whites. It has been our impression that this is the situation in which many of the "disintegrated" tribes find themselves. In this instance, an Indian who may be drinking for a variety of positive rather than retreatist reasons will directly experience the disapproval of whites who will label him as deviant and treat him as such. Unable to retreat to the peace and quiet of a large isolated reservation, this type of Indian will find himself in the position of having to behave toward whites in the deviant manner that they expect. He is, in short, the Indian one sometimes encounters who explains his drunken condition by saying, "I am just a poor drunken Indian."

The effects of such "labeling" may be extensive and may make a large contribution to the personal disintegration so often commented upon. Nevertheless, the question that remains to be answered is whether this type of Indian is drinking because it is expected of him and is the only way that he is permitted to behave and whether, if it is established that his drinking is anomic, it came to be so only after he had been labeled as a drunken Indian. We have often wondered what the initial reaction of whites in Indian country would be if all of the local Indians were suddenly sober, aggressively competing for jobs, shrewd in making purchases of secondhand cars and the like, and calmly but firmly demanding equal treatment.

PRACTICAL ISSUES

Periodically, the Navajo Tribal Council debates the issue of whether to legalize liquor on reservation. In view of the style of drinking on reservation as we have already described it, we think that the increase of the availability of liquor will certainly increase the amount of drinking. How much of an increase this will really represent is hard to say, since it is already easy to get bootlegged liquor even in areas as remote as parts of Kaibito Plateau. Possibly, it will reduce accidents if people do not need to drive long distances while drunk and can carry liquor home without fear of arrest (17). We do not think it will lead to an increase in homicides; as we have already pointed out, the homicide rate has remained constant over the past several generations even with the increasing availability of liquor, and it is constant at the present time from areas with little access to off-reservation sources of supply to the more acculturated areas with ready access to off-reservation towns.

On the other hand, the legalization of liquor and the sale of it only at tribal package stores will increase considerably the tribe's revenue. This is an important factor. The money is spent anyway, and it might be better to keep it in the tribe. It is of interest that, as in other dry parts of the country, liquor store and saloon owners in adjacent areas appear to be in favor of the tribe continuing to prohibit alcohol.

We guess that, if liquor were to be legalized, we would see an increased death rate from alcoholic cirrhosis as a result. At present, the case-fatality rate and death rate are relatively low because most people give up drinking before cirrhosis (if it has developed) is irreversible and fatal. It is likely that with liquor more readily available, people will die of cirrhosis more often than if it were less accessible and they had a chance to stop drinking. The death rate is higher at present in the areas near border towns than in the remote areas, and this is largely a reflection of the availability of alcohol.

We also judge by the White Mountain Apache experience with legalized liquor that the cirrhosis rate might increase. However, we are talking about a relatively few lives being lost as a result of cirrhosis. Whether there would be a reduction in deaths from accidents that would more than outweigh the relatively small increase in deaths from cirrhosis, we do not know.

Ultimately the decision will be made on the basis of considerations other than those we have presented here. However, we think that if alcohol were to be legalized, the changes that would occur would not be as devastating and far-reaching as many people have suggested.

The treatment of alcoholism has increasingly occupied the attention of Indian tribes, the Bureau of Indian Affairs, the Indian Health Service, and the Office of Navajo Economic Opportunity. Despite a general desire to create treatment programs that are consonant with, or at least cognizant of, the dynamics of Navajo drinking, most of these programs are based on the Anglo definition of alcoholism as a disease. The philosophy behind Alcoholics Anonymous most clearly exemplifies the notion that an individual drinks to excess because of an underlying psychological deficit.

Although excessive alcohol consumption is a problem, it is a problem, in our opinion, because of the consequences that follow from it—accidents, the impoverishment of already poverty stricken families, and the like. Many Navajos do, indeed, regard drinking as a problem for just these reasons. It is important, however, that most of the individuals in this study who did become aware that alcohol consumption is more costly than it is worth were apparently able to stop drinking with little difficulty, regardless of whether they were in a treatment program and whether intensive follow-up treatment was provided. This indicates to us that excessive drinking among most Navajos does not originate in the same pathological motives as it does among Anglo alcoholics. The behaviors are labeled the same because they look the same, and often produce the similar end results.

One implication of this, in our opinion, is that an alcohol-treatment program must devise the means to distinguish between persons who require psychotherapy, social case work, and the like and persons who will stop drinking regardless of what is done for them. This approximates the point made by Ferguson when she distinguished "anxiety" from "recreation" drinkers (18). Although we do not agree that the term "recreation" drinker reveals the significance of the most common form of alcohol consumption among the Navajos, it is important to make the distinction between people who drink excessively because they are normal young men in Navajo terms and people who drink because of pathological processes, whether these processes derive from the stresses of acculturation or from more personal difficulties. Our findings indicate that the former group—normal young men—is the vast majority and accounts for most of what is regarded as Navajo problem drinking.

This leads to a consideration of the appropriateness of the disease label for alcohol use as it is seen among the Navajos and the possible effects that treatment programs may have in the foreseeable future. The "disease concept" of alcoholism is relatively new and has not yet gained complete acceptance (19). The results of convincing people that alcoholics are sick and of convincing alcoholics that they are sick raises important issues. In this context, Lemert's distinction between primary and secondary deviance, already alluded to in our discussion of small tribes, is helpful (20). The concept of secondary deviance refers to the results of the labeling process itself. That is, how individuals come to think of themselves and behave after they have been defined by society or some group as being deviant. The implications of the disease label are numerous (21). Most important for our purposes is the fact that it encourages the individual to think of himself as a passive victim.

Insofar as a treatment program conceives its function in strictly medical terms (i.e., the treatment and cure of the sick) and does not espouse larger social and cultural awareness, the labeling of large numbers of normal Navajos as sick can only have untoward consequences. Not only will the health facilities be strained because the overwhelming majority of Navajo men drink, but an ever-increasing number of Navajos will be encouraged to think of themselves as sick and incapable of handling their own affairs. In our opinion, if treatment programs consciously accept the notion of cultural pluralism, they should not emphasize the issue of sickness in their education activities.

If, on the other hand, medical programs are conceived of as agents of change in their own right, then the use of the disease label may be utilized as a means of changing perceptions and values. We have already discussed the role of the Navajo paraprofessional worker as a "moral entrepreneur." These roles provide avenues of success for people who have a small stake in the more traditional system and provide the means by which Navajos may influence other Navajos to accept new cultural norms. In our opinion, this process is well underway on the Navajo Reservation. Whether, however, it is desirable to have Navajos think of themselves as sick and in need of Anglo treatment, as opposed to having them conceive of their problems as existing in the external world—in the job market or political system, for instance—is open to considerable argument.

Another issue of unknown importance is the recent suggestion that Indians metabolize alcohol more slowly than Anglos (22). The work has been criticized on methodological grounds (23) but, nonetheless, represents a potentially significant area of investigation. Although we do not believe that metabolic differences are likely to account for different drinking styles, prolonged clearance time of alcohol from the blood stream (if it turns out to be a real phenomenon) may be related to such important problems as automobile accidents that occur after drinking episodes. In view of the paucity of information available today, it is not useful to go beyond these few suggestions.

The recurrent theme in this study is the argument that economic deprivation alone cannot explain the patterns of alcohol use that we have observed both on and off the Navajo Reservation. Let us make it clear, however, that we do not deny that Indians, including Navajos, are economically deprived. We agree with Aberle's analysis of the Navajo economic situation and his suggestions for its improvement (24). However, poverty cannot explain all of the behavior we have observed and described but poverty, drunk or sober, is not a good thing and should be dealt with on that basis.

The more general theoretical implications of our study should also be mentioned. We said in Chapter One that the interest in acculturation that has been so much a part of both American sociology and anthropology grew out of the generally conservative reaction to the democratic and industrial revolutions of the nineteenth century. Both processes were considered to have destroyed the sense of community that had existed previously and that was typified by the feudal period. We maintain that social scientists have tended to idealize "folk" societies rather than the feudal period but with the same end in view: as a foil for criticizing contemporary "mass" society with its sameness, anomie, alienation, and increasingly powerful central government. We have obviously presented an exaggerated picture, but it is accurate enough.

Traditional societies, which often have no written history, tend to be viewed as harmonious, well-integrated, and *gemeinschaft*like. When deviant behavior is observed, it is attributed to the disintegrating effects of the contact situation, the only reality that we can observe and for which any data exist. The issue we have raised here is that traditional societies appear to have developed their own kinds of deviant behavior and their own ways of controlling deviants prior to white contact. Deviance is usually said to have increased as a result of such contact because of the moral crises that developed. But why such crises should exist only in, or as a result of, contact with civilized societies is not clear and is certainly not provable. We may still ask why white contact was more conducive to social pathology than the great drought in the American Southwest at the end of the thirteenth century, or even the eruption of Sunset Crater about A.D. 1070. All of these events worked changes on the social organization and wellbeing of the peoples affected by them. Do moral crises occur only in civilized and literate societies, or is it only in these societies that people write about them?

We have not denied that Indian societies have changed as a result of the contact situation. We have pointed out, however, that they appear to react in ways that are determined by their own culture and values. Not only do they create their own kinds of deviants, but they deal with external stresses in culturally patterned ways. This does not mean that cultures do not change but, instead, it suggests that there is a remarkable persistence of some cultural constellations over time and despite profound changes in many aspects of life. And it appears to us that many of these enduring constellations are of more value in explaining certain kinds of behavior commonly labeled deviant than has usually been thought.

——————————————— NOTES ———————————————

1. R. J. Havighurst and B. L. Neugarten, *American Indian and White Children* (Chicago: University of Chicago Press, 1955).

2. B. Kaplan and D. Johnson, "The Social Meaning of Navajo Psychopathology and Psychotherapy," in *Magic, Faith and Healing*, A. Kiev, ed. (New York: The Free Press, 1964), pp. 218, 219, 226.

3. Ibid, p. 218.

4. Ibid, p. 219.

5. B. Haile, "A Note on the Navajo Visionary," *American Anthropologist*, 42 (1940): 359.

6. D. F. Aberle, *The Peyote Religion among the Navajo* (Chicago: Aldine, 1966), especially page 219.

7. K. Basso, personal communication.

8. J. Jorgensen, personal communication.

9. R. Jessor, T. D. Graves, R. C. Hanson and S. L. Jessor, *Society, Personality and Deviant Behavior: A Study of a Tri-Ethnic Community* (New York: Holt, Rinehart and Winston, 1968).

10. M. Shepardson and B. Hammond, "Change and Persistence in an Isolated Navajo Community," *American Anthropologist*, 66 (1964): 1029–1050, p. 1045.

11. C. Kluckhohn, *Navajo Witchcraft* (Boston: Beacon Press, 1962), p. 94.

12. D. B. Heath, "Prohibition and Post-Repeal Drinking Patterns among the Navajo," *Quarterly Journal of Studies on Alcohol*, 25 (1964): 119–135, p. 126.

13. S. J. Kunitz and J. E. Levy, "Changing Ideas of Alcohol Use Among the Navajo Indians," *Quarterly Journal of Studies on Alcohol*, in press.

14. M. K. Bacon, H. Barry III, and I. L. Child, "A Cross-Cultural Study of Drinking: II. Relations to Other Features of Culture," in *A Cross-Cultural Study of Drinking: Quarterly Journal of Studies on Alcohol*, Supplement No. 3, April, 1965.

15. E. M. Bruner, "Primary Group Experience and the Process of Acculturation," *American Anthropologist*, 58 (1956): 605–623.

16. E. M. Lemert, "The Concept of Secondary Deviation," in *Human Deviance, Social Problems and Social Control*, E. M. Lemert, ed. (Englewood Cliffs, N.J.: Prentice-Hall, 1967).

17. R. C. Brown, B. S. Gurunanjappa, R. J. Hawk and D. Bitsuie, "The Epidemiology of Accidents among the Navajo Indians," *Public Health Reports*, 85 (1970): 881–888.

18. F. N. Ferguson, "Navajo Drinking: Some Tentative Hypotheses," *Human Organization, 27* (1968): 158–167.

19. E. M. Jellinek, *The Disease Concept of Alcoholism* (New Haven: Hillhouse Press, 1960) and P. W. Haberman and J. Scheinberg, "Public Attitudes Toward Alcoholism as an Illness," *American Journal of Public Health, 59* (1969): 1209–1216.

20. E. M. Lemert, "Secondary Deviation," p. 17.

21. P. M. Roman and H. M. Trice, "The Sick Role, Labelling Theory and the Deviant Drinker," *The International Journal of Social Psychiatry, 14* (1968): 245–251.

22. D. Fenna, L. Mix, O. Scharfer and J. A. L. Gilbert, "Ethanol Metabolism in Various Racial Groups," *Canadian Medical Association Journal, 105* (1971): 472–475.

23. C. Lieber, "Metabolism of Ethanol and Alcoholism: Racial and Acquired Factors," *Annals of Internal Medicine, 76* (1972): 326–327.

24. D. F. Aberle, "A Plan for Navajo Economic Development," in *Toward Economic Development for Native American Communities,* a compendium of papers submitted to the subcommittee of Economy in Government of the Joint Economics Committee, Congress of the United States (Washington, D.C.: U.S. Government Printing Office, 1969).

Appendix I

INTERVIEW FORMS

1. ON-RESERVATION QUESTIONNAIRE
2. OFF-RESERVATION QUESTIONNAIRE
3. FOLLOW-UP ON-RESERVATION QUESTIONNAIRE

Informant No._____   Household No._____
                                            Household Head_____

USPHS FIELD HEALTH TUBA CITY

Alcohol Questionnaire

1. Name_____ 2. Census No._____
3. Date of birth_____ 4. Sex_____
5. Marital status_____ 6. Prior marriages_____
7. Number of surviving children_____ 8. Years education_____
9. Type of school last attended_____
10. Present residence_____
11. Type family unit: matrilocal ext.; patrilocal ext.; neolocal; other; (describe)_____
_____
12. Religious preference: Trad.; NAC; Cath.; LDS; Prot.; other (describe)
_____
13. Number of siblings of respondent_____
14. Occupation_____
15. Cash salary per annum (if any)_____
16. Size of sheep permits (in respondent's name)_____
17. Number of head sold preceding year_____
18. Cash received_____
19. Pounds of wool sold preceding year_____
20. Cash received_____
21. Income from weaving_____ 22. Other income_____
23. Total estimated annual income for household_____
24. Number of people in household_____
25. Have you ever been arrested?_____
26. Where? Local; reservation area; other; off reservation; other state_____
_____

Attitudes

1. In general, what do you think of drinking?

2. What are the good things about drinking?

3. What are the bad things about drinking?

4. Are there occasions when it is proper to drink?

Alcohol Questionnaire
Page 2

Informant No._____
Household No._____

5. Who in this area is a total abstainer?

6. Can you give the names of some people in this area who are thought to drink to excess or whose drinking is causing problems?

7. How would you describe your own use of alcohol?

8. Could you describe a time when you drank? (When, where, with whom, why, how much, etc.)

9. Was this a typical occasion?

Check: age started drinking: steady since then? etc.

Definition of Alcohol
(Check statement you would make)

1. Alcoholic beverages make a social gathering more enjoyable.   + — ?
2. Alcoholic beverages make me feel more satisfied with myself.   + — ?
3. Alcoholic beverages help me overcome shyness.   + — ?
4. Alcoholic beverages help me to get along better with other people.   + — ?
5. Alcoholic beverages make me less self conscious.   + — ?
6. Alcoholic beverages make me more carefree.   + — ?
7. Alcoholic beverages give me pleasure.   + — ?
8. A drink sometimes makes me feel better.   + — ?

Quantity-Frequency

1. How much do you tend to drink at a sitting?

1–5 glasses of beer	6–9 glasses of beer
1–3 bottles of beer	4–6 bottles of beer
1–2 drinks of liquor	3–4 drinks of liquor
1–3 glasses of wine	4–5 glasses of wine
10 or more glasses of beer	Other
7 or more bottles of beer	
5 or more drinks of liquor	
6 or more glasses of wine	

Alcohol Questionnaire   Informant No._____
Page 3   Household No._____

2. How often do you drink?   At most once a month
                               More than once a month
                               Two to four times a month
                               More than once a week

Preoccupation with Alcohol

Which statement would you make about yourself?

1. I stay intoxicated for several days at a time.   + − ?
2. I worry about not being able to get a drink when I need
    one.   + − ?
3. I sneak drinks when no one is looking.   + − ?
4. Once I start drinking it is difficult for me to stop before I
    get completely intoxicated.   + − ?
5. I get intoxicated on work days.   + − ?
6. I take a drink the first thing when I get up in the morning.   + − ?
7. I awaken next day not being able to remember some of the
    things I had done while I was drinking.   + − ?
8. I neglect my regular meals when I am drinking.   + − ?
9. I don't nurse my drinks. I toss them down pretty fast.   + − ?
10. I drink for the effect of alcohol (with little attention to the
    type of beverage or brand name).   + − ?
11. Liquor has less effect on me than it used to.   + − ?

Trouble due to Drinking

1. Has an employer ever fired you or threatened to fire you if
    you did not cut down or quit drinking?   + − ?
2. Has your spouse or other relative ever complained that you
    spend too much money for alcohol?   + − ?
3. Has your spouse ever threatened to leave you if you did not
    do something about your drinking?   + − ?
4. Have you ever been picked up by the police for intoxication
    or other charges involving alcohol?   + − ?
5. Has a physician ever told you that drinking was injuring your
    health?   + − ?

Informant No._____
Household No._____

Medical

1. Have you ever had burning or itching on the soles of your feet?   + − ?
2. Have the whites of your eyes ever turned yellow?   + − ?
3. Has your skin ever turned yellow?   + − ?
4. Have you ever vomited up anything that looked like coffee grounds?   + − ?
5. Have you ever vomited up bright red blood?   + − ?
6. Have you ever passed black, tarry stools?   + − ?
7. After you have been drinking are you shaky and nervous?   + − ?
8. After you have been drinking have you ever heard voices when no one is around?   + − ?
9. After you have been drinking have you ever seen strange things that you couldn't explain, like small animals crawling on the walls?   + − ?

If the answer to either question 8 or 9 is yes, please describe the incidents below. What did you see, hear, etc.? How long after drinking, etc.?

FLAGSTAFF QUESTIONNAIRE

Household No._____   Household head   yes   no
Informant No._____   (circle one)   .
Informant (self or other—specify)_____
Name_____
Date of birth_____
Sex (circle one)   male   female
Marital status_____
Number of prior marriages_____
Number of surviving children_____
Total number of years of education_____
Highest grade achieved_____
Types of schools attended (start from most recent and work backwards)
               School   *Number of years attended*
1. _____   _____
2. _____   _____
3. _____   _____
4. _____   _____
5. _____   _____
6. _____   _____
7. _____   _____
Age at which schooling began?_____
Were you in a special vocational program? (circle one)   yes   no
If so, what trade did you learn?_____
Are you practicing that trade at present (circle one)   yes   no   not applicable
Present occupation_____
Do you work for the federal government? (circle one)   yes   no
Do you work for the city, county, or state government? (circle one)   yes   no
Estimated yearly income_____
Estimated household income_____
Number of people in household on year-round basis?_____
Do you contribute any of your income to anyone not living with you all the
time (on a year-round basis)? (circle one)   yes   no
If so, to whom do you contribute?_____
                              (relation)
How many sheep permits (units) do you have in your name?_____
Do you get any income from sheep or other livestock?_____
Do you own or rent the house you live in?_____

Were you in the military service? (circle one)   yes   no

If so, what branch?_____

Where? (circle one)   stateside,   abroad,   not applicable

Were you in combat?   yes   no   not applicable

Did you volunteer or were you drafted?   volunteer   drafted   not applicable

Did you serve with other Navajos? (circle one)   yes   no   not applicable

Did you serve with any other Indians besides Navajos?   yes   no   not applicable

What years were you in the service?_____

Have you been a patient at a Navajo Sing this past year? (circle one)   yes   no

If so, how many?_____

Which ones?_____

Have you been to any Sing this past year when you weren't a patient? (circle

one)   yes   no

Were you a patient at a Navajo Sing two years ago?   yes   no

Which one?_____

How many?_____

Were you a patient at a Sing three years ago?   yes   no

How many?_____

Which ones?_____

Were you a patient at a Navajo Sing four years ago?   yes   no

How many?_____

Which ones?_____

Were you a patient at a Navajo Sing five years ago?   yes   no

How many?_____

Which ones?_____

Have you been a patient at a peyote meeting this year?   yes   no   No._____

Have you been a patient at a peyote meeting two years ago?

                                                        yes   no   No._____

                               Three years ago?   yes   no   No._____

                               Four years ago?   yes   no   No._____

                               Five years ago?   yes   no   No._____

Have you gone to Anglo doctors this year? (circle one)   yes   no

How often?_____

Which do you prefer, doctors here in Flagstaff or doctors in government hospi-

tals?_____

Why?_____

Home area on reservation:_____

What was family's primary source of support when you were a child? (i.e. livestock, steady wage work, part-time migrant wage work, any combination of
these or any other possibilities)_____

If anyone in the family when you were a child did steady wage work, what relation was he (or she) to you?_____

Who in your home when you were a child attended school? (Use other side if
necessary)

Relation   Number of years of schooling

_____   _____
_____   _____
_____   _____

Are your parents still alive?_____
How old were you when they died?_____
            Age at mother's death?_____
            Age at father's death?_____
If your parents (one or both) died when you were a child, who took care of you
while you were growing up?_____
How many brothers and sisters do you have?_____
How many older than you?   Brothers_____ Sisters_____
How many younger than you?   Brothers_____ Sisters_____
What language was spoken at home when you were a child?_____
If Navajo was spoken mainly, did anyone know English?_____
If English was spoken primarily, did anyone know Navajo?_____
How long have you lived in Flagstaff?_____
Do you vote in the Tribal Elections? (circle one)   yes   no
Whom did you vote for in the last election? (Tribal)_____
Do you vote in local city and county elections?   yes   no
What party?_____
Have you voted in the last Presidential election?   yes   no
For whom? (circle one)   Nixon   Humphrey   Wallace
Religious preference of family when you were a child?_____
What is your present religious preference?_____
Traditional, Traditional-NAC, NAC, Catholic, Protestant (sect)_____

When you were a child, do you remember seeing people drinking?_____
Did people in your home drink?_____
Who were they (i.e. relation to respondent)?_____

What did they drink?_____
Where did they get it?_____
Can you describe a typical drinking situation that you can recall from when you
were a child?

What is your current drinking status (do you still drink, did you drink, did you
give up drinking, etc.?)

If you have ever drunk, how old were you when you had your first drink?

Can you describe the situation when you first drank? (With whom, where, when, etc.)

If you were in the military service, did that have any effect on your drinking? If so, how?

The following questions are not asked of abstainers

What statement would you make about yourself: Answer yes or no to the following questions.

Definition of Alcohol

1. Alcoholic beverages make a social gathering more enjoyable. + − ? (don't know)
2. A drink sometimes makes me feel better. + − ?
3. Alcoholic beverages give me pleasure. + − ?
4. Alcoholic beverages make me more carefree. + − ?
5. Alcoholic beverages help me overcome shyness. + − ?
6. Alcoholic beverages make me less self-conscious. + − ?
7. Alcoholic beverages make me feel more satisfied with myself. + − ?
8. Alcoholic beverages help me get along better with other people. + − ?

Trouble due to drinking:

1. Has an employer ever fired you or threatened to fire you if you did not cut down or quit drinking? + − ?
2. Has your spouse or other relative ever complained that you spend too much money for alcohol? + − ?
3. Has your spouse ever threatened to leave you if you did not do something about your drinking? + − ?
4. Have you ever been picked up by the police for intoxication or other charges involving alcohol? + − ?
5. Has a physician ever told you that drinking was injuring your health? + − ?

Quantity-Frequency

1. How much do you tend to drink at a sitting? (check one)

    | 1–5 glasses of beer | 6–9 glasses of beer |
    | 1–3 bottles of beer | 4–6 bottles of beer |
    | 1–2 drinks of liquor | 3–4 drinks of liquor |
    | 1–3 glasses of wine | 4–5 glasses of wine |

    10 or more glasses of beer
     7 or more bottles of beer
     5 or more drinks of liquor
     6 or more glasses of wine   other_____

2. How often do you drink? (check one)
    At most once a month
    More than once a month
    Two to four times a month
    More than once a week

Preoccupation with alcohol (answer yes or no to the following questions)

1. I don't nurse my drinks, I toss them down pretty fast.   +   —   ?
2. I drink for the effect of alcohol (with little attention to the type of beverage or brand name).   +   —   ?
3. Liquor has less effect on me than it used to.   +   —   ?
4. I awaken next day not being able to remember some of the things I had done while I was drinking.   +   —   ?
5. I neglect my regular meals when I am drinking.   +   —   ?
6. I take a drink the first thing when I get up in the morning.   +   —   ?
7. I get intoxicated on work days.   +   —   ?
8. Once I start drinking it is difficult for me to stop before I get completely intoxicated.   +   —   ?
9. I sneak drinks when no one is looking.   +   —   ?
10. I worry about not being able to get a drink when I need one.   +   —   ?
11. I stay intoxicated for several days at a time.   +   —   ?

Medical Questions

		yes	no	not appli-cable
1.	After you have been drinking, are you very shaky and nervous?	+	–	0
2.	After you have been drinking, have you ever heard voices when no one is around?	+	–	0
3.	Have you ever heard voices when no one is around at times when you haven't been drinking? If yes, please describe:	+	–	0
4.	After you have been drinking, have you ever seen strange things that you couldn't explain, like small animals crawling on the walls? If yes, please describe:	+	–	0
5.	Have you ever seen strange things that you couldn't explain at times when you haven't been drinking? If yes, please describe:	+	–	0
6.	If you used to drink but don't anymore, why did you give it up?	+	–	0

Why did you move to Flagstaff?

Do you think Navajos have special problems in Flagstaff?

If you lost your job, what would you do?
    Move back to reservation
    Stay and look for another job
    Other

How long do you plan to stay in Flagstaff?

Do you plan to return to the reservation when you retire?
If so, where would you live?

FOLLOW-UP RESERVATION QUESTIONNAIRE

Informant No._____ Household No._____

Name_____

Were you in the military service? (circle one)   yes   no

If so, what branch?_____

Where? (circle one)   stateside   abroad   not applicable

Were you in combat?   yes   no   not applicable

Did you volunteer or were you drafted? (circle one)

                                      volunteer   drafted   not applicable

Did you serve with other Navajos? (circle one)   yes   no   not applicable

Did you serve with any other Indians besides Navajos? (circle one)

                                      yes   no   not applicable

What years were you in the service?_____

Did the military service affect your drinking in some way?

                                      yes   no   not applicable

If yes, please describe:

Have you been a patient at a Navajo Sing this past year? (circle one)   yes   no

If so, how many?_____ Which ones?_____

NOTE whether informant was key patient or co-patient. If co-patient, who was the key patient? i.e., relation to informant.

Two years ago? (circle one)   yes   no

How many?_____Which ones?_____

Three years ago?   yes   no

How many?_____ Which ones? (and how many nights)_____

_____

Four years ago?   yes   no

How many?_____ Which ones?_____

Five years ago?   yes   no

How many?_____ Which ones?_____

Have you been to any Sing this past year when you weren't a patient? (circle one)

                                      yes   no

Have you been a patient at a peyote meeting this year?

	yes	no	No.___
Two years ago?	yes	no	No.___
Three years ago?	yes	no	No.___
Four years ago?	yes	no	No.___
Five years ago?	yes	no	No.___

Have you gone to Anglo doctors this year?   yes   no

Did you vote in Tribal Elections?   yes   no

Whom did you vote for in the last Tribal Election?_____

Do you vote in County, State and National Elections (in November, 1968)?

                                                                               yes   no

What party? (Democrat, Republican, etc.) _____

TABULATION OF ARRESTS MADE BY
FLAGSTAFF POLICE DEPARTMENT, 1967

Type of Offense by Race of Offender
(Flagstaff Police Department, 1967)

Offense	White	Negro	Indian	Other
Murder and nonnegligent manslaughter	1	2	0	0
Manslaughter by negligence	0	0	0	0
Forcible rape	3	0	0	0
Robbery	10	0	0	0
Aggravated assault	31	14	11	0
Burglary—breaking or entering	13	1	1	0
Larceny—theft (except auto)	82	3	20	1
Auto theft	6	0	0	0
Other assaults	21	4	5	0
Arson	0	0	0	0
Forgery and counterfeiting	7	0	1	0
Fraud	16	3	2	0
Embezzlement	0	0	0	0
Stolen property (buying, receiving, processing)	0	1	0	0
Vandalism	17	0	2	0
Prostitution and commercialized vice	0	0	0	0

Offense	White	Negro	Indian	Other
Sex offenses (except forcible rape and prostitution)	2	0	1	0
Narcotic drug laws:				
a. Opium or cocaine and their derivatives	0	0	0	0
b. Marijuana	16	0	0	0
c. Synthetic narcotics	0	0	0	0
d. Other dangerous nonnarcotic drugs	7	0	0	0
Gambling	4	0	0	0
Offenses against family and children	34	0	0	0
Driving under the influence	214	14	59	0
Liquor laws	113	7	35	0
Drunkenness	513	65	1,078	0
Disorderly conduct	137	30	53	0
Vagrancy *	655	26	0	0
All other offenses except traffic	47	4	15	0
Suspicion	0	0	0	0

* According to one police informant, Indians as wards of the state cannot be picked up on vagrancy charges as they have a visible means of support—the government.

DEFINITION OF ALCOHOL

SCORES AND RESULTS OF TABULATIONS

Table 1. Definition of Alcohol: Comparison of Scores of Men and Women within Each Group *

Group	Number of Men	Number of Women	p Value
Hospital	29	4	†
Plateau	14	13	Less than .025
South Tuba	17	6	More than .05
Flagstaff	13	7	More than .05

* Calculated by the Mann-Whitney U test.

† Not enough women to make the test worth doing. Women's scores appear no different than the men's.

Table 2. Definition of Alcohol: Comparison of Women's Scores between Groups

Hospital		Plateau		South Tuba		Flagstaff	
Score	Average Rank	Score	Average Rank	Score	Average Rank	Score	Average Rank
0	2.5	0	2.5	1	6	0	2.5
2	9.5	0	2.5	1	6	5	18
4	14	1	6	3	12	5	18
5	18	2	9.5	4	14	6	21.5
		2	9.5	5	18	7	24
		2	9.5	8	28	8	28
		4	14			8	28
		5	18				
		6	21.5				
		7	24				
		7	24				
		8	28				
		8	28				

N = 4
R = 44
Mean score = 2.7

N = 13
R = 197
Mean score = 4

N = 6
R = 84
Mean score = 3.7

N = 7
R = 140
Mean score = 5.5

H = 5
df = 3
p is more than .05

Table 3. Definition of Alcohol: Comparison of
Men's Scores between Groups (Kruskal-Wallis
One-Way Analysis of Variance)

Hospital		Plateau		South Tuba		Flagstaff	
Score	Average Rank	Score	Average Rank	Score	Average Rank	Score	Average Rank
0	6	0	6	0	6	0	6
0	6	0	6	1	13.5	0	6
1	13.5	0	6	1	13.5	1	13.5
2	24	0	6	2	24	2	24
2	24	0	6	2	24	2	24
2	24	0	6	2	24	4	45
2	24	2	24	3	35.5	4	45
2	24	3	35.5	4	45	5	55.5
2	24	4	45	4	45	6	62.5
2	24	4	45	4	45	6	62.5
2	24	5	55.5	5	55.5	7	68.5
2	24	5	55.5	5	55.5	7	68.5
2	24	5	55.5	6	62.5	8	72.5
2	24	7	68.5	6	62.5		
3	35.5			7	68.5		
3	35.5			7	68.5		
3	35.5			8	72.5		
3	35.5						
4	45						
4	45						
4	45						
4	45						
4	45						
4	45						
5	55.5						
5	55.5						
6	62.5						
6	62.5						
7	68.5						

N = 29   N = 14   N = 17   N = 13
R = 1006   R = 420.5   R = 721   R = 553.5
Mean score   Mean score   Mean score   Mean score
  = 3.0   = 2.5   = 3.9   = 4.0

H = 1.68
df = 3
p = more than .05

PREOCCUPATION WITH ALCOHOL

SCORES AND RESULTS OF TABULATIONS

Table 1. Preoccupation with Alcohol:
Differences between Sexes within Groups *

Group	Number of Men	Number of Women	p Value
Hospital	29	4	†
Plateau	17	13	Less than .02
South Tuba	17	6	More than .05
Flagstaff	14	7	More than .05

* By Mann-Whitney U test
† Not enough to make test worthwhile. Responses appear no different from the men's.

Table 2. Preoccupation with Alcohol: Comparison of Women's Scores between Groups (Kruskal-Wallis One-Way Analysis of Variance)

Hospital		Plateau		South Tuba		Flagstaff	
Score	Average Rank	Score	Average Rank	Score	Average Rank	Score	Average Rank
3	6	2	2.5	2	2.5	2	2.5
4	8	3	6	2	2.5	9	18.5
6	11	5	9	3	6	10	20.5
8	16.5	6	11	11	26	10	20.5
		6	11	11	26	11	26
		7	14	11	26	11	26
		7	14			11	26
		7	14				
		8	16.5				
		9	18.5				
		11	26				
		11	26				
		11	26				

N = 4   N = 13   N = 6   N = 7
R = 41.5   R = 194.5   R = 89   R = 140
Mean score   Mean score   Mean score   Mean score
 = 5.25   = 7.15   = 6.66   = 9.14

H = 3.24
df = 3
p = more than .05

Table 3. Preoccupation with Alcohol: Comparison of Men's Scores between Groups (Kruskal-Wallis One-Way Analysis of Variance)

Hospital		Plateau		South Tuba		Flagstaff	
Score	Average Rank	Score	Average Rank	Score	Average Rank	Score	Average Rank
1	4.5	0	1	2	12.5	2	12.5
1	4.5	1	4.5	3	23	2	12.5
1	4.5	1	4.5	4	32	4	32
1	4.5	2	12.5	5	39.5	5	39.5
2	12.5	3	23	5	39.5	6	45
2	12.5	3	23	6	45	8	54
2	12.5	3	23	7	48.5	9	61
2	12.5	3	23	8	54	10	69
2	12.5	3	23	8	54	10	69
2	12.5	4	32	8	54	10	69
3	23	4	32	9	61	10	69
3	23	5	39.5	9	61	10	69
3	23	5	39.5	9	61	11	76
3	23	8	54	10	69	11	76
3	23	8	54	10	69	11	76
4	32	9	61	11	76		
4	32	10	69	11	76		
5	39.5						
5	39.5						
5	39.5						
6	45						
7	48.5						
7	48.5						
7	48.5						
8	54						
9	61						
9	61						
10	69						

N = 29	N = 17	N = 17	N = 15
R = 826	R = 518.5	R = 875	R = 829.5
Mean score = 4	Mean score = 4.2	Mean score = 7.3	Mean score = 7.9

$H = 10.3$
$df = 3$
$p =$ less than .02

Table 4 Preoccupation Scores by Drinking Status for Men in Three Groups

Current Drinking Status	Plateau			South Tuba				Flagstaff			
	0–8	9–10	11	0–8	9–10	11	Unknown	0–8	9–10	11	Unknown
Drinker	6	1	0	7	3	1	2	1	4	3	1
Ex-drinker	9	1	2	3	2	1	0	5	2	0	0

Table 5 Preoccupation Scores by Drinking Status for Women in Three Groups

Current Drinking Status	Plateau			South Tuba			Flagstaff			
	0–8	9–10	11	0–8	9–10	11	0–8	9–10	11	Unknown
Drinker	0	0	1	1	0	0	1	2	3	1
Ex-drinker	10	1	3	2	2	0	0	1	0	2

PREOCCUPATION SCORES OF MEN BY
INCOME, EDUCATION, AND RELIGION

Table 1. Income by Preoccupation Score: Men
(Kruskal-Wallis One-Way Analysis of Variance)

Per Capita Income					
0–499		500–999		1000+	
Score	Rank	Score	Rank	Score	Rank
0	1	3	23	2	12.5
1	4.5	3	23	2	12.5
1	4.5	3	23	4	32
1	4.5	4	32	7	48.5
1	4.5	4	32	7	48.5
1	4.5	4	32	8	54
1	4.5	5	39.5	8	54
2	12.5	5	39.5	9	61
2	12.5	5	39.5	9	61
2	12.5	6	45	10	69
2	12.5	6	45	10	69
2	12.5	7	48.5	10	69
2	12.5	8	54	11	76
2	12.5	9	61	11	76
2	12.5	10	69	11	76
3	23	10	69	11	76
3	23	10	69	11	76
3	23	10	69		
3	23				
3	23				
3	23				
3	23				
3	23				
4	32				
4	32				

Per Capita Income					
0 – 499		500 – 999		1000 +	
Score	Rank	Score	Rank	Score	Rank
4	32				
5	39.5				
5	39.5				
5	39.5				
5	39.5				
5	39.5				
6	45				
7	48.5				
8	54				
8	54				
8	54				
8	54				
9	61				
9	61				
9	61				
9	61				
10	69				
10	69				

$R_1 = 1602$

$N_1 = 43$

$R_2 = 813$ $R_3 = 819$

$N_2 = 18$ $N_3 = 17$

$H = 27.86$

$df = 2$

$p = $ less than .001

Table 2. Education by Preoccupation Score: Men (Kruskal-Wallis One-Way Analysis of Variance)

Years of Education					
0		1–7		8+	
Score	Rank	Score	Rank	Score	Rank
0	1	1	4.5	2	12.5
1	4.5	1	4.5	3	23
1	4.5	1	4.5	4	32
2	12.5	1	4.5	4	32
2	12.5	2	12.5	4	32
2	12.5	2	12.5	6	45
2	12.5	2	12.5	6	45
3	23	2	12.5	7	48.5
3	23	2	12.5	7	48.5
3	23	3	23	8	54
3	23	3	23	8	54
3	23	3	23	8	54
3	23	3	23	8	54
4	32	4	32	8	54
4	32	4	32	8	54
5	39.5	5	39.5	9	61
5	39.5	5	39.5	9	61
5	39.5	5	39.5	9	61
5	39.5	5	39.5	9	61
7	48.5	6	45	10	69

Years of Education					
0		1 − 7		8 +	
Score	Rank	Score	Rank	Score	Rank
9	61	7	48.5	10	69
10	69	8	54	10	69
		9	61	10	69
		9	61	11	76
		10	69	11	76
		10	69	11	76
		10	69		
		10	69		
		11	76		
		11	76		

$R_1 = 927.5$

$N_1 = 22$

$R_2 = 1136$

$N_2 = 30$

$H = 76.7$
$df = 2$
$p = $ less than .001

$R_3 = 1390.5$

$N_3 = 26$

Table 3. Religious Preference by Preoccupation Score: Men (Mann-Whitney U Test)

Traditional *		Christian †	
Score	Rank	Score	Rank
0	1	1	4.5
1	4.5	1	4.5
1	4.5	2	12.5
1	4.5	2	12.5
1	4.5	2	12.5
2	12.5	2	12.5
2	12.5	2	12.5
2	12.5	2	12.5
2	12.5	3	23
3	23	3	23
3	23	3	23
3	23	3	23
3	23	3	23
3	23	4	32
3	23	4	32
4	32	4	32
4	32	5	39.5
4	32	5	39.5
4	32	6	45
5	39.5	6	45
5	39.5	7	48.5
5	39.5	7	48.5
5	39.5	7	48.5
5	39.5	7	48.5
5	39.5	8	54
6	45	8	54

Traditional *		Christian †	
Score	Rank	Score	Rank
8	54	8	54
8	54	8	54
8	54	9	61
9	61	9	61
9	61	9	61
10	69	9	61
10	69	9	61
11	76	10	69
		10	69
		10	69
		10	69
		10	69
		10	69
		10	69
		11	76
		11	76
		11	76
		11	76

$R_1 = 1115$

$N_1 = 34$

$Z = 2.30$

$p = .0107$

$R_2 = 1966$

$N_2 = 44$

* Includes traditional, traditional + NNAC, and NNAC.
† Includes all Christian denominations and LDS.

ABERLE, D. F.

1966 *The Peyote Religion among the Navajo.* Chicago: Aldine.

1967 The Psychological Analysis of a Hopi Life-History. In *Personalities and Cultures.* R. Hunt, ed. American Museum Sourcebooks in Anthropology. Garden City, N.J.: Natural History Press.

1969 A Plan for Navajo Economic Development. In *Toward Economic Development for Native American Communities.* A compendium of papers submitted to the subcommittee on Economy in Government of the Joint Economic Committee, Congress of the United States. Washington, D.C.: U.S. Government Printing Office.

ABLON, J.

1964 Relocated American Indians in the San Francisco Bay Area: Social Interaction and Indian Identity. *Human Organization, 23:296–304.*

ADAMS, R. D.

1959 Nutritional Diseases of the Nervous System in the Alcoholic Patient. *Transactions of the American Clinical and Climatologic Association, 71:59–61.*

ADAMS, W. Y.

1963 *Shonto: A Study of the Role of the Trader in a Modern Navajo Community.* Smithsonian Institution, Bureau of American Ethnology, Bulletin No. 188. Washington, D.C.: U.S. Government Printing Office.

ADDAMS, J.

1927 *Twenty Years at Hull House.* New York: Macmillan.

AMERICAN SOCIOLOGICAL SOCIETY
1914   Proceedings of the Eighth Annual Meeting of the American Sociological Society. Chicago: University of Chicago Press.

ARIZONA CHAMPION
1884   Flagstaff, Arizona, March 1 and September 20.

ARIZONA COMMISSION OF INDIAN AFFAIRS
1966   Reservation Survey of Health. Phoenix.

ARIZONA STATE EMPLOYMENT SERVICE
1969   An Arizona Resource Study: Flagstaff, 1969. Research and Information Series No. ECO-3-19. Phoenix, May.

ARRINGTON, L. J.
1963   The Changing Economic Structure of the Mountain West, 1850–1950. Monograph Series, Vol. X. Logan: Utah State University Press.

BACON, M. K., H. BARRY, III, and I. L. CHILD
1965   A Cross-Cultural Study of Drinking: II. Relations to other Features of Culture. In A Cross-Cultural Study of Drinking. Quarterly Journal of Studies on Alcohol, Supplement No. 3, April.

BAILEY, L. R.
1964   The Long Walk: A History of the Navajo Wars, 1846–68. Los Angeles: Westernlore Press.

BASSO, K. H.
1969   Western Apache Witchcraft. Anthropological Papers of the University of Arizona. Tucson: University of Arizona Press.

BECKER, H. S.
1966   Outsiders, Studies in the Sociology of Deviance. New York: The Free Press.

BENEDICT, R.
1961   Patterns of Culture. New York: Houghton Mifflin, Sentry Edition.

BERGMAN, R. L.
1967   Boarding Schools and the Psychological Problems of Indian Children. Unpublished report to the Committee of Indian Health of the American Academy of Pediatrics.

BERRY, B.
1969   *The Education of American Indians, A Survey of the Literature.* A report prepared for the Special Subcommittee of Indian Education of the Committee on Labor and Public Welfare, U.S. Senate. Washington, D.C.: U.S. Government Printing Office.

BLACK, R. A.
1969   Personal communication, August.

BOYER, L. B.
1962   Remarks on the Personality of Shamans: With Special Reference to the Apache of the Mescalero Indian Reservation. In the *Psychoanalytic Study of Society,* Vol. 2. W. Muensterberger and S. Axelrad, eds. New York: International Universities Press.

BROPHY, W. A., and S. D. ABERLE
1966   *The Indian, America's Unfinished Business.* Norman: University of Oklahoma Press.

BROWN, D. N.
1965   A Study of Heavy Drinking at Taos Pueblo. Mimeographed. Department of Anthropology, University of Arizona.

BROWN, R. C., B. S. GURUNANJAPPA, R. J. HAWK, and D. BITSUIE
1970   The Epidemiology of Accidents among the Navajo Indians. *Public Health Reports, 85:*881–888.

BRUNER, E. M.
1956   Primary Group Experience and the Process of Acculturation. *American Anthropologist, 58:*601–623.

BUCKLEY, W.
1967   *Sociology and Modern Systems Theory.* Englewood Cliffs, N.J.: Prentice-Hall.

CAHALAN E., and I. H. CISIN
1968a   American Drinking Practices: Summary of Findings from a National Probability Sample, I. Extent of Drinking by Population Subgroups. *Quarterly Journal of Studies on Alcohol, 29:*130–151.
1968b   American Drinking Practices: Summary of Findings from a National Probability Sample, II. Measurement of Massed versus Spaced Drinking. *Quarterly Journal of Studies on Alcohol, 29:*642–656.

CLOWARD, R. A.
1959   Illegitimate Means, Anomie and Deviant Behavior. *American Sociological Review, 24:164–176.*

CLOWARD, R. A., and L. E. OHLIN
1960   *Delinquency and Opportunity: A Theory of Delinquent Gangs.* New
York: The Free Press.

CLUM, J. P.
1929   The San Carlos Apache Police. *New Mexico Historical Review,*
4:203–219.

COLLIER, J.
1962   *On the Gleaming Way.* Denver: Sage Books.
1963   *From Every Zenith.* Denver: Sage Books.

COLLIER, J. and E. M. BARROW
1914   *The City Where Crime is Play.* New York: The People's Institute.

COLTON, H. S.
1934   A Brief Survey of Hopi Common Law. *Museum of Northern Arizona,
Museum Notes, 7:21–24.*

CRANE, L.
1915   Narrative Section of the Annual Report for the Moqui Indian Reservation. Xeroxed. U.S. Department of Interior, Indian Service.

CRESSY, D. R. and D. A. WARD, eds.
1969   *Delinquency, Crime, and Social Process.* New York: Harper and Row.

DAVIS, A. F.
1967   *Spearheads for Reform: The Social Settlements and the Progressive
Movement, 1890–1914.* New York: Oxford University Press.

DIZMANG, L. H., J. WATSON, P. A. MAY, and J. BOPP
1970   Adolescent Suicide at Fort Hall Indian Reservation. A paper presented before the Annual Meeting of the American Psychiatric Association. San Francisco, May.

DOWNS, J. F.
1964   *Animal Husbandry in Navajo Society and Culture.* University of California Publications in Anthropology, Vol. 1. Berkeley and Los
Angeles: University of California Press.

DOZIER, E. P.

1966　Problem Drinking among American Indians: The Role of Sociocultural Deprivation. *Quarterly Journal of Studies on Alcohol* 27:72–87.

DRIVER, H. E.

1961　*Indians of North America.* Chicago: University of Chicago Press.

DYK, W.

1947　*A Navajo Autobiography.* Viking Fund Publications in Anthropology, No. 8.

1966　*Son of Old Man Hat, A Navajo Autobiography.* 2nd ed. Lincoln: University of Nebraska Press.

EGGAN, F.

1950　*Social Organization of the Western Pueblos.* Chicago: University of Chicago Press.

1966　*The American Indian: Perspectives for the Study of Culture Change.* Chicago: Aldine.

ERIKSON, E. H.

1963　*Childhood and Society.* New York: W. W. Norton.

ERIKSON, K. T.

1962　Notes on the Sociology of Deviance. *Social Problems,* 9:307–314.

1967　Notes on the Sociology of Deviance. Revised ed. In *The Other Side,* H. S. Becker, ed. New York: The Free Press.

EVERETT, M.

1969　Cooperation in Change? Western Apache Evidence. A paper presented at the Annual Meeting, Society for Applied Anthropology, Mexico City, April.

EULER, R. C.

1948　An Economic History of Northern Arizona During the Territorial Period, 1863–1912. M. A. Thesis, Arizona State College, Flagstaff.

1960　Havasupai Ethnohistory. A report prepared for Marks and Marks, attorneys. Phoenix.

FELDMAN, H.

1968　Ideological Supports to Becoming and Remaining a Heroin Addict. *Journal of Health and Social Behavior,* 9:131–139.

FENNA, D., L. MIX, O. SCHAEFER, and J. A. L. GILBERT
1971 Ethanol Metabolism in Various Racial Groups. *Canadian Medical Association Journal, 105:472–475.*

FERGUSON, F. N.
1965 The Peer Group and Navajo Problem Drinking. *Abstracts of papers of the American Anthropological Association,* 64th Annual Meeting.
1968 Navajo Drinking: Some Tentative Hypotheses. *Human Organization,* 27:159–167.
1969 Community Treatment Plan for Navajo Problem Drinkers. Final report for Grant MH-01389. McKinley County Family Consultation Services. Gallup, New Mexico.

FIELD, P. B.
1962 A New Cross-Cultural Study of Drunkenness. In *Society, Culture and Drinking Patterns.* D. J. Pittman and C. R. Snyder, eds. New York: Wiley.

FRANCISCAN FATHERS
1910 *Ethnological Dictionary of the Navajo Language.* St. Michaels, Arizona: The Franciscan Fathers.

GARDNER, R. E.
1969 The Role of the Pan-Indian Church in Urban Indian Life. *Anthropology UCLA, 1:14–26.*

GIBBS, J. P.
1966 Conceptions of Deviant Behavior: The Old and the New. *Pacific Sociological Review, 9:9–14.*

GILLETTE, J. M.
1914 Discussion of F. A. McKenzie's Paper, "The Assimilation of the American Indian." In *Proceedings of the Eighth Annual Meeting of the American Sociological Society.* Chicago: University of Chicago Press.

GOFFMAN, E.
1961 *Asylums, Essays on the Social Situation of Mental Patients and other Inmates.* Garden City, N.J.: Doubleday Anchor Books.

GOODLUCK, C. T.
1970 Some Problems Resulting from Acculturative Stress in a Navajo Com-

238   Bibliography

munity. Senior paper, Department of Anthropology, Prescott College, Prescott, Arizona.

GRAVES, T. D.
1967 Acculturation, Access, and Alcohol in a Tri-Ethnic Community. *American Anthropologist, 69:306–321.*
1970 The Personal Adjustment of Navajo Indian Migrants to Denver, Colorado. *American Anthropologist, 72:35–54.*
1971 Drinking and Drunkenness among Urban Indians. In *The American Indian in Urban Society.* J. O. Waddell and O. M. Matson, eds. Boston: Little, Brown, and Company.

GRAVES, T. D. and M. VAN ARSDALE
1966 Values, Expectations and Relocation: The Navaho Migrant to Denver. *Human Organization, 25:300–307.*

GREGG, J.
1954 *Commerce of the Prairies.* M. L. Moorehead, ed. Norman: University of Oklahoma Press. First published in 1845.

GROSS, M. M., E. HALPERT, L. SABOT,
and P. POLIZONS
1963 Hearing Disturbances and Auditory Hallucinations in the Acute Alcoholic Psychoses. I: Tinnitus: Incidence and Significance. *Journal of Nervous and Mental Disease, 137:455–465.*

HAGAN, W. T.
1966 *Indian Police and Judges.* New Haven: Yale University Press.

HAILE, B.
1940 A Note on the Navajo Visionary. *American Anthropologist, 42:359.*

HARSHBARGER, J. W., C. A. REPENNING,
and J. T. CALLAHAN
1953 Part IV: The Navajo Country, Arizona—Utah—New Mexico, of the Physical and Economic Foundation of Natural Resources. *Interior and Insular Affairs Committee, House of Representatives, United States Congress.*

HAVIGHURST, R. J., and B. L. NEUGARTEN
1955 *American Indian and White Children.* Chicago: University of Chicago Press.

HEATH, D. B.
1964 Prohibition and Post-Repeal Drinking Patterns among the Navajo. *Quarterly Journal of Studies on Alcohol, 25:*119–135.

HESTER, J. J.
1962 *Early Navajo Migrations and Acculturation in the Southwest.* Museum of New Mexico Papers in Anthropology, No. 6. Santa Fe: Museum of New Mexico Press.

HIPPLER, A. E.
1969 Fusion and Frustration: Dimensions in the Cross-Cultural Ethnopsychology of Suicide. *American Anthropologist 71:*1074–1087.

HOCHDERFFER, G.
1965 *Flagstaff Whoa! The Autobiography of a Western Pioneer.* Flagstaff: Museum of Northern Arizona.

HODGE, W. H.
1969 *The Albuquerque Navajos.* Anthropological Papers of the University of Arizona, No. 11. Tucson: University of Arizona Press.

HOLLINGSHEAD, A. H.
1957 *Two-Factor Index of Social Position.* New Haven: Department of Sociology, Yale University.

HORTON, D.
1943 The Functions of Alcohol in Primitive Societies. *Quarterly Journal of Studies on Alcohol, 4:*199–320.

HRDLICKA, A.
1908 *Physiological and Medical Observations among the Indians of Southwestern United States and Northern Mexico.* Bureau of American Ethnology, Bulletin 30.

HUNTER, R.
1965 *Poverty.* New York: Harper and Row Torchbook. First published in 1904.

INDIAN HEALTH SERVICE TASK FORCE ON ALCOHOLISM
1969 *Alcoholism: A High Priority Health Problem.* Washington, D.C.: U.S. Public Health Service, Indian Health Service.

ISBELL, H., H. F. FRAZER, R. E. BELLEVILLE,
and A. J. EISENMAN
  1955   An Experimental Study of the Etiology of "Rum Fits" and Delerium
         Tremens. *Quarterly Journal of Studies on Alcohol, 16:1–33.*

JELLINEK, E. M.
  1960   *The Disease Concept of Alcoholism.* New Haven: Hillhouse Press.

JESSOR, R., T. D. GRAVES, R. C. HANSON,
and S. L. JESSOR
  1968   *Society, Personality and Deviant Behaviour: A Study of a Tri-Ethnic
         Community.* New York: Holt, Rinehart and Winston.

JOSEPH, A., R. SPICER, and J. CHESKY
  1947   *The Desert People.* Chicago: University of Chicago Press.

JUDD, B. I.
  1968   Tuba City, Mormon Settlement. *The Journal of Arizona History,
         9:37–42.*

KAPLAN, B., and D. JOHNSON
  1964   The Social Meaning of Navajo Psychopathology and Psychotherapy.
         In *Magic, Faith and Healing,* A. Kiev ed. New York: The Free Press.

KELLER, M.
  1960   Definition of Alcoholism. *Quarterly Journal of Studies on Acohol,
         21:125–134.*

KELLY, R. E., and J. O. CRAMER
  1966   *American Indians in Small Cities.* Rehabilitation Monograph No. 1.
         Flagstaff: Department of Rehabilitation, Northern Arizona University.

KESSEL, H., and H. WALTON
  1965   *Alcoholism.* Baltimore: Penguin Books.

KITUSE, J. I.
  1962   Societal Reaction to Deviant Behavior: Problems of Theory and
         Method. *Social Problems, 9:247–256.*

KLUCKHOHN, C.
  1962   *Navaho Witchcraft.* 2nd ed. Boston: Beacon Press.

KLUCKHOHN, C., and D. C. LEIGHTON
  1946   *The Navaho.* Cambridge: Harvard University Press.

KNEAL, A. H.
1950   *Indian Agent*. Caldwell, Idaho: Caxton Press.

KNUPFER, G.
1967   The Epidemiology of Problem Drinking. *American Journal of Public Health*, 57:973–986.

KUNITZ, S. J.
1970   Benjamin Rush on Savagism and Progress. *Ethnohistory, 17:*31–43.
In   The Social Philosophy of John Collier. *Ethnohistory*.
press

KUNITZ, S. J., and J. E. LEVY
1970   Navajo Voting Patterns. *Plateau, 43:*1–8.
In   Changing Ideas of Alcohol Use Among the Navajo Indians.
pre: *Quarterly Journal of Studies on Alcohol*.

KUNITZ, S. J., J. E. LEVY, P. BELLET, and T. COLLINS
1969   A Census of Flagstaff Navajos. *Plateau, 41:*156–163.

KUNITZ, S. J., J. E. LEVY, and M. EVERETT
1968   Alcoholic Cirrhosis among the Navajo. *Quarterly Journal of Studies on Alcohol, 30:*672–685.

KUNITZ, S. J., J. E. LEVY, and C. L. ODOROFF
1970   A One Year Follow-Up of Navaho Migrants to Flagstaff, Arizona. *Plateau, 42:*92–106.

KUNITZ, S. J., J. E. LEVY, C. L. ODOROFF, and J. BOLLINGER
1971   The Epidemiology of Alcoholic Cirrhosis in Two Southwestern Indian Tribes. *Quarterly Journal of Studies on Alcohol, 32:*706–720.

LAMAR, H. R.
1966   *The Far Southwest, 1946–1912, A Territorial History*. New Haven: Yale University Press.

LANTERNARI, V.
1963   *The Religions of the Oppressed*. New York: Alfred A. Knopf.

LAUTZENHEISER, E. L., S. H. KERR, and E. J. LINCOLN
1953   Flagstaff and Bellemont, Arizona. In *Indians in Non-Indian Communities*. Window Rock, Arizona: Bureau of Indian Affairs, Welfare Placement Branch.

LEIGHTON, A. H.
1968   The Governing of Men. Princeton: Princeton University Press. First published in 1945.

LEIGHTON, A. H., and D. C. LEIGHTON
1944   The Navaho Door. Cambridge: Harvard University Press.

LEIGHTON, D. C., and JOHN ADAIR
1966   People of the Middle Place. New Haven: Human Relations Area Files Press.

LEIGHTON, D. C., and C. KLUCKHOHN
1948   Children of the People. Cambridge: Harvard University Press.

LEMERT, E. M.
1958   The Use of Alcohol in Three Salish Indian Tribes. Quarterly Journal of Studies on Alcohol, 19:90–107.
1967   The Concept of Secondary Deviation. In Human Deviance, Social Problems and Social Control. E. M. Lemert, ed. Englewood Cliffs, N. J.: Prentice-Hall.

LEVY, J. E.
1962   The Community Organization of the Western Navajo. American Anthropologist, 64:781–801.
1965   Navajo Suicide. Human Organization, 24:308–318.

LEVY, J. E. and S. J. KUNITZ
1969   Notes on Some White Mountain Apache Social Pathologies. Plateau, 42:11–19.
1971   Indian Reservations, Anomie and Social Pathology. Southwestern Journal of Anthropology, 27:97–128.
In   Indian Drinking: Problems of Data Collection and Interpretations. In
press   Research on Alcoholism, I. Clinical Problems and Special Populations. M. E. Chavetz, ed. Washington, D.C.: U. S. Government Printing Office.

LEVY, J. E., S. J. KUNITZ, and M. EVERETT
1969   Navajo Criminal Homicide. Southwestern Journal of Anthropology, 25:124–152.

LEVY, J. E., S. J. KUNITZ, C. L. ODOROFF,
and J. BOLLINGER
n.d.   Hopi Deviance: An Historical and Epidemiological Survey.

LIEBER, C.
1972 Metabolism of Ethanol and Alcoholism: Racial and Acquired Factors. *Annals of Internal Medicine*, 76:326–327.

LUEBBEN, R. A.
1964 Anglo Law and Navaho Behavior. *Kiva, 29:*60–75.

LYON, W. H.
1968 The Corporate Frontier in Arizona. *The Journal of Arizona History*, 9:1–17.

MacANDREW, C.
1969 On the Notion that Certain Persons Who are Given to Frequent Drunkenness Suffer from a Disease Called Alcoholism. In *Changing Perspectives in Mental Health*. S. C. Plog and R. B. Edgerton, eds. New York: Holt, Rinehart, and Winston.

MacANDREW, C., and R. B. EDGERTON
1969 *Drunken Comportment: A Social Explanation.* Chicago: Aldine.

MacANDREW, C., and H. GARFINKEL
1962 A Consideration of Changes Attributed to Intoxication as Common Sense Reasons for Getting Drunk. *Quarterly Journal of Studies on Alcohol, 23:*252–266.

MacGREGOR, G.
1946 *Warriors without Weapons.* Chicago: University of Chicago Press.

MARJOT, D. H.
1970 The Length of the Drinking Bout Preceding Alcohol Withdrawal States. *British Journal of Addiction, 64:*307–314.

MARTIN, H. W.
1964 Correlates of Adjustment among American Indians in an Urban Environment. *Human Organization, 23:*290–295.

MARX, L.
1964 *The Machine in the Garden.* New York: Oxford University Press.

MAXWELL, M. A.
1952 Drinking Behaviour in the State of Washington. *Quarterly Journal of Studies on Alcohol, 13:*219–239.

McCLELLAND, O.C., W. DAVIS, E. WANNER,
and R. KALIN
1966   A Cross-Cultural Study of Folk-Tale Content and Drinking. *Sociometry, 29:*308–333.

McCLELLAND, D. C., W. DAVIS, R. KALIN,
and E. WANNER
1972   *The Drinking Man: Alcohol and Human Motivation.* New York: The Free Press.

McNITT, F.
1962   *The Indian Traders.* Norman: University of Oklahoma Press.

MERTON, R. K.
1968   *Social Theory and Social Structure.* New York: The Free Press.

MILES, GENERAL N. A.
1896   *Personal Recollections and Observations.* Chicago: Werner Co.

MILLER, N. E.
1969   Learning of Visceral and Glandular Responses. *Science, 163:*434–445.

MITCHELL, E. B., and T. D. ALLEN
1967   *Miracle Hill, The Story of a Navajo Boy.* Norman: University of Oklahoma Press.

MIZEN, M. L.
1966   *Federal Facilities for Indians: Tribal Relations with the Federal Government.* Report to the Committee on Appropriations, United States Senate. Washington, D.C.: U.S. Government Printing Office.

MOORE, H. C.
1967   Culture Change in a Navajo Community. In *American Historical Anthropology, Essays in Honor of Leslie Spier.* C. L. Riley and W. W. Taylor, eds. Carbondale: Southern Illinois University Press.

MORGAN, H. G.
1968   Acute Neuropsychiatric Complications of Chronic Alcoholism. *British Journal of Psychiatry, 114:*85–91.

MOTT, R. H., I. F. SMALL, and J. M. ANDERSON
1965   Comparative Study of Hallucinations. *Archives of General Psychiatry, 12:*599.

MULFORD, H. A.
1964   Drinking and Deviant Drinking, U.S.A. 1963. *Quarterly Journal of Studies on Alcohol, 25:634–650.*

MULFORD, H. A., and D. E. MILLER
1960a Drinking in Iowa, III. A Scale of Definitions of Alcohol Related to Drinking Behaviour. *Quarterly Journal of Studies on Alcohol, 21:267–278.*
1960b Drinking in Iowa, IV. Preoccupation with Alcohol and Definitions of Alcohol, Heavy Drinking and Trouble Due to Drinking. *Quarterly Journal of Studies on Alcohol 21:279–291.*

MULFORD, H. A., and R. W. WILSON
1966   *Identifying Problem Drinkers in A Household Health Survey.* National Center for Health Statistics, P. H. S. Publication No. 1000, Series 2, No. 16. Washington, D.C.

NAGATA, S.
1970   *Modern Transformations of Moenkopi Pueblo.* Bloomington: University of Indiana Press.

PEARCE, R. H.
1967   *Savagism and Civilization.* Baltimore: Johns Hopkins University Press.

PHELPS STOKES FUND
1939   *The Navajo Indian Problem.* New York: Phelps Stokes Fund.

PRICE, J. A.
1968   The Migration and Adaptation of American Indians to Los Angeles. *Human Organization, 27:168–175.*

REEVE, F.
1941   The Government and the Navajo, 1878–1883. *The New Mexico Historical Review, 16:278.*

REICHARD, G. A.
1963   *Navajo Religion, A Study of Symbolism.* 2nd ed. Bollingen Foundation, No. 18. New York: Pantheon Books.

RILEY, J. W., JR., and C. F. MARDEN
1947   The Social Pattern of Acoholic Drinking. *Quarterly Journal of Studies on Alcohol, 8:265–273.*

ROBINS, L. N., G. E. MURPHY, and M. B. BRECKENRIDGE
1968   Drinking Behaviour of Young Urban Negro Men. *Quarterly Journal of Studies on Alcohol*, 29:657–684.

ROBINSON, H. E.
1954   *Some Economic Implications of the Tourist Industry for Northern Arizona.* Phoenix: Stanford Research Institute, Mountain States Division.

ROMAN, P. M., and H. M. TRICE
1968   The Sick Role, Labelling Theory and the Deviant Drinker. *The International Journal of Social Psychiatry*, 14:245–251.

RUBIN, E., and C. LIEBER
1971   Alcoholism, Alcohol, and Drugs. *Science*, 172:1097–1102.

RUBENSTEIN, A., J. BOYLE, C. L. ODOROFF, and S. J. KUNITZ
1969   Effect of Improved Sanitary Facilities on Infant Diarrhea in a Hopi Village. *Public Health Reports*, 84:1093–1097.

SASLOW, H. L., and M. J. HARROVER
1968   Research on Psychological Adjustment of Indian Youth. *American Journal of Psychiatry*, 125:224–231.

SAVARD, R. J.
1968   Effects of Disulfiram Therapy on Relationships within the Navajo Drinking Group. *Quarterly Journal of Studies on Alcohol*, 29:909–916.

SCHOENWETTER, J., and A. E. DITTERT, JR.
1968   An Ecological Interpretation of Anasazi Settlement Patterns. *Anthropological Archaeology in the Americas.* Washington, D.C.: The Anthropological Society of Washington.

SCHUR, E. M.
1969   Reactions to Deviance: A Critical Assessment. *American Journal of Sociology*, 75:309–322.
1971   *Labeling Deviant Behavior.* New York: Harper and Row.

SHEPARDSON, M.
1963   *Navajo Ways in Government.* American Anthropological Association Memoir, No. 96.

SHEPARDSON, M., and B. HAMMOND
1964   Change and Persistence in an Isolated Navajo Community. *American Anthropologist*, 66:1029–1050.

SIEGEL, S.
1956   *Nonparametric Statistics for the Behavioural Sciences*. New York: McGraw-Hill.

SMITH, C. S.
1908   *Working with the People*. New York: A. Wessels Co.

SNYDER, P. Z.
1971   The Social Environment of the Urban Indian. In *The American Indian in Urban Society*. J. O. Waddell and O. M. Watson, eds. Boston: Little, Brown.

SPICER, E. H.
1962   *Cycles of Conquest*. Tucson: University of Arizona Press.

STEWARD, J. H.
1955   *Theory of Culture Change, the Methodology of Multilinear Evolution*. Urbana: University of Illinois Press.

STEWART, O. C.
1964   Questions Regarding American Indian Criminality. *Human Organization*, 23:61–66.

STRAUS, R. and S. D. BACON
1953   *Drinking in College*. New Haven: Yale University Press.

SUTHERLAND, E. H., and D. R. CRESSEY
1966   *Principles of Criminology*. Philadelphia: J. B. Lippincott.

SZUTZER, C. F., R. J. SAVARD, and J. H. SAIKI
n.d.   *The Use of Disulfiram in Treatment of Alcoholic Problems in an American Indian Population*. Fort Defiance, Arizona: U. S. Public Health Service, Fort Defiance Indian Hospital.

TAYLOR, B. J.
1968   Indian Manpower Resources: The Experience of Five Southwestern Reservations. *Arizona Law Review*, 10:579–596.

TAYLOR, B. J., and D. J. O'CONNOR
1969   *Indian Manpower Resources in the Southwest: A Pilot Study.* Bureau of Business and Economic Research, College of Business Administration. Tempe: Arizona State University.

THOMPSON, L.
1948   Attitudes   and   Acculturation.   *American   Anthropologist,* 50:200–215.
1950   *Culture in Crisis: A Study of the Hopi Indians.* New York: Harper Brothers.

THOMPSON, L., and A. JOSEPH
1945   *The Hopi Way.* Chicago: University of Chicago Press.

TYLER, C. W., JR., and A. L. SAEGER, JR.
1968   Maternal Health and Socioeconomic Status of Non-Reservation Indians. *Public Health Reports, 83:465–473.*

UCHENDU, V. C.
1966   *Navajo Harvest Hands: An Ethnographic Report.* Food Research Institute, Stanford University, Stanford, California.

UNDERHILL, R.
1948   *Ceremonial Patterns in the Greater Southwest.* American Ethnological Society, Monograph 13. Seattle: University of Washington Press.
1965   *The Navajos.* Norman: University of Oklahoma Press.

U.S. DEPARTMENT OF HEALTH, EDUCATION AND WELFARE
1966   *Indian Health Highlights.* Public Health Service, Division of Indian Health. Washington, D.C., June.

U.S. DEPARTMENT OF THE INTERIOR
1883   *Report of the Secretary of the Interior, Annual Report of the Com-*
–90   *missioner of Indian Affairs.* Washington, D.C.: Government Printing Office.

VALLEY NATIONAL BANK
1967   *Arizona Statistical Summary.* Phoenix.

VAN VALKENBURGH
1937   Navajo Common Law: Navajo Law and Justice. *Museum of Northern Arizona, Museum Notes, 9:51–54.*
1948   Navajo Naat'aani. *The Kiva, 13:14–23.*

VOGT, E. Z.
1951   *Navajo Veterans, A Study of Changing Values.* Papers of the Peabody
       Museum of American Archaeology and Ethnology, Vol. 41, No. 1. Re-
       ports of the Rimrock Project Values Series, No. 1. Cambridge: Har-
       vard University.
1961   Navajo. In *Perspectives in American Indian Culture Change.* E. H.
       Spicer, ed. Chicago: University of Chicago Press.

WASHBURN, W. E.
1968   Philanthropy and the American Indian. *Ethnohistory, 15:43–56.*

WASHBURNE, C.
1961   *Primitive Drinking,* New Haven: College and University Press Pub-
       lishers.

WEPPNER, R. S.
1971   Urban Economic Opportunities: The Example of Denver In *The
       American Indian in Urban Society.* J. O. Waddell and O. M. Watson,
       eds. Boston: Little, Brown.

WILSEY and HAM
1967   *Flagstaff Arizona, Planning Reports.* Flagstaff.

WOLFE, S., and M. VICTOR
1970   The Physiological Basis of the Alcohol Withdrawal Syndrome. A
       paper presented at the Symposium on Recent Advances in Studies on
       Alcoholism, sponsored by the National Center for Prevention and
       Control of Alcoholism, National Institute of Mental Health, Washing-
       ton, D.C., June 25–27, 1970. To be published in the proceedings of
       the symposium.

WOODS, R. A.
1898   *The City Wilderness, A Settlement Study.* Boston: Houghton, Mifflin.

WYMAN, L., and C. KLUCKHOHN
1938   *Navajo Classification of Their Song Ceremonials.* American Anthropo-
       logical Association Memoir 50.

WYMAN, L. C., and B. THORNE
1945   Notes on Navajo Suicide. *American Anthropologist, 47:278–288.*

YOUNG, R. W.
1961   *The Navajo Yearbook.* Window Rock, Arizona: The Navajo Agency.